MW00810661

NARRATIVE PERSPECTIVE IN FICTION

DANIEL FRANK CHAMBERLAIN

Narrative Perspective in Fiction: A Phenomenological Mediation of Reader, Text, and World

UNIVERSITY OF TORONTO PRESS
Toronto Buffalo London

© University of Toronto Press 1990
Toronto Buffalo London
ISBN 0-8020-5838-8
University of Toronto Romance Series 59

Printed on acid-free paper

Canadian Cataloguing in Publication Data

Chamberlain, Daniel Frank, 1951–
   Narrative perspective in fiction

   (University of Toronto romance series ; 59)
   Includes bibliographical references.
   ISBN 0–8020–5838–8

   1. Point of view (Literature).   2. Fiction – History and
   criticism.   3. Narration (Rhetoric).   4. Phenomenology and
   literature.   5. Hermeneutics.   I. Title.   II. Series.

   PN3383.P64C48 1990   808.3   C89-094869-0

This book has been published with the help of a grant from the Canadian
Federation for the Humanities, using funds provided by the Social Sciences
and Humanities Research Council of Canada.

Again and forever to Mónica

Contents

Acknowledgments

The following pages are the result of a great deal of effort and dedication on the part of family, friends, and faculty. Although I am indebted to all, a few deserve special mention. I would like to thank my mother and father for their encouragement and constant faith in me. I would also like to express my deep gratitude to Professor Mario J. Valdés, whose patient guidance has taught me much more than this inquiry could ever hope to reveal. My readers and editors, particularly Ron Schoeffel of the University of Toronto Press and copy-editor John St James, merit special thanks for their careful reading and tactful advice. My wife Mónica deserves much more than thanks. Without her unfailing support this book would not have been possible.

DANIEL FRANK CHAMBERLAIN

NARRATIVE PERSPECTIVE IN FICTION

Introduction

Narrative perspective has been described as the essence of the narrative art (Scholes and Kellogg 240). It plays an essential role in the writing and reading of texts and has become a major issue in the theory that narrative gives rise to. Different theoretical approaches have sought to define it with terms such as 'person,' 'point of view,' 'reflector,' 'voice,' 'central consciousness,' and 'focalization.' Despite the variety of approaches and the ongoing debate concerning the essence of narrative perspective, most theories agree that perspective is in one way or another involved in the more general process of perception. Perception, however, is often understood as an impression upon the senses of data proceeding from the outside world. When understood as an impingement upon the senses, perception is often reduced to one of its essential dimensions. The concept of data from the world falling upon the senses and marking an otherwise blank mind gives the spatial dimension of perception an 'objective' and 'unquestionable' authority to which theorists often appeal. The temporal dimension and the selection of meaningful data in the experience of perception are often left unheeded. Thus, narrative perspective is often approached from the presupposition of a passive reader and an active author or text. The aim of this study is to inquire into the nature of narrative perspective in a manner that does not presuppose a passive definition of perception. I shall depart from an understanding of perception as an 'opening' through which one's self-awareness and an awareness of the world are correlated. Thus, I understand perception as also being an active 're-creation or re-construction of the world at every moment' (Merleau-Ponty 1962, 207). In this way the temporal dimension is not ignored and perception can be related to both language and experience in a more general process of consciousness.

From this understanding of perception as a dialectic of space and time and of the role it plays in the process of consciousness, I intend to address the specific question, 'Can narrative perspective provide a medium through which to disclose potential meanings and through which to share the lived experience of narrative texts from both familiar and culturally different worlds today?' I shall address this question by organizing my inquiry according to a process of understanding, explanation, and comprehension. At the first level of this process I follow the hermeneutics of Hans-Georg Gadamer and particularly his notion of consciousness as being exposed to the effects of history.[1]

This notion of consciousness exposed to the effects of history in turn is divided into four interrelated parts proceeding from language to perception, experience, and concept. Language, understood as a mode of being in the world rather than as a closed system, is 'prior to everything else' in the hermeneutical study of narrative perspective (Gadamer 1975, 340).[2] The structure and character of consciousness can be understood in terms of a dialectic of question and answer as well as a conversation with the world through discourse. Following the phenomenology of Maurice Merleau-Ponty, awareness is also divided into four levels.[3] Perception, representation, illusion, and hallucination vary in degree from an open and shared awareness of the world and one's self to a closed and private one. Perception's essential dimensions of time and space are correlated to two senses and two perspectives that have played important roles as media of narrative transmission. Perception gives way to experience. Paul Ricoeur's notion of narrative as both emplotment (temporal muthos) and the imitation of action (mimesis) provides an understanding of the character and structure of the narrative experience. The 'essence of narrative art' functions at all moments of the narrative experience. The different dimensions of perception and the different moments in the process of narrative can provide various points of departure for the concept of narrative perspective. While this study does not intend to provide a critique of philosophical traditions, it is only by delving into philosophical questions presupposed by 'narrative' and 'perspective' that a greater appreciation of the creative potential and impact of narrative perspective can be achieved. An exploration of the concept of narrative perspective fulfils the primary level of understanding and opens to the second level of explanation.

The explanation of narrative perspective concentrates on three dimensions: that of the narrative voice, that of the narrative world, and that of the reader's perspective. Each of these dimensions is divided into four interrelated facets. These facets are in turn related to language and perception through the tropological character of discourse, on the one hand, and the particular sense brought to the fore by the predominant medium of cultural transmission, on the other. The similarity and difference of narrative perspective can then be comprehended as an interplay of facets.

The understanding and explanation of this 'essence' is not fully realized until the process includes a comprehension of texts recognized as moments of achievement in 'narrative art.' The comprehension of *Cien años de soledad* and *Jacob's Room* brings together two texts representative of narrative achievement in their respective linguistic milieus as well as two narrative perspectives representative of the dialectic of perception's temporal and spatial dimensions. The comprehension of these texts is accomplished through the interplay of facets of narrative perspective in the reading experience itself. I do not intend to provide a survey of critical evaluations concerned with the texts or their authors. This level of comprehension, therefore, presupposes a careful reading of the texts.

The intention of this investigation is, then, to offer an understanding, explanation, and comprehension of narrative perspective to a community of readers who share their experience of texts through the 'tradition of textual commentary' (Valdés 1987, 54). The design of my inquiry is necessarily complex. There is very little in the narrative art upon which its essence does not come to bear. This concern for the essential may lead, however, to a misunderstanding that the study intends to close the issue by way of an implicit claim to universality or absolute truth. Once an inquiry proposes the perception and experience of texts as its point of departure, any claim to universality, any claim to absolute truth, is dismissed in favour of a deeper level of understanding, a level in which communication between different perspectives becomes the rule. Any study of narrative perspective, including the present inquiry, can represent but one of many possible standpoints in language and history. With this in mind I offer the reader my experience with the question of narrative perspective. It is my hope that it will contribute to the never-ending process of appropriation through narrative as well as to the tradition we esteem and continue to celebrate.

Part One

THE MEANING OF NARRATIVE PERSPECTIVE

1

Language of Experience: Hans-Georg Gadamer and Consciousness Exposed to the Effects of History

The starting point for a consideration of narrative perspective in terms of the reader's encounter with a text lies in the structure and character of consciousness itself. Hans-Georg Gadamer's concept of 'consciousness exposed to the effects of history,' is well suited for an examination of the relationship between narrative perspective and reader because it is constituted by a hierarchy of four levels common to both: language, perception, experience figured by history, and concept.[1] Gadamer's philosophy starts 'from the basic ontological view, according to which being is language, ie [sic] self-presentation, as revealed to us by the hermeneutical experience of being' (1975, 443). His hermeneutic ontology is concerned with understanding as a 'mode of being' and being 'that can be understood is language' (xviii, xxii).[2] From this 'fundamental linguistic quality' of humanity, Gadamer establishes an indivisible relationship between language and world (401).

The 'linguistics' that interests Gadamer is not so much that of Ferdinand de Saussure but rather that of Wilhelm von Humboldt. Gadamer concentrates on the inner tendency to be communicative rather than on language as a system. He is concerned with language as a moment that continually presents itself, a moment in which our doubts begin to come forth as a vague stimulus that tends towards communication. He shares Humboldt's recognition that language 'is no product (*Ergon*), but an activity (*Energeia*). Its true definition can therefore only be a genetic one' (Humboldt 49). If language is the energy of the human power to have and to disclose a world, then every particular language represents a point of view of the world (Humboldt 49 and Gadamer 1975, 397ff).[3] The 'essence of language,' which is 'the living act of speech, linguistic energeia,' and the world-view handed down in language as tradition, is of primary concern to Gadamer because its elements, rather than exclusive formal differences, come to bear upon experience (401). The nature of language 'is one of the most mysterious questions that exist for man to ponder on' because we 'cannot see a linguistic world from above ... there is no point of view outside the experience of the world in language from which it could itself become an object' (340, 410). Language, like history, does not provide an exterior standpoint from which to examine the problem of its identity: 'The standpoint that is beyond any standpoint, a standpoint from which we could conceive its true identity, is a pure illusion' (339).

Gadamer seeks to approach this 'universal mystery of language that is prior to everything else' from the 'conversation that we ourselves are,' from the putting into play of language, and from the living act of speech that is its essence (340, 91, 446). A conversation that is built upon questions and answers presupposes a common language between the listeners and speakers in the occasionality of human speech, as well as an agreement concerning what the object under discussion is to be.[4] In a conversation 'something is placed in the centre, as the Greeks said, which the partners ... both share, and concerning which they can exchange ideas' (341). Conversation is concerned with an understanding of the object placed between the listeners and speakers without claiming to express its meaning absolutely, and it creates a bond and sense of belonging between them from which an understanding of the world takes place (341). Within a dialogue individual words do not occur in isolation. Every word 'causes the whole of the language to which it belongs to resonate and the whole of the view of the world which lies behind it to appear' (415–16).[5]

The role that perception plays in Gadamer's theory of language and hermeneutic ontology is made apparent by his frequent use of the terms 'standpoint,' 'view,' and 'point of view.' Language and perception intermingle in the fourfold process of consciousness. The relationship of being, language, and world in its variety and continuity is explored in terms of the part-to-whole character of perception:

The variety of these views of the world does not involve any relativisation of the 'world'. Rather, what the world is, is not different from the views in which it presents itself. The relationship is the same in the perception of things. Seen phenomenologically, the 'thing-in-itself' is, as Husserl has shown, nothing other than the continuity with which the shades of the various perspectives of the perceptione [sic] of objects pass into on another ... In the same way as

with perception we can speak of the 'linguistic nuances' that the world undergoes in different linguistic worlds. (1975, 406)

Perception differs from language, according to Gadamer, in that each
nuance of the object of perception is exclusively different from the
others and the thing in itself constitutes a continuum (406). Each linguistic nuance, however, contains potentially within it every other one.
This quality of language makes a view of the world belonging to another
language accessible without leaving or negating one's own linguistic
world. Gadamer holds that 'the connection with language which belongs to our experience of the world does not involve an exclusiveness
of perspectives. If, by entering into foreign linguistic worlds, we overcome the prejudices and limitations of our previous experience of the
world, this does not mean that we leave and negate our own world'
(406).[6] The experience of different world-views creates a fundamental
'contingency of all human thought concerning the world, and thus of
our own contingency' as well (406). He emphasizes that this consciousness of contingency is not presented in search of 'an absolute position'
but in search of living yet often contradictory relationships (406).

In the fourfold process that is consciousness, perception occupies an
intermediary position between language as energy and Gadamer's crucial notion of experience as event. He explains that the one unity of
the hermeneutical experience 'proceeds from various individual perceptions through the retention of many individuals' (314). It is true
that language 'precedes experience' but it does not do so immediately,
for the hermeneutical experience 'occupies a remarkably indeterminate
intermediate position between the many individual perceptions and
the true universality of the concept' (313, 314). An *order* and a *direction*
is, therefore, implicit in the process of consciousness.

Perception is not alone in this intermediary position between language and experience. It appears to share this level with the 'question.'
On the one hand, 'the linguistic nature of conversation,' or language,
forms 'the basis of the question' and on the other, 'we cannot have
experiences without asking questions' (341, 325). The question, like
perception, is of 'constitutive significance ... for the hermeneutical
phenomenon' (341). It will be of importance that perception and question lie between language and experience in the consideration of
Merleau-Ponty's theory. The fundamental similarity that emerges between the structure of perception and the structure of question can
help reveal the structure of narrative perspective.

Experience is undoubtedly the axis from which Gadamer considers consciousness. His notion of experience provides a counterbalance to positivistic knowledge. Both perception and questioning give way to an experience exposed to the effects of history. This experience has the character of the hermeneutical experience and the structure of a question. Experience in general is born of an event in which one plays a part yet over which one has no absolute control. It is an openness to further experience and leads to an awareness of both human finitude and reality. It forms an antithesis to positivistic knowledge. Because experience runs counter to our expectations it contains 'an essential element, a fundamental negativity that emerges in the relation between experience and insight [that is, self-knowledge]' (1975, 319). Experience is an essentially productive process that negates both previous and dogmatic opinion while giving way to a more comprehensive knowledge.

The hermeneutical experience in particular is concerned with tradition and its transmission (350). Tradition is the persistence in consciousness of a 'variety of voices in which the echo of the past is heard' (252). This persistence is the result of freely chosen acts of reason that affirm, cultivate, and share the 'multifariousness of such voices' (252–3). Tradition, then, is linguistic in character and 'is a genuine partner in communication, with which we have fellowship as does the "I" with the "Thou" ' (321). The character of the hermeneutical experience is outlined first negatively and then positively in terms of an *attitude* between the 'I' and the 'Thou' in dialogue. It is not characterized by a search for human nature in order to achieve control over another as a means to a subjective end. Such an 'I ← thou' relation, which directs the other towards the self, 'contradicts the moral definition of man' and, as will be noted later, the nature of perception of the other (322). Nor is it an attitude characterized by a search for historical consciousness. This is the structure that recognizes the 'thou' as a 'person' but still in 'a form of self-relatedness' (322). The 'I' in such cases claims to 'transcend its own conditionedness completely in its knowing of the other, it is involved in a false dialectical appearance, since it is actually seeking to master, as it were, the past' (323). The 'I ← thou' attitude and this 'I → Thou' attitude are displaced by an 'I ↔ Thou' attitude in which 'the important thing is, as we have seen, to experience the 'Thou' truly as a 'Thou', ie not to overlook his claim and to *listen* to what he has to say to us' (324); emphasis added). It is not the other that we listen to but rather what he has to say. In this way 'understanding does not at all understand the "Thou", but what the "Thou" truly says to us' and it is thus that Gadamer affirms. 'Being that can be understood is language' (xxiii, xxii). Unlike romantic hermeneutics, understanding is not based on getting 'inside another person' but rather on language as a 'middle ground in which understanding and agreement concerning the object takes place between two people' (345–6). Tradition, as the material of hermeneutical experience, is understood not as 'an expression of life of a "Thou", but as a meaningful content detached from all bonds of the meaning individual, of an "I" or a "Thou" ' (321).

The personal pronouns play an important role in Gadamer's characterization of experience. Its structure, however, is that of the question, which is implicit in each experience. Each question like each experience takes place within a context. The form of the question is that of 'a radical negativity: the knowledge of not knowing' (325). While the centre of the question is a radical negativity, a 'not knowing,' it is also the beginning of a search for an answer. In this question-answer dialectic it is 'of the essence of the question to have sense. Now sense involves direction,' as the question seeks an answer among many possibilities (326). Thus, around the not-knowing core lies an indeterminate state in which an openness to this and that direction, yes and no, exists. To ask a question is to first bring it into this openness and the 'sense of every question is realised in passing through this state of indeterminacy, in which it becomes an open question' (327). Around the state of indeterminacy lies the hermeneutical horizon of the question. Here the 'fluid indeterminacy of the direction in which [the question] is pointing is overcome by a specific alternative being presented' (327). Once the indeterminacy is overcome and a specific alternative is established, then 'the sense of the question [becomes] the direction in which alone the answer can be given if it is to be meaningful. A question places that which is questioned within a particular perspective' (326). The answer, in turn, reflects the question. The answer's 'sense lies in the sense of the question' because the 'sense of what is correct must be in accordance with the direction taken by a question' if a meaningful relation of question and answer is to be achieved (326, 327). An answer may lead to a reconstruction of the question, but in this event the direction of the question-and-answer process 'is, in fact, reversed' (337). It is the question that takes priority in Gadamer's hermeneutics. The reader's hermeneutic task is to carry out the dialectic of question and answer with a text. Behind the answer lies a dissolution of counter-arguments leading to knowledge and eventually to further questions lying behind the text.

The structure of the question, then, is composed of six intervals radiating from the standpoint of consciousness in tradition. The first period of not knowing forms a dialectic with a second moment of knowing one does not know. This trough and ridge, as it were, give way to a period of indeterminacy that is overcome by a fourth moment of determinacy in which a specific alternative is presented. The question is then concentrated into a fifth period in which a specific sense takes precedence over all others and is fully directed towards an answer. A sixth moment is achieved when the directed sense rises to find the question's answer. While the very possibility of an answer comes into being at the same moment as the question, it remains to be realized. Although the answer may resolve its question satisfactorily by overcoming counter-arguments it can, in turn, lead to further questions. The first three levels of this process, then, radiate from the centre of consciousness in all directions and the second three levels are committed to a specific direction that makes sense.

The question has a radical negativity at its core yet it does not proceed from an absolute vacuum nowhere. Each question proceeds from a standpoint in history and is affected by it. Gadamer refers to 'effective-history' as the effectivity of history within understanding itself' (267). A methodological consciousness can be achieved through the analysis of consciousness open to the effects of history. The crucial point of Gadamer's historically trained consciousness is that it helps decide what phenomenon will prompt further inquiry. If one tries 'to understand a historical phenomenon from the historical distance that is characteristic of our hermeneutical situation, we are always subject to the effects of effective-history. It determines in advance both what seems to us worth enquiring about and what will appear as an object of investigation, and we more or less forget half of what is really there' (1975, 267–8). Gadamer criticizes historical 'objectivism' that, while itself being subjected to historical conditions, claims a truth of fact that is not available to the finite nature of understanding. This objectivism 'resembles statistics, which are such excellent means of propaganda because they let facts speak and hence simulate an objectivity that in reality depends on the legitimacy of the question asked' (268). Consciousness that is subject to the effects of history strives to be aware of its own hermeneutical situation through a process of question and answer. An absolute consciousness of the effects of history is not possible because they 'are already operative in the choice of the right question to ask' (268).

Awareness of the effects of history in shaping a situation is a difficult achievement. It is nevertheless the responsibility of a disciplined mind to cultivate an awareness of the essential role played by the past in present situations. The task of reflection is the never-ending 'illumination' of this hermeneutical situation (269). A situation develops around a 'standpoint that limits the possibility of vision' (269). This standpoint, in turn, rests upon a historically given 'understanding' or 'substance,' used in an etymological sense. A standpoint finds the limit of its vision in a horizon, that is, 'the range of vision that includes everything that can be seen from a particular vantage point' (269). An 'expansion of horizon' is an achieved distance of vision that does not limit the observer to the immediacy of the substance underlying the standpoint (269). A narrow horizon is limited to what is close at hand and may cause an over-evaluation of its importance. Distance, then, is not necessarily a negative factor. It is essential to an adequate methodology. The awareness of an attentive mind works out a hermeneutical situation by achieving 'the right horizon of enquiry for the questions evoked by the encounter with tradition' (269). Coming to know another through conversation is very much an effort 'to discover his standpoint and his horizon' (270).

Gadamer does not limit his explanation of historical effects to spatial metaphors. A standpoint also has a temporal horizon of the the past, that is, a 'historical horizon out of which tradition speaks' (270). This horizon of the past is in constant movement because human life is not bound to one fixed standpoint. Understanding the past, like understanding another, involves placing oneself in the past's (or the other's) position in order to become aware of its individuality. In this way a new horizon is opened, revealing not only the other's individuality but one's own particularity as well.

Standpoint also includes a horizon of the present. This horizon involves a 'process of distinguishing' that makes one aware of both the otherness present and the 'prejudices that we bring with us' (272). These prejudices, which help constitute a present horizon, are not to be confused with rigid opinions, dogma, or fixed evaluations. They are the present functioning of an inherited tradition. These prejudices come under scrutiny and are continually tested as they ceaselessly form present horizons. An understanding of the past and the substance of tradition is a result of the fusion of, and the tension between, the present horizon and the horizon of the past. In this way every 'encounter with tradition that takes place within historical consciousness involves the experience of the tension between text and the present. The hermeneutic task consists in not covering up this tension by attempting a naive assimilation but consciously bringing it out' (273). Past horizon and present horizon, background and foreground reveal each other. Understanding implies projecting a historical horizon in order that it become a living part of one's horizon of the present. The task of hermeneutics is, then, to 'discover in all that is subjective the substantiality that determines it' (269). A hermeneutics exposed to the effects of history assumes responsibility for the role of the past in selecting the questions that structure present experience. It also responds for the present view of history as it tests the criteria and prejudices made apparent through the process of distinguishing the phenomena of our experience.

The final level in Gadamer's fourfold hierarchy consists of concept formation. A concept is the result of a dialectic that manages to see things in the unity of an aspect. As with dialogue it is 'the working out of common meaning ... the process of question and answer, giving and taking, talking at cross purposes and seeing each other's point' (331). This conversation takes place between individuals in the present and with texts from the past. In the dialogue with texts, 'that which is handed down in literary form is brought back out of the alienation in which it finds itself and into the living presence of conversation, whose fundamental procedure is always of question and answer' (331).

Four themes then, converge in Gadamer's concept of consciousness exposed to the effects of history. (Ricoeur 1981a, 74–5). First, the notion of *distance* as historical distance is not to be seen only in problematic terms. It is a necessary methodological attitude more than a disruptive break with the past. Distance does not put an end to our collusion with the past but mediates present and past. Second, historically efficacy is a concept that belongs to an ontology of *finitude*, for there is no 'overview' from which the totality of effects can be grasped at once. Third, while there can be no absolute knowledge, there is no standpoint in history that is absolutely restricted either. Each situation has a *horizon* that is organized into near and far and that may contract or expand. Finally, while a previous historical standpoint can be occupied, this cannot be achieved completely because one cannot leave behind or negate completely one's own historically formed attitude to the world. As Paul Ricoeur puts it, the *fusion of horizons* is brought about by 'restoring the dialectic of points of view and the tension between the other and the self' (1981a, 75).

Gadamer's philosophy of language as the horizon of an understanding of Being, and specifically this concept of consciousness exposed to the effects of history, is invaluable for the study of literary texts. It is important that while the notions of standpoint, horizon, overview, point of view, perspective, perception, and substance are freely used throughout his major work *Truth and Method*, little attention is given to the process of perception itself. This is surprising, for not only does perception embrace these frequently used notions, it also constitutes the essential mediation between language and experience. This lack of a fully developed notion of the nature and function of perception itself may lead to confusion concerning the modes of perception in the hermeneutical process. The notion of standpoint and horizon points to the concept of ' "point of view" which grounds why we see a thing in one way and not in another, a concept from optics' (Gadamer 1975, 160–1). It is this notion of standpoint and horizon that has recently played an important role in the literary theory concerned with the act of reading and an optical focus is often used to help understand the relation between the present (as self) and the past (as text) (Iser 1978a). Nevertheless, when Gadamer accounts for that particular dialectic through which the essential idea of a 'belongingness' between subject and object is achieved, then the 'optical' focus is left behind in favour of the 'ancient insight into the priority of hearing over sight' and

we must take account of the particular dialectic that is contained in hearing. It is not just that he who hears is also addressed, but there is also the element that he who is addressed must hear, whether he wants to or not. When you look at something, you can also look away from it, by looking in another direction, but you cannot 'hear away'. This difference between seeing and hearing is important for us because the primacy of hearing is the basis of the hermeneutical phenomenon, as Aristotle saw. There is nothing that is not available to hearing through the medium of language (1975, 419–20)

By giving hearing priority in the hermeneutical situation Gadamer distinguishes it from the other senses. They 'have no immediate share in the universality of the linguistic experience of the world, but only offer the key to their own specific fields' (1975, 420). Hearing is not understood only in terms of an awareness of external phenomena. It is also the sense through which one listens to the voice of tradition as it speaks to us from the past. Hearing plays a key role in tradition for it helps mediate a text's past origins and present functions, its past significance and present meaning (Weimann 1976, 18–51, 89–145). This role of hearing is vital to language, experience, and literature: 'The language in which hearing shares is not only universal in the sense that everything can be expressed in it. The significance of the hermeneutical experience is rather that, in contrast with all other experience of the world, language opens up a completely new dimension, the profound dimension whence tradition comes down to those now living. This has always been the true essence of hearing, even before the invention of writing, that the hearer may listen to the legends, the myths and the truth of the ancients' (Gadamer 1975, 420).

Renewed questions can, of course, be found behind the answers proposed by Gadamer's notion of consciousness. If the 'truth of tradition is like the present that lies immediately open to the senses,' what is the role of the senses in the perception of hermeneutical phenomena and specifically of the literary text? (1975, 420). If point of view involves 'seeing' a narrative world from a certain standpoint, what does the reader 'hear' in this standpoint? What are the consequences of a hearing and seeing dialectic, and from what standpoint can it be examined? If the optical model of standpoint and horizon is used to outline the past and present relationship, is an auditive model more adequate in coming to terms with contemporary hermeneutical phenomena? Does Gadamer privilege difference with the present and similarity with the past? Do the different modes of literary transmission, oral or written, have an 'effect' on the 'impact' of literature through perspective, which is bound up in perception?[7] The present formation and opening of new questions is but a limited indication of the potential that Gadamer's notion of consciousness presents. As long as narrative perspective is understood as point of view, justice will not be done to the voice speaking from a tradition to the reader listening in a tradition. It will be equally impossible to project the historical understanding or substance from which proceeds the reader's vital questioning of the text. As long as narrative perspective is understood only as a voice representing a traditional or ideological position, justice will not be done to the textual strategies that help constitute its standpoint and horizon and contribute to the eventual fusion of horizons in the present experience of the text. What appears to be called for, then, is a co-ordination of both point of view and voice, which together give rise to the experience of a narrative world.

2

Perception of Language: Maurice Merleau-Ponty and the Phenomenology of Perception

It is clear from the outset that sense, attitude, and direction play a fundamental role in human consciousness. This role can be seen at all three levels of Gadamer's investigation: structure, character, and situation. He is not concerned with a dichotomy but with a dialectic involving three moments and three interrelated notions. First, at the level of structure, the sense of a question points to an answer. Second, an answer's sense reveals its question. Third, if the relation between a question and answer is to be valid, it must achieve a sense of reciprocity between the two terms. Together, they must 'make sense.' At the level of character, Gadamer is not concerned with a dichotomy either. Here a dialectic of attitudes mediates first and second person. A search for subjective control of human nature through knowledge is surpassed by a search for objectivity through a form of self-relatedness. These two attitudes, then, give way to a reciprocal attitude in which belonging 'together always also means being able to listen to one another' (1975, 324). This essential, mediative dimension is related to the physical sense of hearing and to the spiritual sense that listens to a traditional substance. At the level of situation, Gadamer is not concerned with a dichotomy of standpoint and horizon but with a dialectic of directed awareness. First, the voice of tradition underlying a standpoint helps direct the observer's gaze and helps establish what will or will not be realized within a field of vision. It is by first understanding the voice of tradition that one can then explain what is seen in a situation. Second, what is distinguished as a foreground against the background of a horizon in turn directs the observer's awareness to his or her own traditional point of view. Finally, the bilateral awareness of an attentive mind comprehends the relation between a tradition and a present situation. Sense, attitude, and direction, then, come together as a mediative principle that can be fully appreciated within that dimension mediating language and experience: perception itself.

Being as Perceiving

Philosophy, says Maurice Merleau-Ponty, 'is not a "higher point of view" from which one embraces all local perspectives. It seeks contact with brute being ... [by plunging] into the perceptible, into time and history toward their articulations.'[1] This philosophy, which is 'the exact opposite of a ... God-like survey,' speaks not of 'being and nothingness' but rather of the 'visible and the invisible' (M.M-P. 1964c, 21, and 1964b, 71–82). It seeks to lay bare what the intellect perceives as a 'chiasma,' a bottomless 'abyss' from which the 'intertwining' of self and world emerges (1964c, 21). The notion of 'being,' for Merleau-Ponty, is not something unrestricted, 'self-identical and unquestioned,' nor does it face a 'zero in every respect,' a nothingness that annihilates (21). The invisible constitutes the outline and the depth of the visible and it is from the 'environs and edges,' around the 'void' that an 'opening out' into perception is developed (14, 20, 21).

His phenomenology of perception rejects a dichotomy in favour of a productive dialectic, and he also approaches his subject in terms of four different levels: a primary level of faith, a level of the senses, a level of experiencing the world, and a level of concepts. If Gadamer explains his point of departure in negative terms as a 'not knowing,' Merleau-Ponty moves to include a positive description of his first level by using metaphor. Here his metaphors bring together notions of 'art,' 'soul,' 'tradition,' and 'language.' At the core of perception, below the senses, lies a fundamental 'non' sense. This primary level is not Hegel's ' "hole in being" but a hollow, a fold,' in the texture of existence (M.M-P. 1962, 215). It is not speech but the silence from which speech emerges. It is an awareness, an experience prior to any subject/object opposition. It precedes even such basic dichotomies as birth/death:

Activity takes place on the periphery of my being. I am no more aware of being the true subject of my sensations than of my birth or my death. Neither my birth nor my death can appear to me as experiences of my own, since if I thought of them thus, I should be assuming myself to be pre-existent to, or outliving, myself, in order to be able to experience them, and I should therefore not be genuinely thinking of my birth or my death. I can, then, apprehend myself only as 'already born' and 'still alive' – I can apprehend my birth and my death only as prepersonal horizons ... Each sensation, being strictly speaking, the first, last and only one of its kind is a birth and a death. The subject who experiences it begins with and ends with it. (1962, 215–16)

This level of ' "primary faith," which binds us to a world as to our native land,' is similar to Gadamer's notion of language in that it has the character of tradition (M.M-P. 1962, 321). A 'tradition of perception' precedes any particular sense perception because the *person who* perceives ... has historical density, he takes up a perceptual tradition and is faced with a present' (1964c, 70, and 1962, 238). This tradition of perception is the material of 'an operative intentionality already at work before any positing or any judgement, a "Logos of the aesthetic world," an "art hidden in the depths of the human soul" ' (1962, 429). It is a spiritual centre that 'ratifies and renews in us a "prehistory" ' (240). Any 'personal existence must be the resumption of a prepersonal tradition' and this prepersonal existence, from which perception issues forth is 'always in the mode of the impersonal One' (254 and 240). This third, non-personal 'One,' appears similar to the standpoint in language from which Gadamer examines the attitudes (or directions) mediating a dialogue between 'I' and 'Thou.' What is more, perception also has the character of a dialogue in that 'the whole of nature is the setting of our own life, or our interlocutor in a sort of dialogue ... To this extent every perception is a communication or a communion' (320).

Although primary faith is bound to a tradition, it is not a passive core into which external sense data are poured. Perception is not an impingement on the senses by the outside world.[2] Merleau-Ponty states that 'underlying perception properly understood, there is, then, sustaining them a deeper function without which perceived objects would lack the distinctive sign of reality ... It is the momentum which carries us beyond subjectivity which gives us our place in the world prior to any science and any verification through a kind of "faith" or "primary opinion" ' (1962, 343). This 'momentum' appears similar to the 'energy' and 'power' of language of which Humboldt and Gadamer speak. The primary core is *directed* outward from an eternal 'Now' through the senses towards the world. This temporal quality is not an empirical succession of states. On the contrary, it is ' "timeless" (*zeitlose*) in the sense that it is not intratemporal. "In" my present, if I grasp it while it is still living and with all that it implies, there is an *ek-stase* towards the future and towards the past which reveals the dimensions of time not as conflicting, but as inseparable: to be now is to be from always and for ever.' (422).

This *ek-stase* or centrifugal 'direction' of existence is essential to Merleau-Ponty's phenomenology of perception 'since the perceived world is grasped only in terms of direction, [and therefore] we cannot dissociate being from orientated being [*sic*]' (1962, 253). It is this impulse of existence towards things that permits a differentiation between perception and representation on the one hand and illusion and hallucination on the other. While perception is temporal in character and is by nature in the present of its primary faith, representation is a drawing of the past and the future, 'former experience' and 'coming experience,' 'recollection' and 'imagination' into the present of primary awareness (424). The act of representation makes no claim to be anything but a recalling into the present. It is not to be confused with the historical event that is represented. Hallucination and illusion comprise precisely such a confusion. Hallucination is an event alienated from the world with no path to connect it to the world. It is divorced from the actual environment. While perception deals with the common-property world of intersubjective fact, hallucination involves an alienated, 'private world' as well as the disintegration of both sensory content and of the world (287, 334, 343). While perception is an 'opening upon the world,' hallucination is a closure to the world (297). In the case of illusion the whole perceptual and motor field endows an unreality with reality, for 'the nature of illusion is not to present itself as such' (295). Illusion makes possible a subsequent perception that crosses it out, makes it void, and corrects it. Illusion unlike hallucination is not a total closure. Thus, in 'the very moment of illusion this possibility of correction was presented ... Illusion too makes use of this belief in the world and is dependent upon it while contracting into a solid appearance, and because in this way, always being open upon a horizon of possible verifications, it does not cut [the perceiver] off from the truth' (297).

Hallucination, illusion, representation, and perception form a hierarchy, each level of which 'has the value of reality' (1962, 342). The character of each can be observed only from an experiential level. Merleau-Ponty clarifies that 'the difference between perception and dream not being an absolute, one is justified in counting them both among "our experiences," and it is above perception itself that we must seek the guarantee and the sense of its ontological function' (1968, 6). Hallucination is primarily a *reversal* of direction for it 'brings us back to the pre-logical bases of our knowledge' (1962, 334). In the case of hallucination the world takes precedence over the temporal quality of being and 'invades' being by directing it into itself. In his final works, Merleau-Ponty emphasizes that reversibility between self and world, between 'the seeing and the visible ... [is] a reversibility always imminent and never realized in fact' (1968, 147). In this way, the 'normal person does not find satisfaction in subjectivity, he runs away from it, he is genuinely concerned with being in the world and his hold on time is direct and unreflecting, whereas the sufferer from hallucinations simply exploits his being in the world in order to carve a private sector for himself out of the common property world, and constantly runs up against the transcendence of time' (1962, 342–3). Hallucination transgresses the momentum of perception as it reaches out to the world by running contrary to its temporal quality and into the primary level of faith. In faith there is no empirical proof. Perception is possible only because the 'flesh (of the world or my own) is not contingency, chaos, but texture that returns to itself and conforms to itself ... And finally [because] I believe it – I believe that I have a man's senses, a human body' (1968, 146). The victim of hallucination, says Merleau-Ponty, 'enjoys no such belief' (1962, 339). This second level of the senses, then, must be understood before the experience of time, space, and direction can be further developed.

Perceiving as Body

The organization of the world begins with the body and language (M.M-P. 1964c, 18, 19). Merleau-Ponty's notion of sense is primarily concerned with the former, yet his intertwining of body and language is synonymous with that of perception and world: 'Every external perception is immediately synonymous with a certain perception of my body just as every perception of my body is made explicit in the language of external perception' (1962, 206). Language is not considered in abstract terms but as realized speech. Speech is explained using the same metaphor as that used for 'primary faith.' It is 'always only a *fold* in the immense fabric of language' (1964c, 42; emphasis added). Language, body, and culture are interpenetrating:

It is my body which gives significance not only to the natural object, but also to cultural objects like words. If a word is shown to a subject for too short a time for him to be able to read it, the word 'warm,' for example, induces a kind of experience of warmth which surrounds him with something in the nature of a meaningful halo. The word 'hard' produces a sort of stiffening of the back and the neck, and only in a secondary way does it project itself into the visual or auditory field and assume the appearance of a sign or a word. Before becoming the indication of a concept it is first of all an event which grips my body, and this grip circumscribes the area of significance to which it has reference ... The word is then indistinguishable from the attitude which it induces. (1962, 235)[3]

If the theory of the body is already a theory of perception, it is so because on this second level of sense, external 'perception and the perception of one's own body vary in conjunction ... they are the two facets of one and the same act' (1962, 205). The body is 'at once phenomenal body and objective body ... [that is], the body as sensible and the body as sentient ... a being of two leaves ... belonging to the order of the "object" and to the order of the "subject" ' (1968, 136–7). Again, there is something distinctly metaphoric in Merleau-Ponty's theory. The body is Subject and again it is not. It is Object and again it is not. What is more, Merleau-Ponty insists that the body is not to be compared 'to a physical object, but rather to a work of art' (1962, 150). Works of art such as 'a novel, poem, picture or musical work are individuals, that is, beings in which the expression is indistinguishable from the thing expressed, their meaning, accessible only through direct contact, being radiated with no change of their temporal and spatial situation' (151–2). The continuity of its temporal and spatial arrangement is what permits a work of art to be recognized as one and the same throughout its changing historical context. The continuity of temporal and spatial situation is in the same way provided by the here and now dimension of the body. It is this radiated continuity which gives the text priority over its changing context just as it is the continuous now and here of experience that takes priority over memory of the past and expectation for the future. This continuity is the very unity of the body that permits the unity of an object to be grasped. It is the fixed point, 'an absolute "here" ' from which Space is made possible (247). As the introduction to *Sense and Non-sense* points out, the body 'set-to-explore' is 'precisely that organizing activity which has been called "ex-istence" ' (xii).

The senses begin on the outer border of the negative 'non-sense' of primary faith. It is on this horizon of natural perception that the positive elements of time, tradition, and the momentum of reaching out to the world can be sensed. Natural perception is achieved 'with our whole body all at once, and ... opens on a world of inter-acting senses' (1962, 225). Beyond this horizon lies the field of sensation where the unity of senses is broken, yet where each individual sense lies in synaesthetic communication with the others. Here 'synaesthetic perception is the rule,' not the exception (229).[4] This sensible quality is 'an attitude of curiosity or observation ... a certain kind of *questioning*' (226; emphasis added). It is within this field that 'perception brings together our sensory experiences into a single world, [however] it does not do so in the way that a scientific colligation gathers together objects or phenomena, but in the way that binocular vision grasps one sole object' (230). The horizon of the perceptual field marks both the limit of sensations and the temporal horizon on the one hand and the primordial level of space on the other. At this horizon the interchange and communication between the senses begin to concentrate into a 'highly particularized attitude' (225). Here 'the body, when it escapes from dispersion, pulls itself together and tends by all means in its power toward one single goal of its activity, and when one single intention is formed in it through the phenomenon of synergy' (225, 232). This synergy or combined, cooperative action of all the senses breaks through the indeterminate level of synaesthesia. The eyes' convergence on an object is a prospective activity in that the object is anticipated in the very act of looking. This aim of a *sense* must be understood in a way that is not readily available through the English lexical term, but through the French *sens* or the Spanish *sentido*: 'In all uses of the word *sens*, we find the ... notion of a being orientated or polarized in the direction of what he is not and thus we are always brought back to a conception of the subject as *ek-stase*, and to a relationship of active transcendence between the subject and the world,' (430). Sense and direction are interchangeable in Merleau-Ponty's use of *sens*. This synergy or directed concentration of the senses towards a goal runs contrary to the reflective or speculative focusing of space as developed in figure 1 on page 27 below. Here it proceeds from a pre-personal selection, not from analytic thought; from a question within, not without.

The senses, in that they tend towards and meet the world, are spatial. Each sense, when it contacts the world, forms 'concrete "moments" of a comprehensive configuration' that is space (222). This unity of space, like the unity of objects within it, is experienced as 'the correlate of our body's unity' (204). The notions of Space, direction, and position cannot be divorced from the sense one makes of the world.

Space

When Merleau-Ponty states that the essence of space is 'to be always "already constituted," ' its more objective quality is made evident (1962, 252). Existence is spatial in that 'through an inner necessity it opens on to an "outside" ' (293). Although space always precedes itself it is not a prearranged setting. It is rather 'the means whereby the position of things becomes possible' through the relationships admitted between objects (243, 280). In this way Merleau-Ponty can affirm that 'spatial perception is a structural phenomenon' involving the body anchored in a world and 'gearing' onto its world (280, 251). Three principles are essential to perceived space: (1) being, which is synonymous with being situated, constitutes an 'actual starting-point, an absolute "here" '; (2) an object in the relationships of the perceptual field is 'not conceived' unless elaborated or traced as a figure against a background, and (3) while 'no direction' is 'no space,' spatial direction cannot be gleaned from the synaesthetic, 'labyrinthine' mosaic of sensation that is the body (247, 277, 249). Direction emerges with a body in action: 'What counts for the orientation of the spectacle is not my body as it in fact is, as a thing in objective space, but as a system of possible actions, a virtual body with its phenomenal 'place' defined by its task and situation. My body is wherever there is something to be done' (249). A virtual body or system of possible actions is projected into space by the anchored actual body. Perceived space is made available when direction is established. The latter comes about when 'my actual body is at one with the virtual body required by the spectacle, and the actual spectacle with the setting which my body throws round it' (250). A situation is bound up with action. 'By action,' says Merleau-Ponty, 'I make myself responsible for everything' (1964c, 72).

The two elements of a situation are motive and decision. Motive looks back in time to an antecedent while decision looks forward in time to the completion of an undertaking. Space 'itself' without the presence of a perceiver has 'no direction, no inside and no outside' (1962, 204). Motion, as opposed to action, is the 'modulation of an already familiar setting,' yet this setting itself presupposes a background or field against which a certain entity is selected as mobile, that is, as a 'figure' (275). Movement, then, does not exist between objects alone but rather what 'makes part of the field count as an object in motion, and another as the background is the way in which we establish our relations with them by the act of looking' (278).

Depth, size-distance, scope, and focus give the dimensions of space. It is from direct experience that these dimensions emerge. Depth is the 'most "existential" of all dimensions because ... it belongs to the perspective and not to things' (1962, 256). It is the distance along the axis of the perceiving subject and the thing selected from a background to be perceived. It precedes both breadth and height. Depth constitutes an intersection from which both time and space proceed. For Merleau-Ponty, the relation between the depth of being (understood metaphorically as a fold or hollow in the world) and the body is a relationship of question and answer. Depth and body, not knowing and knowing one does not know, both have the same trough and crest structure of 'waves' of being. Thus, the body is 'that which answers each time to the question "Where am I and what time is it?"' (1970, 51). The question proceeds from the not-knowing centre. Depth is the hub of time and space and is so only in a lived present that holds a past and a future within itself: 'Things co-exist in space because they are *present* to the same perceiving subject and enveloped in one and the same temporal wave. But the unity and individuality of each temporal wave is possible only if it is wedged in between the preceding and the following one, and if the same temporal pulsation which produces it still retains its predecessor and anticipates its successor' (1962, 275). Depth's retention and anticipation become important factors in the point-horizon structure of perspective.

The size of an object, that is, its breadth and height, might appear at first sight to be a primary relationship between things. This relationship, however, already presupposes the same selection of a figure against a field carried out in depth. Depth is a 'contraction into one perceptual act of a whole possible process ... It is the dimension in which things or elements of things envelop each other, whereas breadth and height are the dimensions in which they are juxtaposed' (1962, 264–5). The distance between an object with height, breadth, and depth and a perceiving subject is experienced as increasing when 'the thing is beginning to slip away from the grip of our gaze and is less closely allied to it' (261). Distance is 'the situation of the object in relation to our power of grasping it' (261). Thus proximity is a complete grip or hold on an object. Size and distance are two features 'of a comprehensive organization of the field' (259). Distance and size appear to hold a cause-effect relationship between them, yet this in itself is 'nothing other than a way of expressing our vision of depth' (259). Depth is 'born beneath [the] gaze' as a directed purpose or intention that brings monocular, disparate images into a stereoscopic unit (262). Distance and size emerge from the organization of dispersed elements into one whole, and give a 'lived distance' that 'measures the "scope" of my life at every moment' (286).

Scope is closely related to depth in that it also helps sustain time and perception against both the onslaught of hallucination and the disintegration of space. When scope is lost the body loses its capacity to bring together distanced objects into a consistent whole. It becomes 'atomized or dislocated' (1962, 282). This occurs when the body 'has ceased to draw together all objects in its one grip; and this debasement of the body into an organism must itself be attributed to the collapse of time, which no longer rises towards a future but falls back on itself' (283).

Depth, which allows for a 'perceptual faith' in a single thing, emerges when being 'tries to see *something*' and the thing is seen in its unity (262). The unity and organization of depth perception can be destroyed by the ambiguity of paradox. When faced with a paradox, being does not grasp the thing seen in the unity of depth, but grasps it through a speculative gaze. This gaze involves reflective focusing. Focusing is 'indicated or recommended by phenomena' (263). The figure presents the question and the subject's speculative focus is the reply. This spatial focusing runs against the senses back towards the non-sense. It is fundamentally a reversal in direction that challenges the escape from dispersion achieved by the phenomenon of synergy. In the case of this spatial focusing, 'my act is not primary or constituting, but called forth ... Every focus is always a focus on something which presents itself as to be focused upon. When I focus upon the face ABCD of the cube, that does not only mean that I bring it to the state of being clearly visible, but also that I make it count as a figure and as nearer to me than the other face [EFGH]; in a word I organize the cube, and the gaze is that perceptual genius underlying the thinking subject which can give to things the precise reply that they are awaiting in order to exist before us' (1962, 264, 263).

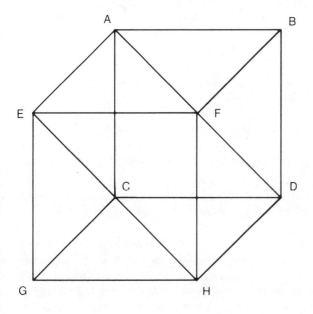

Figure 1

This phenomenon of disintegration cannot be grasped as one single figure except by consciously centring the gaze. One must look at nothing, in no particular direction, and permit a mosaic to emerge if a whole is to be achieved. The gaze of a 'thinking subject,' and the 'mental inspection' involved in this divergent act of focusing runs up against the 'grasp' of depth perception (1962, 264).

Merleau-Ponty emphasizes that all the senses are spatial. Nevertheless, it is beyond the synaesthetic level of intersensory communication, that is, in the spatial level, that vision comes into its own. The 'difference ... between seeing and hearing' is a tacit distinction that he does not fully develop (1962, 213). Direction is essential to all senses yet hearing lacks the precision of sight in determining spatial direction. He points out that a change of 'direction in acoustic phenomena is extremely difficult to bring about' (251n). The reversal of focus is, therefore, more readily available to the sense of sight as it functions in space (251n). Hearing can give space a sense of depth but cannot function with the same precision. The world of space is an objective 'world of silence' (1968, 145). The audio-oral system is more subjective because it is 'bound to the mass of my own life as is the voice of no one else' (144). The eye, understood in Rilke's words, is 'la fenêtre de l'âme' that opens to space: 'Le "quale visuel" me donne et me donne seul la présence de ce qui n'est pas moi, de ce qui est simplement et pleinement. Il le fait parce que, comme texture, il est la concrétion d'une universelle visibilité, d'un unique Espace qui sépare et qui réunit, qui soutient toute cohésion' (M.M-P. 1964a, 84–5). The direction of hearing and sound seems, by nature, to be centred either around the subject or as radiating from a vibrating source. The diaeretic or divergent phe- nomenon of a 'gaze,' focusing on a single thing that points paradoxi- cally in either one direction or another successively, can be more easily associated with the sense of sight and space than with the other senses. As Merleau-Ponty notes, 'renverser un objet c'est lui ôter sa signifi- cation. Son être d'objet ... [est] un être-pour-le-regard qui le rencontre sous un certain biais et ne le reconnaît pas autrement' (1945, 292). Of all the spatial dimensions, visual focusing appears to point towards an axis of contiguity where the juxtaposition of different directions is more easily realized. This contiguity of things in the world, accessible through vision, comes together in a relationship of causality: 'In the world there is the thing itself and outside this thing itself there is that other thing which is only reflected light rays and which happens to have an ordered correspondence with the real thing; there are two individuals, then, bound together externally by causality' (M.M-P. quoted in Schmidt, 97).

This reversal in the question-answer dialectic stems from the more objective 'otherness' of space's 'centripetal' or 'concrete movement.'[5] As noted by James Schmidt, vision is for Merleau-Ponty 'a process of interpretation, a process of reflection and judgement' rather than initial awareness (91–3). It is related to grasping things as in Hegel's divergent expression: 'an sich oder für uns' (M.M-P. 1968, 199). Here Merleau- Ponty's 'chiasm' does not open to an 'intertwining' but rather the intertwining of seen and seer looks back upon and through itself (130– 55). It is 'this reversal,' therefore, that brings to light the 'fundamental narcissism of all vision' (199, 139).

To this point, space has been considered in its dimensions of depth, size-distance, scope, and focus. These dimensions constitute 'geo- metrical space' (M.M-P. 1962, 292). Geometrical space is accompanied by a 'mythical space' that appears to lie between the two extremes of the hallucination, illusion, representation, and perception hierarchy

(292). Again Merleau-Ponty underscores the notion that 'insanity and perception,' 'dream-like' and 'mythical' consciousness 'are not small islands of experience cut off from each other, and from which there is no escape ... Mythical consciousness does indeed open on to a horizon of possible objectifications' (292). As with geometric space, the 'mythical world' is constituted by a relationship between things: 'The myth itself, however diffuse, has an identifiable significance ... simply because it does form a world, that is, a whole in which each element has meaningful relations with the rest' (292). Mythical space is 'a projection of existence and an expression of the human condition' (292–3). Myths function in two directions simultaneously. Subjectively, they 'function in arriving at awareness' and through a more reflective objectivity, they base 'their own significance on the significance they have for the philosopher' (293).

Both mythical space and geometric space come together in a 'space directly experienced' (1962, 291). In both cases, depth remains the most existential of all spatial dimensions. Unlike focus, depth provides a perspective that does not posit the multiplicity 'made explicit by analysis' (265). A depth perspective understands multiplicity in terms of stability and vice versa. This dialectic in space of stability and multiplicity, of constancy and variance, of concordance and discordance can be grasped 'if we understand it as temporal ... [because] co-existence, which in fact defines space, is not alien to time, but is the fact of two phenomena belonging to the same temporal wave' (265).

The relationship obtained between the characteristics of this process of spatial perception are summarized by Merleau-Ponty:

And there are determinate shapes like 'a square' or 'a diamond shape,' or any actual spatial configuration, because our body as a point of view upon things, and things as abstract elements of one single world, form a system in which each moment is immediately expressive of every other. A certain way of directing my gaze in relation to the object signifies a certain appearance of the object and neighbouring objects. In all its appearances the object retains invariable characteristics, remains itself invariable and is an object because all the possible values in relation to size and shape which it can assume are bound up in advance in the formula of its relations with the context. What we are affirming in the specific being of the object, is in reality a *facies totius universi* which remains unchanged. (1962, 301)

It is then, an integrated, deep perspective that constitutes the hub of space and time in perception and it is now time itself that must be understood.

Time

One of Merleau-Ponty's best descriptions of time, according to Samuel Mallin, is that it is the 'thrust' or 'the power that holds events together by distancing them from one another' (96). This distancing-assimilation, this thrust of energy is nothing less than 'that "body of the spirit" Valéry used to talk about' (1964c, 15). If space leans towards objectivity and otherness, 'subjectivity, at the level of perception, is nothing but temporality, and this is what enables us to leave to the subject of perception his opacity and historicity' (1962, 239). Subjectivity for Merleau-Ponty 'is not motionless identity with itself; as with time it is of its essence, in order to be genuine subjectivity, to open itself to an Other and to go forth from itself' (426). Thus, direction is again of the essence to perception and again, as with primary faith, it is towards the world that it makes sense. If space consists of the relationships possible between things, time 'arises from *my* relation to things' (412). If the concrete movement of space is centripetal, time's centrifugal 'flight out of the Itself … [is], as Heidegger says, an *ek-stase*' (419).

The structure of this centrifugal movement is that of a 'rhythmic cycle' for time 'restarts itself' (1962, 423). As a centrifugal movement it tends outward, in the form of a 'fold' and an 'upsurge' creating a wave (428, 265). The centre of time is an ever-present 'Now.' Although the past and future exist only in the present, it is their distancing from the present that sustains the very notion of subjectivity. They withdraw 'of their own accord from being' and although mediated by the present, this past-future dichotomy 'present in the world' comes into a dialectic relationship with the present (412). Thus temporalization is not a series of discrete 'nows,' nor does it reach out to the world in a series of discrete moments. Temporality 'temporalizes itself as future-which-lapses-into-the-past-by-coming-into-the-present' (420).

If time is for Merleau-Ponty 'the body of the spirit,' then the 'living use of language' is nothing less than the 'voice of [this] spirit' (1964c, 77). This relation between time and speech is also found on the structural level. While time is an 'upsurge' in being, speech is a 'fold in the immense fabric of language' (42). This fabric of language is itself 'more like a sort of being than a means' (43). Time and language come together in speech as dialogue. Phenomenological philosophy, which estab-

lishes itself in 'the order of instructive spontaneity,' is revealed best
by the phenomenology of speech:

When I speak or understand, I experience that presence of others in myself
or of myself in others which is the stumbling-block of the theory of intersubjectivity, I experience that presence of what is represented which is the stumbling-block of the theory of time, and I finally understand what is meant by
Husserl's enigmatic statement, 'Transcendental subjectivity is intersubjectivity.' ... Now it is at the heart of my present that I find the meaning of those
presents which preceded it, and that I find the means of understanding others'
presence at the same world; and it is in the actual practice of speaking that I
learn to understand. (97)

This intertwining of speech, understanding, time, and spirit becomes
a pole within a dialectic of *l'oeil* and *l'esprit*. If space, as a more objective
pole, appears to give priority to the senses of sight and touch, then
time, as subjectivity, is entangled with speech, intersubjective dialogue, understanding, and voice. Two major perspectives emerge as
modes of world formation: the visual and the audio-oral. The former
appears as a more 'objective' and the latter as a more subjective pole.
The subjectivity of the voice is not located anywhere in space: 'Among
my movements, there are some that go nowhere ... these are the facial
movements, many gestures, and especially those strange movements
of the throat and mouth that form the cry and the voice ... I am a
sonorous being, but I hear my own vibration from within' (M.M-P.
1968, 144). It is through subjectivity that the most intimate link between
voice and time is established. The voice as speech is inseparable from
both thought and dialogue. As the consciousness of the body 'immediately signifies a certain landscape about me,' so speech reverses 'my
ordinary relationship to objects,' giving certain ones 'the value of
subjects' in a dialogue (1964c, 89, 94). Through the intersubjectivity of
language, ideas are 'emancipated but not freed' for they come to live
only in other 'horizon structures' of language (1968, 153). In the same
way, the combined action of the senses breaks out of dispersion and
concentrates into one directed sense that reaches out to the world so
all of language concentrates and breaks forth into speech that reaches
out to another. In other words, speech is to language as the synergetic
concentration of sense is to perception. It is that 'moment when the
significative intention (still silent and wholly in act) proves itself capable
of incorporating itself into my culture and the culture of others – of

shaping me and others by transforming the meaning of cultural instruments' (1964c, 92).

The spiritual nature of language is also a locus of truth in time. Truth
occurs when 'an inner communication is established in the density of
personal and interpersonal time through which our present becomes
the *truth* of all other knowing events' (1964c, 96). It is 'like a wedge
we drive into the present' that comes to be when 'an experience has
been transformed into its meaning' (96). Truth is driven into the present
but the 'wedge' also opens to a resounding past because truth 'is another name for sedimentation' and sedimentation, in turn, is 'a single
view' founded on a 'personal and interpersonal tradition' that enables
the speaking subject 'to think farther' (96, 92).

The present is privileged by Merleau-Ponty not only because it is
when being and consciousness coincide but also because it mediates
past and future. Former experience is 'recollected' or gathered together
by memory and then brought into the present anew or 'represented.'
Coming experience can be made present through imagination. Both
representation of the past and imagining the future presuppose a 'recognition' in the present of what is already potential and latent in one's
primary level of faith and one's tradition (1962, 413). Neither representation nor imagination can be understood 'unless [one has] a sort
of direct contact with the past in its own domain' (413). Merleau-Ponty
appears to give the past priority over the future by stating that 'the
future has not even been in existence and cannot, like the past, set its
mark upon us' (413–14). Imagining the future does not take place in
some situation ahead of the present but rather somewhere between
the present and the past because looking ahead into the future is in
reality a 'retrospection, and the future a projection of the past' (414).

The past and the future exist, then, only 'when a subjectivity is there
to disrupt the plenitude of being in itself, to adumbrate a perspective,
and introduce a non-being into it' (1962, 421). Merleau-Ponty's notion
of temporality disregards both the realist perspective and the idealist
perspective of past, present, and future worlds. The question of a deep
understanding through a perspective rooted in the present is formulated as 'the relation between *meaning* and the *absence of meaning*,' between 'non-sense and sense' (428, 430). Significance is much like scope.
It comes into being both when an intention is fulfilled and 'conversely,
when a number of facts or signs lend themselves to our taking them
up and grasping them inclusively, or, at all events, when one or more
terms exist *as* ... [sic] representative or expressive of something other

than themselves' (428). This metaphoric and unifying quality of meaning and significance is possible only through a perspective: 'We have
no way of knowing what a picture or a thing is other than by looking
at them, and their *significance* is revealed only if we look at them from
a certain point of view, from a certain distance and in a certain *direction*
[*sens*], in short only if we place, at the service of the spectacle, our
collusion with the world ... The meaning of a sentence is its import or
intention, which once more presupposes a departure and arrival point,
an aim and a point of view' (429–30). The notion of meaning and
understanding are thus wrapped up with time (430). In this way time,
sens, meaning, and perspective are intertwined along with speech and
voice in subjectivity.

This fundamental notion of *sens* as a polarization away from the self
and towards the world is prevalent in Merleau-Ponty's major early
work *Phenomenology of Perception*. His final work *L'Oeil et l'Esprit* and
his posthumous *The Visible and the Invisible* explore this notion of direction, which is so essential to the emergence of understanding, in a
different manner. Rather than moving through *sens* to the world, he
reverses the direction of his inquiry. He introduces a mirror, as it were,
and proceeds to explain the invisible world of non-sense from the
visible world of sense. This possibility of reversal is explored first and
foremost through the sense of sight and the world of the painter: 'Entre
[le peintre] et le visible, les rôles inévitablement s'inversent. C'est pour-
quoi tant de peintres ont dit que les choses les regardent ... Ce qu'on
appelle inspiration devrait être pris à la lettre: il y a vraiment inspiration
et expiration de l'Etre, respiration dans l'Etre, action et passion si peu
discernables qu'on ne sait plus qui voit et qui est vu, qui peint et qui
est peint' (1964a, 31-2). This entry into the 'not knowing,' from the
sense into the non-sense is explored first and foremost through a reversal in sight's direction. In Merleau-Ponty's final notes and articles,
however, this 'new reversibility' is extended from sight to include sound
as well (1968, 144). His chapter 'The Intertwining – The Chiasm' marks
a clear move in this direction: 'As there is a reflexivity of the touch, of
sight and of the touch-vision system, there is a reflexivity of the movements of phonation and of hearing; they have their sonorous inscription, the vociferations have in me their motor echo' (144). Through
reflexivity the audio-oral system becomes a type of inscription. This
more subjective audio-oral dimension of reversibility makes discourse
itself an important medium of 'self' knowledge. The three dimensions
of spoken language – that is, voice, audience, and world – also witness

an 'echo coming from everywhere [which] makes it such that in speaking to others we also speak to ourselves, and speak of what exists' (1964c, 20). Reversibility rebounds back along the process of perception into the depths of a 'non-sense' core of being. The rebound does not begin with a first-hand experience of the world, although it does presuppose this experience. It begins in knowing, in thought, in what is described by the full semantic value of the term *reflection*. The reversal in direction back towards the centre of the self, in order to know it, begins with what Merleau-Ponty calls 'that *I think*, that must be able to accompany all our experiences ... [as we proceed] toward the center ... seeking to comprehend how there is a center' (1968, 145). The moment of reflection is a reversal parting from the concept of 'laws' and 'forces' that can explain perception in terms of cause and effect (149). 'Literature, music and the passions,' says Merleau-Ponty, become instruments in 'the *exploration* of an invisible and the disclosure of a universe of ideas' (149; emphasis added). The cause and effect relations established by a structural exploration are not, however, the source of meaning in discourse: 'If my words have meaning, it is not *because* they present the systematic organization the linguist will disclose, it is because that organization, like the look, refers back to itself: the operative Word is the obscure region whence comes the instituted light' (154).

When the process of perception bounces back upon itself and 'reflects' upon the representation of literature through some notion of laws, it would follow that the illusion of an 'objective' standpoint is achieved. A reversal in the perception-hallucination hierarchy is therefore also implied. An 'objective' comprehension born in reflection, thought, and ideas is an illusion because man cannot, in fact, begin outside of himself. Man cannot approach his central or primary level of faith from a standpoint outside of himself. The reflection in a mirror is, in fact, not a standpoint but an illusion. Once again Merleau-Ponty warns that 'reversibility [is] always imminent and never realized in fact' (1968, 147).

If living language returns to the self as an *echo* then the structure of reversibility must be similar to the concave or parabolic walls of a cave. The central 'fold,' 'wedge,' or 'obscure region' of the 'operative Word' into which reflective thought peers is outlined in terms of the same concave form. When dealing with this primary level of faith Merleau-Ponty leaves behind the reflective language of structural analysis. In this primary centre, metaphor replaces cause-and-effect explanation. Once again it is important to note that he describes this deep level in terms much the same as Gadamer's radical negativity, that is, as a 'negativity that is not nothing,' but he also adds a positive aspect to his description (1968, 151). Metaphor at this central point becomes an important heuristic device. In positive terms it is 'a furrow that traces itself out magically under our eyes without a tracer, a certain hollow, a certain interior' (151). As Merleau-Ponty proceeds 'toward the centre,' the direction moves into the 'pyramid of time which has been me' (1964c, 14) into 'the leaves' (1968, 131), into the 'temporal wave ... wedged in between the preceding and the following one' (1962, 275) and into 'the wedge we drive into the present,' which is truth itself (1964c, 96). It is from within this wedge, or 'vault of language,' that meaning reverberates when non-sense emerges into sense (20).

If significance and meaning emerge from the opening of non-sense into sense, *signification* is 'what comes to seal, to close' the 'retrograde' movement of reversibility (1968, 154). This reversibility of perception does not open itself to the interpersonal meaning and understanding of significance. These are realized through dialogue with others. Much like paradox, reversibility is a reflection that looks back on and listens to the self, not others. While it presupposes a reaching out to the world, it forms a backwash along the same wave into subjectivity, into isolation, in order to explore '[how] it sees itself and hears itself' (155). Much like the notion of spatial focusing seen in figure 1 on page 27 above, reversibility gives sight priority and juxtaposes two divergent or diaeretic phenomena that can be mediated only by a forced centring of the gaze on a mosaic. The reversibility of sense and non-sense is ultimately mediated by the stable unity of the body in existence itself. Here 'there is no dialectical reversal from one of these views to the other; we do not have to reassemble them into a synthesis' (155). Thus, for Merleau-Ponty it is incorrect to affirm 'that *everything has a significance* or that *everything is nonsense*, but only that *there is significance*' (1962, 296). The duality of reaching out to the world and reversibility does not invoke an 'either-or' dilemma characteristic of spatial dichotomies. It is a 'both-and' duality of time and space, voice and vision. Vision, nevertheless, has the advantage in the reflective phenomenon of reversibility. Vision is the sense Merleau-Ponty chooses to set at a *distance* in order to reflect on one's self. Voice tends towards interpersonal communication and the *assimilation* of others through dialogue. The difference is one of degree, not exclusion: 'Already our existence as seers (that is, we said, as beings who turn the world back upon itself and who pass over to the other side ...) and especially our existence as sonorous beings for others and for ourselves contain everything required for there to be speech from the one to the other, speech about the world. And, in a sense, to understand a phrase is nothing else than to welcome it in its sonorous being' (1968, 155). A duality of sense is again brought into play. One is distanced *to* 'the other side,' in order to reflect. The other speaks *from 'one to* the other' about the world in order to achieve an understanding in time. Reversibility lies along the axis of sense and non-sense and this axis is, for Merleau-Ponty, 'the ultimate truth' (155). If his late texts explain the painter's world of sight and space, this is so because the priority of time and language has already been clearly established in his early writing: 'But, once more, my human gaze never *posits* more than one facet of the object, even though by means of horizons it is directed towards all the others. It can never come up against previous appearances or those presented to other people otherwise than through the intermediary of time and language' (1962, 69).

Time, then, is a subjective understanding from the continuous 'Now.' It can be explained objectively as a discontinuous past, present, and future. Time, like space, also counts on at least four outstanding qualities. First, it is personal in its subjectivity and interpersonal through language. Second, it involves the stable duration of a present that, when broken, causes the succession of events. Language as tradition and faith helps create events through speech. Third, it involves a standpoint capable of drawing disperse moments into a temporal scope and unity that has significance. Finally, through sense and non-sense, it presents the fundamental notion of reversibility.

Understood from a phenomenological standpoint, perception's six interrelated levels function together in a 'wave' of awareness. The structure and character of this wave bear a distinct resemblance to the dialectic of question and answer found at the heart of hermeneutics. The first level or core of the perceptive process is a level of primary faith and intention that reaches out to the world as awareness. This pre-personal level of faith cannot be defined by means of rational categories because it is a level where non-sense prevails. It is a level below the senses, a not knowing that intertwines with the tradition into which 'one' is born. It can be sensed as a centrifugal direction of time as it flows from within itself towards the world. This fold, trough, or chiasm at the core of perception rises up to crest at the second level of primary or natural perception. It is this crest that mediates the non-sense and the senses, one's tradition and the ever-present world, the out-flow of time and one's echo from space. This crest falls into a third level of senses in synaesthetic communication. The intersensory level recalls the first fold or trough because it is a region of indeterminate sense. Much in the same way that the question concentrates its indeterminacy and rises to establish a direction towards an answer, so this field of intersensory, synaesthetic communication rises to a crest that mediates the experience of time, on the one hand, and a primordial level of space, on the other. These two sides of the same wave provide a standpoint in a situation. It is here that the phenomenon of synergy overcomes the indeterminacy of synaesthetic communication between the senses, concentrates fully on a specific sense, grasps the world in a particular direction, and endows it with significance. This specific sense constituting the fifth level is what is called a perspective. It mediates the subject anchored through the body to a traditional substance or understanding, on the one hand, and an object made available through time and the spatial coordinates of direction, on the other. This fifth level of perspective rises to meet an object at a sixth level. The object cannot be perceived in its totality because no one perspective can make all of its facets available at any particular time and from any particular standpoint. What is available is the object selected as a foreground from a background and the particular facets of that foreground facing the perceiver at a particular moment. These facets are figured to create an integrated totality that can be grasped as an object by the particular perspective in keeping with its tradition. No object is totally available to our senses from any one standpoint. There are always aspects hidden from our senses. There is, therefore, an ipseity or presence of the object as well as an aseity or absence of the object inherent in all objects perceived. The aseity or absence of facets guarantees the unavailability of a total perception of knowing of any object.

The fifth level or level of perspective, then, plays an essential role in constituting the object, in figuring out what it is from the facets available. Perspective, in that it is set at the crest of a single wave of time and space, brings both into play when it falls into its figuring function. The intention of perspective functions as both a protension in that it projects a future and as a retention in that it holds a past. It is also prospective in that it leans towards figuring an object and retrospective in that it already carries the sense of the object from the moment of synergy. Much like the answer that echoes its question and the effect that reflects its cause, the phenomenon of reversibility also plays a role in perspective. It runs back against the direction of perspective in order to abstract the paradox underlying its sense. Perspective is the medium through which perception achieves an object, and it is now the specific sense of perspective itself that must be fully grasped.

Perspective

Time and space do not exist independently of each other. They are two sides of a single wave. They are co-existent. Temporality is 'spatial since its moments co-exist spread out before thought, [and] it is a present because consciousness is contemporary with all times' (M.M-P. 1962, 415). Perception, says Merleau-Ponty, 'provides me with a "field of presence" in the broad sense, extending in two dimensions: the here-there dimension and the past-present-future dimension' (265). The dual character of *sens* is corresponded by a dual structure of perspective. Point of view functions as a here relative to which space exists. Intention functions as a 'Now' aimed at the future or the past. Merleau-Ponty speaks of this spatial and temporal perspective in terms of a point-horizon structure. Spatial perspective is founded on the 'exploration' of an object as a foreground (1962, 68). It is selected from a landscape that functions as a horizon or background and that guarantees the object's identity. What is explored from a specific standpoint is a display of objects: 'The object-horizon structure, or perspective, is no obstacle to me when I want to see the object: for just as it is the means whereby objects are distinguished from each other, it is also the means whereby they are disclosed. To see is to enter a universe of beings which *display themselves* ... In other words to look at an object is to inhabit it, and from this habitation to grasp all things in terms of the aspect which they present to it' (68).

This same point and horizon structure extends into the temporal dimension. Here, exploration becomes a reporting or carrying back into the present. Each present is a point in time calling for recognition of all others. An object is 'seen at all times as it is seen from all directions and by the same means, namely the structure imposed by a horizon' (M.M-P. 1962, 69). The immediate past is held in the present without being posited as an object. Since the immediate past similarly holds its predecessor, past time, for Merleau-Ponty, is 'wholly collected up and grasped in the present.' The same can be said of the imminent future. It will also have its 'horizon of imminence.' The past has a horizon of future around it as well. It is through the past's 'horizon of futurity' that 'I have my actual present seen as the future of that past.' The intention of a temporal perspective functions 'through the double horizon of retention and protention.' The present moment can become 'a fixed and identifiable point in objective time' when the flow of lived, present duration is interrupted (1962, 69).

This objectification of duration results in an event, and a subsequent succession of events, yet it is not the discrete event that interests Merleau-Ponty. He is concerned with the communication and relation between events, that is, the way each event as a 'moment of time calls all others to witness.' The notion of event as an 'advent' connects each event to the past and future. It shows ' "how things were meant to turn out" and "how it will all finish." ' Advent is the cohesion of 'temporal relations [making] possible the events in time.' With advent in mind, Merleau-Ponty states: 'Let us no longer say that time is a "datum of consciousness"; let us be more precise and say that consciousness deploys or constitutes time' (1962, 69, 414).

At first glance, the term perspective may appear closer to a notion of space than to one of time. In the same way temporal perspective is structured as protension and retention, so spatial perspective is structured as 'prospective' and 'retrospective.' Spatial perspective is prospective in that an object lies 'in the final stages' of focusing and is retrospective 'since [the object] will present itself as preceding its own appearance, as the "stimulus," the motive or the prime mover of every process since its beginning' (1962, 239). Nevertheless, Merleau-Ponty points out that again the spatial dimension of perspective presupposes the temporal dimension: 'The spatial synthesis and the synthesis of the object are based on this unfolding of time. In every focusing movement my body unites present, past and future, it secretes time, or rather it becomes that location in nature where, for the first time, events instead of pushing each other into the realm of being, project round the present a double horizon of past and future and acquire a historical orientation' (239–40).

The standpoint of a perspective is its 'perceptual *ground*, a basis of my life, a general setting in which my body can co-exist with the world' (250). From this standpoint an orientation becomes possible, allowing an action to be performed and a situation to arise. The standpoint is a 'when' and a 'where' that permits the congealing of perspectives into a whole. It is the standpoint in a tradition that gives a perspective its scope and unity.

Perspective, for Merleau-Ponty is 'much more than a secret technique for imitating reality' (1964c, 50). He describes it as nothing less than 'the invention of a world' (50). To see perspective as being distinct from perception is to take away both its sense and its world. Each perspective, as a sense, is different from other perspectives but related to them through the intersensory function of perception. It is, however, 'distinct from intellection' (1962, 225). As a sense, perspective 'can never be exactly transposed,' but to the very degree that a perspective makes sense, it communicates with other perspectives (225). Perspective is a question that asks *'what precisely it is that I see'* (226). Perception is its unifying force. Although perception brings sense experiences or different perspectives 'into a single world, it does not do so in the way that scientific colligation gathers together objects or phenomena, but in the way that binocular vision grasps one sole object' (230). To the degree that perspective is a sense and an attitude, it is a 'will' towards the object in question, not just a desire for it: 'I must find the attitude which *will* provide it with the means of becoming determinate (214). The separation of perspective from perception is limited in meaning. It would answer questions of difference such as 'Do we know whether tactile and visual experiences can, strictly speaking, be joined without an intersensory experience?' yet ignore the equally pressing question concerning the assimilation of experience through non-visual perspectives, that is, 'Whether my experience and that of another person can be linked in a single system of intersubjective experience?' (220). This second question is linked more to the subjectivity of time and oral 'reporting' than to spatial and visual 'exploration.' The experience of a thing and the sharing of an experience 'is not to coincide with it, nor fully embrace it in thought' (325). As noted above in Gadamer's experience of another language, it is 'without relinquishing his place and his point of view ... [that the perceiving subject must] reach out towards things to which he has, in advance, no key, and for which he nevertheless carries within himself the project, and open himself to an absolute Other which he is making ready in the depths of his being' (325–6).

In the same way that Merleau-Ponty speaks of sense and reversibility, his study *L'Oeil et l'Esprit* (1964a) distinguishes between a *perspectiva artificialis* and a *perspectiva communis* or *naturalis* (48–50). The former searches for 'une construction exacte' and pretends to 'clore la recherche et l'histoire de la peinture, fonder une peinture exacte et infaillible' (49). This 'Renaissance' perspective breaks with the earlier view in that it tries to lock perspective into the spatial dimension of distance and size by rejecting the previous importance given to a shared stand-point (49). The previous *perspectiva naturalis* or *communis* is based on a *spherical* field 'qui lie la grandeur apparente non à la distance, mais à l'angle sous lequel nous voyons l'objet' (49). The common perspective is not centred on a spatial criteria of distance but rather on a communal experience. It is also *expérience* that objected to the Renaissance search for an artificial exactness: 'Les peintres, eux, savaient *d'expérience* qu'aucune des techniques de la perspective n'est une solution exacte ... qu'il n'y a pas de projection du monde existant qui le respecte à tous égards et mérite de devenir la loi fondamentale de la peinture' (50; emphasis added). The artificial 'perspective linéaire' is not a common or shared point of departure but, on the contrary, 'un point d'arrivée,' a specific window on the world (50). It was from a standpoint in 'ex-perience' that perspective was considered an opening to 'plusieurs chemins' rather than a closure (50). The community of experience is achieved precisely by reporting through a perspective, in language. Others' perception is not an inaccessible mystery. Merleau-Ponty ex-plains that 'for me to have not an idea, an image, nor a representation, but as it were the imminent experience of them, it suffices that I look at a landscape, *that I speak of it with someone*. Then, through the *concordant* operation of his body and my own, what I see passes into him ... [into] his vision without quitting my own' (1968, 142; emphasis added). Ex-perience itself is the only standpoint from which the two perspectives can be mediated and again it is in language that the difference is over-come and world is perceived in communion. Common perspective, language, and experience are intertwined. The common perspective is temporal to the degree that it is concerned with sharing an ever-chang-ing meaning and making a 'common sense.' Much like time, it strives 'to open itself to an Other and to go forth from itself' (M.M-P. 1962, 426).

Artificial perspective, language, and precise thought are also inter-twined. To the degree that it is linear rather than spherical, that it strives to escape time and history and that it seeks infallibility, artificial perspective belongs to space. Space is 'l'en soi par excellence, sa déf-inition est d'être en soi' (M.M-P. 1964a, 47). The infallibility it seeks can be found only in some standpoint on high, in objectified thought that is divorced from a point of departure in time. Artificial perspective, as a plane projection, never reaches this exact infallibility because it is 'à notre point de vue qu'elle renvoie' and this, in turn, 'n'est qu'un cas particulier, une date, un moment dans une information poétique du monde qui continue après elle' (50, 51). Again, for Merleau-Ponty as for Gadamer, even a highly conceptualized reflection of the most precise consciousness presupposes a temporal, common perspective: 'The fact that even our purest reflection appears to us as retrospective in time, and that our reflection on the flux is actually inserted into that flux, shows that the most precise consciousness of which we are capable is always, as it were, affected by itself or given to itself, and the word consciousness has no meaning independently of this duality' (1962, 426).

It must be stressed that it is not against reflection itself that Merleau-Ponty argues nor is it against the 'point of arrival' in turn becoming a 'point of departure' through reversibility. It is against the classical, Cartesian separation of perspectives that cuts the 'point of arrival' loose from its mooring in time, closes it, makes it discrete and absolute as 'objective truth.' If existence can be considered in 'three planes of signification or three forms of unity' understood as 'matter, life, and mind,' then Cartesian dichotomies take *mind*, not life, as their point of departure (M.M-P. 1969, 156). This focus creates a major problem because the intellect can account 'for the thought of seeing, but the fact of vision and the ensemble of existential knowledges remain outside of it' (151). The very operations of thinking by means of discrete units in a closed structure lack the central unity or 'essence' that would integrate 'the optic or auditive regions in a functional whole' (163). Existence would then become a structure visible from the outside for there 'is no essence of thinking which would receive the particular forms of "visual thought" and "auditive thought" ' (163). A Cartesian approach meets only half the problem; it conforms the contingencies and variables of existence but does not express its inner unity.

Naturalism, however, is also rejected by Merleau-Ponty. A determinism of cause and effect would take *matter* as its point of departure. The sum of psychological and physiological events may constitute a whole but this 'whole can be only the condition of existence of such and such a sensible scene; it accounts for the fact that I perceive but not for that which I perceive' (1969, 161). Thinking in terms of material cause and effect does not provide an objective view of history or of a social milieu because 'before having conceptualized our class or milieu, we *are* that class or milieu' (179). If the Cartesian mind provides a rigid and eternal structure by cutting it off from being in time, the 'proof' provided by objective matter of cause and effect is, in life itself, only a 'contingency of lived perspectives [that] constitutes, alters and reorganizes itself before us like a spectacle' (180). Merleau-

Ponty calls for a point of departure resting neither in 'mind' nor in 'matter,' but parting from the experience of *life*. It is not a problem of logical or illogical resolution. Life presents alogical 'categories of an original experience' that can be understood only by means of 'a special dialectic' (171, 156).

Different perspectives, then, can be different only by degrees of sense and direction because they are still integrated into the whole of life. A priority is recognized in the direction *from* non-sense *to* sense, from the human being to the world. In either direction there is still a connection between them. Therefore, both the perspective *from* a standpoint made communal through speech and the perspective *to* a standpoint through a particular view, a 'fenêtre' or 'dans le miroir,' should be mediated by a consideration of perspective in narrative (M.M-P. 1964a, 47, 39). Whereas the significance of speech lies in the interpersonal communication of understanding within a shared standpoint, the 'signification' of a particular view occurs 'when we submit the data of the world to a "coherent deformation" ' (1964c, 54). As in figure 1 on page 27 above, it is concerned with the 'convergence of all the visible and intellectual vectors ... towards the same signification, X,' already intended in the act of perception (54). It 'concentrates the still scattered meaning of ... perception and makes it exist expressly' (55).

A text's perspective may privilege the sense of sight or the sense of hearing. This is a defining quality of 'the work of art ... which often addresses itself to only one of our senses and never hems us in on all sides as our lived experience does' (1964c, 57). The reader of a text 'responds to [the writer's] appeal and joins him at the virtual center of the writing *even if neither one of them is aware of it*' (76–77). Fiction does not pertain to the realm of analytical thought but to an experience in this virtual centre of the text:

> As for the novel, although its plot can be summarized and the 'thought' of the writer lends itself to abstract expression, this conceptual significance is extracted from a wider one, as the description of a person is extracted from the actual appearance of his face. The novelist's task is not to expound ideas or even analyze characters, but to depict an inter-human event, ripening and bursting it upon us with no ideological commentary, to such an extent that any change in the order of the narrative or in the choice of viewpoint would alter the *literary* meaning of the event. (1962, 151).

The novelist's function is to make ideas 'exist for us in the way that things exist' (1964b, 26). While the work of a great novelist 'rests on two or three philosophical ideas,' the task of criticism is not to show a work of literature as an example of some philosophical Realism or Idealism (26). Criticism 'may well compare one novelist's mode of expression with another's' but this work 'is legitimate only if it is preceded by a perception of the novel in which the particularities of "technique" merge with those of the overall project and meaning, and only if it is intended to explain what we have already perceived' (1964c, 78). Thus critical explanation presupposes a perceptive understanding. Analytical criticism alone is not sufficient. As a 'reflective' endeavour, criticism must look back in search of self-understanding, to the central core of tradition, language, and primary faith. The meaning of a text does not originate in an analysis of the organized structure but, on the contrary, in the sense that emerges from perception's centre. The primary level of faith or centre of non-sense can be approached with reflective thought by way of negative definition and it can be approached in positive terms by way of the heuristic tool of metaphor. Metaphor marks the transition from non-sense to sense, from primary faith to significance, from the soul to the body. As Merleau-Ponty puts it, in none of these cases 'is it a question of a causal relation between the two terms' (1969, 141). This level 'beneath the separated products' is the essential question (166).

Maurice Merleau-Ponty describes the 'constituting operation' mediating the levels of perception as 'the living *word* which is its unique actualization, in which the meaning is formulated for the first time and thus establishes itself as meaning and becomes available for later operations' (1969, 166). While this description may answer questions concerning perception's unity, it also leads to further questions. What constitutes the *living* word? In other words, if Merleau-Ponty rejects causal categories in favour of 'structural metaphors,' then what is the structure of metaphor (177)? If the event of a literary text exists for us in the way that things exist, what process is followed in order to *sense* the 'virtual center' (1964c, 77)? What role does the standpoint of the reader play in the process? If a *'coherent deformation'* is 'imposed on the visible,' what emerges from the community of speech in the stability of time (78)? If 'style is the system of equivalences [the artist] makes for himself for the work which manifests the world he sees,' how is the reader's perspective to be considered (54)? Again, if the author's style 'is the universal index of "coherent deformation," ' what is the reader's stylistic sense of the text (54)? If the ties between philosophy and literature 'have been getting closer' since the end of the nineteenth century, then it is in a phenomenology of hermeneutics that these questions may find an answer (1964b, 27).

3

The Experience of Perception: Paul Ricoeur and Phenomenological Hermeneutics

In Hans-Georg Gadamer's fourfold process of consciousness, Being that can be understood is language in the living act of speech. For Maurice Merleau-Ponty, Being is perception as a grasping the world through the body in action. The two notions are not only compatible but complementary.[1] As two levels of a single process there is a moment when the sense of a word is an attitude of the body and an attitude of the body already the sense of a word spoken. Both levels share similar structures and characteristics. A question is directed through its sense to an answer as one enters into dialogue with others. So also the body opens through the senses to an object as it enters into a dialogue with the world. Gadamer outlines the centre of the question as a not-knowing and Merleau-Ponty describes the experiential core of the body as a non-sense. To this negative outline Merleau-Ponty adds a positive dimension through the heuristic use of metaphor. The single notion of consciousness brings together language, perception, experience, and concept in a hierarchy that proceeds from a prepersonal, open tradition to a unique definition enclosing a principle. The single value of reality brings together perception, representation, illusion, and hallucination in a hierarchy that proceeds from an open faith in a shared, public world to an enclosed private world of individual disbelief.

Explained in terms of levels, perception proceeds from a primary faith, that is, a level of spirit, language, and tradition, a belief in the world. This level lies below the very dualities or dichotomies the rational mind must employ to define it. It is both a 'non-sense' and a reaching out to the world in the time of an eternal 'Now.' At the horizon of primary perception the intention of this level opens to the senses in a field of intersensory or synaesthetic communication. This horizon mediates the chiasm of faith and the intertwining of senses. The level of intersensory communication concentrates into a specific sense that opens to an object in the world. In so doing a dialectic of Subject as time and Object in space is made possible. A situation arises. A standpoint 'here' is realized together with a horizon 'there,' and a foreground and background are accommodated within the horizon. Perspective mediates the subject-object poles of the dialectic. It is inseparable from the sense that the phenomenon of synergy concentrates in the subjective act of perceiving an object. The sense of hearing is tied closely to the subject's standpoint in language and tradition, while the sense of sight is more free to explore space with greater precision. Distance is created by the body's power to grasp the object. Space begins with the act of perception and exists as a relationship between things created by a body in action. Prospection projects a virtual body into space that the body then enacts. Action objectified is movement, that is, the modulation of a familiar setting. Height and breadth are achieved through the primary and most subjective dimension of space, which is depth. As primary faith allows an object to exist in its unity, so depth permits objects to be brought into a consistent whole. Depth mediates geometric space and mythical space. The former is a projection of our virtual body into action, the latter is the projection of existence and an expression of the human condition into a world of meaningful relations. Once the object is achieved in space, it reflects the depth of the process of its perception. Perspective mediates Subject and Object retrospectively in self-understanding.

If this process of perception is itself to be reversed then the reversal must be achieved artificially. It would have to give priority to an illusion of objectivity provided by a concept. The unity provided by depth would be lost to the abstraction and disintegration inherent in mental inspection and explanation. A display of movement would displace action. Difference rather than unity and signification rather than meaning would become governing laws or principles. In turn, answer would displace question; object would displace subject; focusing displace perspective; sight displace hearing; and space would displace time in order of priority. This illusion of objectivity would, of course, have the value of reality but it would not share with perception the community of fact.

Time is the subjectivity that all space as meaningful relations presupposes. It is a metaphoric incorporation of that spiritual level that flows out of itself in order to grasp the world. It is the *energeia* or thrust of language and perception that proceeds from a dynamic dialectic of distance and togetherness, of non-sense and sense, of chiasm and intertwining. It is the depth of a common tradition or sedimentation and the scope of a single view. Much like sound waves or ripples extending form the centre of an otherwise tranquil pool, time radiates from an eternal 'Now.' It provides a past, present, and future when an event disrupts the simplicity of being fully absorbed in the immediacy of life. As sight leans to space, so hearing leans to time. Time opens into an event through perspective. The protention and retention of the event through a temporal perspective make it an advent. It is understood as meaningful through the depth of the perspective and as significant through the perspective's scope. The meaning and significance an event is given in turn echoes the perceiving subject, thus giving way to self-understanding and a recalling of his or her traditional standpoint in time.

Once again, if this process is itself to be reversed it must part from an abstract concept of disintegrated or diaeretic time. The concepts of past, present, and future would provide the illusion of an objective time and a point of departure for the exploration of the Subject. Once cut off from that metaphoric sense directed towards the world, this invasion of the subject would be faced with an intersensory hallucination on the one hand and a vacuum on the other. The subject would close in on itself within a time of private signification and perception's meaningful dialogue with the common-property world would be lost. The objectivity inherent in space facilitates reversibility, while the subjectivity inherent in time counteracts it. Thus, sight lends itself to the illusion of absolute reversal with an ease that is not shared by hearing.

Perspective mediates all interactions between subject and object in time and space. It is inseparable from the notions of sense as meaning, direction, attitude, and also as hearing and sight. Perspective mediates the abstract analysis of an illusive object and the concentrated will of a perceptive subject. A perspective that leans towards precise exploration through reflective thought may be designated an artificial perspective. The sense of sight lends itself to this artificial perspective and the linear exploration of space. A perspective that is inclined to report a common experience, or shared tradition, through dialogue is called a natural or common perspective. The sense of hearing lends itself to this common perspective and the circular report of time. A change in sense, in direction, in attitude or, more simply, in perspective is directly correlated to an alteration in the experience of being in the world. To the degree that narrative perspective is narrative, it is language and inevitably interwoven with the hermeneutics of Hans-Georg Gadamer. To the degree that narrative perspective is perspective it is perception and inextricably intertwined with the phenomenology of Maurice Merleau-Ponty. It is Paul Ricoeur who celebrates the alliance of phenomenology and hermeneutics in the experience of the literary text. With phenomenological hermeneutics this inquiry passes to a third level, that of experience itself.[2]

It is necessary at this third level to return to Hans-Georg Gadamer's principle of experience in order to co-ordinate language and perception in a manner that will clarify the character and structure of perspective in discourse itself. If the body stands at the junction of time and space, it does not do so alone but inseparably with language. It is important to reiterate the understanding of 'language' being used here. It is language in the sense put forth by Humboldt and taken up by Gadamer (Gadamer 1975, 397ff.). It is that *tertium quid* that precedes both *langue* and *parole*. Albert Riedlinger's notes on the Saussure course interpret it as 'une puissance, faculté, l'organisation prête pour parler' (Saussure 1:31, col. 2).[3] Saussure states that 'language' is not to be understood in its origin but in its life: 'Il n'y a aucun moment où la genèse diffère caractéristiquement de la *vie* du langage, et l'essentiel est d'avoir compris la vie' (1:30, col. 6). It is well known that Saussure insists upon approaching *langage* by means of *langue*. He felt that the latter provided 'la meilleure plateforme' or 'point de départ' from which to operate (1:30, col. 5). Language, in its generality, underlies all of the human sciences and yet 'on ne sait comment lui conférer l'unité' (1:32, col. 2). Abstract thought, working with binary oppositions of discrete units, breaks down when faced with the 'amas confus de choses hétéroclites sans lien entre elles' that is *langage* (1:30, col. 1). It is that faculty preceding *langue*, which is 'plein de mirage' and which appears as non-sense to the logics of positivistic thought (1:23, col. 4). This prelogical faculty, however, does not appear to contradict the notion of synaesthetic communication within the third level of perception. Before the phenomenon of synergy defines a specific sense, there are no closed categories or logical classifications, and experience itself comes to the fore. It might be asked why Saussure chose the closed, abstract system as the 'phénomène concret' upon which to base his course (1:24, col. 5). Language is also accessible by means of the living, direct path of *parole*. It is *parole* that provides a point of departure from within the continuity of lived experience as an act of discourse.

This angle of approach appears to have interested Merleau-Ponty. For him the phenomenon of speech is a 'miraculous' emergence of words from a prehistory and primary faith (M.M-P., quoted in Wood 126). For Hans-Georg Gadamer the concrete realization of language provides the 'mysterious' questions upon which his hermeneutics is constructed (1975, 340). The fundamentally open nature of discourse precedes 'l'objet intégral' and 'autonome' of *langue* (Saussure 1:24, col. 3, 31, col. 1). Nevertheless, discourse too can furnish 'un point d'appui satisfaisant pour l'esprit,' which is language (1:31, col. 1). The steadfast closure of *langue* as a system is opened by discourse to a hermeneutical experience that frustrates any attempt at absolutism.

It is Paul Ricoeur who rises to meet the challenge of approaching the fact of language in terms of a hermeneutics. While maintaining the formal rigour demanded by systematic, scientific study, he opens the question of producing meaning in and beyond the unit of the word. By moving from the word as a discrete unit opposing others within a system to the intertwining of words in concrete acts of usage, Ricoeur's tension theory of metaphor aims to open the heart of consciousness and perception in order to shed light on what has been, to this point, call a 'mystery,' 'energy,' a 'miracle,' 'prehistory,' and 'primary faith.' Rather than shunning the non-sensical aspects of semantic phenomena and the never-ending conflict of interpretations, he celebrates the polysemantic nature of language in terms of productive hermeneutic experience. Ricoeur, like Gadamer, looks to Humboldt for a point of departure: 'Language as discourse (Rede) lies on the boundary between the expressible and the inexpressible' (Humboldt, quoted in Ricoeur 1981a, 176). Ricoeur situates phenomenological hermeneutics on this same frontier. It is through the life of the expressible that the origin of the inexpressible is revealed.

Language as discourse is also a 'phénomène total' (Saussure 2:172, col 1). It brings to the fore the dialectic of event and meaning that is essential to Ricoeur's phenomenological hermeneutics. All discourse is realized as a meaningful event. The event of discourse is but a fleeting moment, yet the meaning of discourse endures. Ricoeur takes particular care in clarifying this point:

This point demands the greatest clarification, for it may seem that we are reverting from the linguistics of discourse to the linguistics of language [*langue*]. But that is not so; it is in the linguistics of discourse that the event and meaning are articulated. This articulation is the core of the whole hermeneutical problem.

Just as language, by being actualised in discourse, surpasses itself as system and realises itself as event, so too discourse, by entering the process of understanding, surpasses itself as event and becomes meaning. The surpassing of the event by the meaning is characteristic of discourse as such. (1981a, 134)

Discourse as an event has an act as its mode of presence (Ricoeur 1974, 86). Ricoeur appeals to the work of Austin and Searle in order to explain the three related levels of the speech act that give way to the event of discourse: the locutionary act, the illocutionary act, and the perlocutionary act.[4] The 'locutionary or propositional act [is] the act *of* saying' (Ricoeur 1981a, 134 and Austin 94). By creating an utterance a speaker also does something, that is, he or she states, describes, asserts, warns, commands, requests, promises, and so on (Austin 98 and Searle 23). This 'what we do *in* saying' constitutes the 'illocutionary act (or force)' that accompanies the act of saying something (Ricoeur 1981a, 134, and Austin 99). The act of saying something is also directed towards someone upon whom it is intended to have an impact or effect. This act that exerts 'influence upon the emotions and effective attitudes of the interlocutor' or listener is the perlocutionary act (Ricoeur 135 and Austin 101). All levels are inherent in the event of discourse and come to bear on its meaning.

The acts of speech are realized by uttering words. According to Austin, '["sentences" form a class of "utterances," which class is to be defined, ... grammatically' (Austin 6). Utterances, however, are not only formal units of, say, a conjugated verb and a noun but are also propositions, that is, they express something about something or someone. Propositions both predicate about someone or something and refer to something or someone (Searle 24, 29–33). The same predication and reference can occur in a variety of grammatical structures and on a number of different occasions. In this way propositions are marked by an endurance and stability that is not shared by grammatically defined sentences in the event of speech. The content of the proposition (predication + reference) is, then, meaning.

Ricoeur points out that meaning in turn involves a dialectic. He explains that 'to mean is both what the speaker means,' that is, his or her intended meaning, and it is also 'what the sentence means' (1976, 12). The aspect of meaning intended by the speaker is called 'noesis' and constitutes the 'noetic' pole of the dialectic of meaning. The aspect of meaning expressed by the utterance is called the 'noema' and it constitutes the 'noematic' pole of the dialectic of meaning. Ricoeur insists that in 'an objective phenomenology, every intentional act without exception must be described from its noematic sides as the correlate of a corresponding noetic act' (90).

Discourse is a process whereby private experience is made public (Ricoeur 1976, 15). This process brings experience, which is also born in an event, together with language as an event (Gadamer 1975, 316). Discourse, both in what it says and in what it does, is linked to the character and structure of experience. First, it has an act as its mode of presence that is of the nature of an event (Ricoeur 1974, 86). Each saying something or locutionary act is also a goal-oriented doing something or illocutionary act. This illocutionary act is bound to the structure of experience in a manner that recalls Gadamer. It 'is a kind of question [because to] assert something is to expect agreement' (Ricoeur 1976, 15). Speech acts are meaningful in that they predicate and refer, that is, they constitute propositions. A proposition's content is meaning and meaning is that which is transferred from one sphere of life to another. There is, therefore, an intentionality in speech. In the same manner, experience is always contextual, so spoken language takes place in a dialogue situation characterized by 'the possibility of showing the thing referred to as a member of the situation common to both speaker and hearer' (Ricoeur 1976, 34). In other words, spoken language has a situational reference that is ostensive in character and that is made available through the coincidence of the speaker's intended meaning, or noesis, and the meaning of what is said, or noema.

In experience both question and answer are mediated by sense and direction. In discourse the noematic aspect or meaning of what is said reflects or points back to the noetic aspect or speaker's intention, while at the same time it points to the world by means of sense and reference. Sense is the 'immanent pattern of discourse' (Ricoeur 1981a, 171). Sense is what is stated, while reference is that part of the world towards which the sense is directed. The reference also reverses back along the sense to the self in the same way that an answer reveals a question and a perceived object or perceived world reveals the perceiving subject. Every reference, then, is also a self-reference. Sense is carried by the meaning of a proposition. Sense is the content of meaning. Sense is in turn a dialectic of the universal and the singular. It is universal by means of the predication of the verb and singular by means of identification in the noun. There is no absolute knowledge of the meaning of a proposition. In this way it is similar to the central negativity of the question, the knowing one does not know. This lack of absolute knowledge of a proposition's meaning is made obvious in writing. A written proposition has semantic autonomy, for it outlives the event in which it is born and creates new events. In the same way that experience is born as an event over which one has no control, so the proposition is free from any absolute control (Gadamer 1975, 316).

The realization of discourse in a new context is an act and constitutes an event. As the character of experience is founded on an 'I' and a 'Thou' partnership in communications, so 'dialogue is an essential structure of discourse. Questioning and answering sustain the movement and the dynamic of speaking' (Ricoeur 1976, 15). Dialogue connects at least two physical events; speaking and listening. This 'intersubjective exchange' of experience creates a transformation of the speakers and listeners, or interlocutors, by means of communication (Ricoeur 16 and Gadamer 1975, 197, 341). Behind every dialogue is found a fundamental intention of communicability and an intention of being recognized as communication. This intention or noetic aspect on the part of those involved in a dialogue is the counterpart to the aim of the hermeneutical experience, that is, the understanding of the other person. Ricoeur's dialectic of discourse is therefore constituted by notions both of Being and of language, event and meaning, noema and noesis, reference and sense.

It is upon these ontological and linguistic dimensions of discourse that Ricoeur constructs a second, epistemological dimension, which is concerned with the communication process of written texts that involves a dialectic of understanding and explanation.[5] While sense permits an understanding to take form, understanding emerges through a selection of parts from the immanent pattern of discourse. Understanding, which begins as a series of guesses, leads to a subsequent explanation. The explanation is a part-by-part reconstruction of the whole of a text. This circular dialectic of part to whole, in turn, gives way to a third dimension, that of critical comprehension and validation. The comprehension of a text requires that the reader grasp it as an entire unit. Because a text 'involves potential horizons of meaning, which may be actualized in different ways' a text generates 'multiple' meanings (1976, 78). Literary texts are not concerned with first-order, primary, or literal meanings but rather with second-order, metaphoric meanings. The 'secondary meanings, as in the case of the horizon, which surrounds perceived objects, open the work to several readings' (78). This context or horizon can only be understood in terms of the standpoint and traditional substance that helps form the guesses of the understanding. Thus, a comprehensive grasp of the text depends on an in-depth understanding. Validation follows comprehension. It is the 'argumentative discipline' founded on a 'logic of uncertainty and of qualitative probability' much like that governing juridical procedures and legal interpretations (78). Validation opens the process by returning it to dialogue and the communication of experience in a new event.

This entire process finds its fulfilment and its fundamental principle in the existential dimension of appropriation. Appropriation is a dialectic of assimilation and distanciation. Assimilation makes sense in two directions. First, it points away from the self to the other. Like experience it makes a foreign mode of being in the world one's own (Ricoeur 1981a, 185, and 1976, 94). Second, it turns back to the self. Like experience it negates the ego, opinion, and dogma in order to reveal the self in its ongoing struggle for self-understanding. The order and the direction of assimilation is essential. One who sets off to find the self rarely does. It is by first wilfully overcoming the narcissistic ego and reaching out to the world through language in order to make another's mode of being in the world one's own that the self is both realized and revealed.

The assimilation of another mode of being in the world is also accompanied by a distanciation. Distanciation has two directions as well. On the one hand, it looks for objectivity, which is the prerequisite for a productive methodology. As with experience, distance is necessary 'to look beyond what is close at hand ... to see it better within a larger whole and a truer proportion' (Gadamer 1975, 272). Distanciation underlies the disjunctive or diaeretic principle of abstraction and analysis. Much like aseity in the process of perception, distanciation guarantees the 'absence of absolute knowledge' (Ricoeur 1976, 44). On the other hand, distanciation is that undeniable 'solitude of life' and the alienation underlying cultural estrangement. Distanciation is assimilation's very reason for being because assimilation exists only to overcome distanciation (19, 43). This fundamental dialectic of appropriation as assimilation and distanciation is the essence of an event. Discourse and experience come together in this dialectic of appropriation.

Ricoeur's approach to language, then, can be understood as a helix of dynamic productivity. In lieu of discrete units of opposition, he proposes functions co-ordinated by degrees of difference and similarity. This circular process of language as discourse begins in an event and leads to a new event. Experience, which has the character of dialogue and the structure of question and answer, is intertwined with the event of discourse. The event of discourse is brought about by acts of speech that present utterances. Utterances are not only grammatically defined sentences but also meaningful propositions. While the actualization of the vent of discourse is but a transitory moment, the proposition, understood as meaning, is more stable and enduring. The act of discourse is a meaningful dialogue that presents the speakers' intended meaning or noesis by means of the noema or utterance meaning. The noema or utterance meaning has both sense and reference. While the sense can reflect the speaker, it is the reference that points to the world. Reference itself is divided into two orders. First-order reference is univocal, or what we call literal reference, while second-order reference is split. Split reference is divided into symbol, which maintains simultaneous meanings without tension, and metaphor, which maintains simultaneous meanings mediated by a dynamic tension.

This ontological level of event and linguistic level of discourse give way to an epistemological level of understanding and explanation. Understanding, which relies on guesswork, begins with hearing and seeing the essential parts of a text. Explanation of a text's sense involves putting the parts together into a consistent whole. This epistemological dimension may become part of a critical dimension constituted by comprehension and validation. Comprehension involves grasping the parts of the text as a whole that reveals a world as a possible way of perceiving things. Validation, by contrast, is an integral part of an argumentative discipline exercised within a community of readers.

This dialectic progression from sense and reference to understanding and explanation, and then to comprehension and validation, is already part of an existential dimension of assimilation and distanciation. Assimilation is the work of resemblance that plays with degrees of similarity and dissimilarity. Assimilation forms the basis for cultural belonging. Distanciation is the basis of cultural solitude and historical alienation, as well as a condition for achieving scientific status. These various dimensions return to the initial notion of an event upon reaching the essential principle of appropriation. Appropriation is a renewed event that involves dispossessing the narcissistic ego and repossessing the self as well as making one's own a foreign mode of being in the world through a transformation brought on by play (Ricoeur 1981a, 182–93). While all these dimensions meet their point of departure in the notion of an event, the process is not a closed circle. It is similar to a helix that returns to its starting point but at a different level.

The Medium of Discourse and Its Transformation

The transition of discourse from the audio-oral situation of speaking and listening to the visual world of writing and reading is 'much more than mere material fixation' (Ricoeur 1976, 28). It alters the degree of emphasis placed on the different poles involved in the dialectic. A change in the 'medium or channel' affects not only the message but 'irradiates in every direction' (26). Following Aristotle, Ricoeur states that '*technê* generates individuals ... whereas *epistêmê* grasps species' (77). A technical change will necessarily affect the epistemological understanding and explanation of the world. Inscription both limits and liberates the possibilities of discourse. The ostensive reference 'which can be indicated "around" the speakers, "around" ... the instance of discourse itself,' disappears (1981a, 148). The shape of discourse is affected. Sense in the speech situation 'fades into' the ostensive reference in the circumstantial 'reality which surrounds the instance of discourse' (148). In the case of the written text, what is fixed and preserved over temporal and spatial distance is not the event of discourse but 'the intentional exteriorization constitutive of the couple "event-meaning" ' (1976, 27). What is inscribed is 'the noema of the act of speaking, the meaning of the speech event' (27). The writer's intention and the meaning of the text do not coincide to the same degree as does the speaker's subjective intention and the meaning of what is said in the personal context of a dialogue. A speaker has authority over the meaning because what is said and what is meant overlap. An author does not have authority over the meaning of the text. The text breaks with its 'moorings to the psychology of the author' and is no longer limited to her or his finite temporal and spatial horizon (30). The text achieves semantic autonomy. 'Circumscription of a set of meanings' takes the place of circumstance, and the interpretation of scripture or exegesis begins (30). The author 'stands in the space of meaning traced and inscribed by writing' and it is within the text that the author appears (1981a, 149).

The reader is not determined by the unique situation of a particular dialogue. The listener is a specific second-person, a particular 'you' while the reader to whom the text is addressed is potentially anyone who can read. The pole of reception is universalized. A text also 'initiates new modes of communication' and 'creates its public' (1976, 31). It is, however, the 'response of the audience which makes the text important and therefore significant' (31). A text, whether written or memorized, is a product of work. Production is understood as a form applied to something in order to shape it (33). The technical conditions and strategies presiding over the production of a text will help create its individual shape. While memory 'appears as the support of an inscription similar to that provided by [the] external marks' of writing, Ricoeur is careful to point out that the rules of oral and written composition may 'coincide without being identical processes' (33–4).

These changes in the medium with repercussions in the speaker, hearer, and code have their most complex impact on the functioning of discourse between the message and its reference in the world. Writing, as a literary work, introduces a dialectic more complex than that of event and meaning. Here 'the meaning itself, as immanent "sense," is externalised as transcendent reference' (1976, 34). It is in the situation surrounding the two modes of discourse that important changes occur. Ricoeur explains that

in spoken discourse the ultimate criterion for the referential scope of what we say is the possibility of showing the thing referred to as a member of the situation *common to both speaker and hearer*. This situation *surrounds* the dialogue ... [Landmarks of the situation] can be described in such a definite way that one, and only one, thing may be identified within the common framework of reference ... Singular identifications ultimately refer to the here and now determined by the interlocutionary situation. There is no identification which does not relate that about which we speak to a unique position in the spatio-temporal network, and there is no network of places in time and space without a final reference to the situational here and now. In this ultimate sense, all references of oral language rely on monstrations, which depend on the situation *perceived* as common by members of the dialogue. (34–5; emphasis added)

The perception of a situation from within the spherical field of what Merleau-Ponty calls the *perspectiva communis* or *naturalis* is ultimately linked to the nucleus of perception's temporal pole, which is the here and now. This pole in turn is directly linked to the audio-oral medium of discourse. The impact of writing on this common situation is shattering in that 'a *gap* appears between identification and monstration. The *absence* of a common situation generated by the spatial and temporal *distance* between writer and reader; the cancellation of the absolute here and now ... and the semantic autonomy of the text, which severs it from the present of the writer and opens it to an indefinite range of potential readers in an indeterminate time' are all brought on by the impact of writing (Ricoeur 1976, 35; emphasis added). The impact of writing on discourse does not centre on the temporal constitution of perception but on its counterpart, space. The scope of reference is extended in space to allow for a world. It is 'thanks to writing [that] man and only man has a world and not just a situation' (36). The 'strategy of certain modes of discourse' is also affected, allowing the 'as if' of fictional narrative greater possibilities for 'projecting a world' rather than simply describing a situation (36). Ricoeur looks to the 'optic alphabet of the painter' to illustrate the spatial impact of writing on discourse. It is because 'the painter could master a new alphabetic material … [that] he was able to write a new text of reality' (41). Painting became progressively more abstract and moved closer to science. Abstract art 'challenges perceptual forms by relating them to non-perceptual structures' (41). It is in this same way that writing abstracts. The 'invention of notational systems presenting analytical properties: discreteness, finite number [and] combinatory power' can be seen to create what Merleau-Ponty called a *perspectiva artificialis*, and the sense of the reference moves from the ear to the eye (42). The importance of this change in emphasis from one sense to another, from one perspective to another, and from time to space cannot be over-emphasized. Through writing, perception centres on

the space-structure not only of the bearer, but of the marks, themselves, of their form, position, mutual distance, order, and linear disposition. The transfer from hearing to reading is fundamentally linked to this transfer from the temporal properties of the voice to the spatial properties of the inscribed marks. This general spatialization of language is complete with the appearance of printing. The visualization of culture begins with the dispossession of the power of the voice in the proximity of mutual presence. Printed texts reach man in solitude, far from the ceremonies that gather the community (42–3)

When Ricoeur speaks of the 'non-perceptual structures' brought out by visual art's abstraction, he is not speaking of an absence of perception or of an unperception. What is not perceived cannot contribute to experience. The 'non-perceptual' structures indicate a reverse in direction. The direction of perception appears to proceed *from* a spatialized perspective located in the structures of the object, and to move against the 'sense' of perception *towards* the 'non-sense.'

This change in the medium of discourse has resulted in 'an immense range of effects' in society (1976, 28). Some of the effects suggested by

Ricoeur are those of political imperialism, the birth of market relationships, the standardizing of laws and juridical codes, as well as the
archiving of history (28). Changes in literary production run parallel
to these socio-political and economic changes. To approach these changes
from the standpoint of the socio-political or economic impact, rather
than from the change in the literary medium itself, is a valid though
more indirect method. Socio-political or economic changes do not have
direct access to the text. They must pass through discourse to exercise
their effects. Discourse itself and its media provide a direct platform
from which to approach literary production. A change in medium is
quite literally a change in the *sense* of discourse and this change must
directly affect the possibilities of reference.

Sense, Perception, and the Productive *Figure* of Discourse

Ricoeur's theory of discourse establishes at least four qualities: (1) discourse has an act as its mode of presence that is in the nature of an
event; (2) it consists of a series of choices whereby certain meanings
(which have 'sense') are selected over others; (3) the choices produce
new combinations (which can never be exhausted); and (4) 'it is in the
instance of discourse that language has a reference. To speak is to say
something about something ... [showing] precisely that the aim of language is double: the aim of an ideal sense or meaning (that is, not
belonging to the physical or psychic world) and the aim of reference,'
(1974, 87). While (2) and (3) are shared with semiotics, (1) and (4) bridge
a gap between the ideal and the real, between the sense and the reference to the world. This bridge, in turn, splits open Merleau-Ponty's
view of the body as expression and speech. It creates the stereoscopic
vision he suggested but did not develop (M.M-P. 1962, 174ff.). As James
E. Eddie has noted, Ricoeur offers 'the only important attempt up to
now to develop Merleau-Ponty's theory of speech act further than he
himself did,' by going beyond the 'word' to the 'sentence' (xxxii). Eddie
sees in Ricoeur's 'Structure, Word, Event' a decisive development of
Merleau-Ponty's theory of perception (Ricoeur 1974, 79ff.). Ricoeur's
standpoint on a bridge of 'transcendence of the sign' that links ideal
to real adds a vital third dimension to the perspective: that vital dimension of depth that is the living metaphor (Ricoeur 1974, 87). Thus,
it is no accident that the one noun Merleau-Ponty uses to fill the 'gap'
in perception is the same one used by Ricoeur to shed light on Gadamer's 'universal mystery of language' (Gadamer 1975, 340):

We are ... wholly active and wholly passive because we are the upsurge of time. (M.M-P. 1962, 428)

The upsurge of saying into our speaking is the very mystery of language. Saying is what I call the openness, or better, the opening-out, of language. (Ricoeur 1974, 96)

In both cases the upsurge, or energy, is the product of a dialectical process. Metaphor, which lies at the root of Ricoeur's theory of narrative as an event in time, is the point of a 'crystallization' of all exchanges between the structure and the function of language (1974, 95). It has its base in three areas of tension: (1) 'tension within the statement: between tenor and vehicle, between focus and frame';[6] (2) 'tension between a literal interpretation that perishes at the hands of semantic impertinence and a metaphorical interpretation whose sense emerges through non-sense'; and (3) 'tension in the relational function of the copula: between identity and difference in the interplay of resemblance ... between an "is" and an "is not" ' (1977, 247–8). This interplay of resemblance (or 'is like') of the copula in its relational function affects the copula in its existential function, thereby creating the key notion of metaphorical truth. Metaphorical truth 'preserves the "is not" within the is' and 'says *that* things really are this way' (249, 248). The notion that metaphor passes through non-sense, that is, semantic impertinence, into the sense of a metaphorical figure locates its point of origin at the very centre of language, tradition, and primary faith. This 'question' of metaphor is summed up by Ricoeur: 'The question is precisely whether poetic language does not break through to a pre-scientific, ante-predicative level, where the very notions of fact, object, reality, and truth, as delimited by epistemology, are *called into question* by this very means of the vacillation of literal reference' (254). I take the emphasized phrase literally and understand Ricoeur's theory as the recalling of metaphor into the structure and function of the question, which, as has been pointed out, mediates Gadamer's philosophy and that of Merleau-Ponty.

The principal characteristics of metaphor are, then, tension, an openness to the world, a questioning, non-sense and sense, context, focus and frame. Metaphor also manifests itself as a 'figure' that, as is evident in the polysemic value of the French *figure*, refers in two directions: to the trope and to the character of a 'human face' reflected in a mirror (Ricoeur 1981b, 229). Ricoeur explains that metaphor gives 'discourse a quasi-bodily externalization' (229). The heuristic fiction that metaphor puts into play by 'facing' reality through representation, brings together 'sensa – sounds, images, feelings that adhere to the "sense" ' (1977, 238). Ricoeur places metaphor on the most intimate sense level, that of feeling. As stated above, this intimate relation between language and perception is developed by Merleau-Ponty but only on a secondary semiotic level of the word, not in the primary semantic sphere: 'The word "hard" produces a sort of stiffening of the back and the neck, and only in a secondary way does it project itself into the visual or auditory field and assume the appearance of a sign or a word ... The word is then indistinguishable from the attitude which it induces, and it is only when its presence is prolonged that it appears in the guise of an external image and its meaning as a thought. Words have a physiognomy because we adopt towards them, as towards each person, a certain form of behaviour' (M.M-P. 1962, 235). Quoting Werner, Merleau-Ponty emphasizes that ' "the word as read is not a geometrical structure in a segment of visual space, it is the presentation of a form of behaviour and of a linguistic act in its dynamic fullness" ' (236).

Ricoeur elevates this intimate relation to the vital dimension of the sentence, where Merleau-Ponty's 'word' in fact works. The metaphor is also 'appropriate' in the full sense of this word. Metaphorical discourse appropriates a world in that what it creates, it discovers; and what it finds, it invents (1977, 239). The attitude or perspective adopted towards the figure is not only an appropriation of the world, but a reflection of the self and its standpoint in a tradition from which the metaphor surges forth. This ' "perpectival" [*sic*] character of poetic language'[7] is not born at the outer level of perception but at its core:

Metaphor's power of reorganizing our perception of things develops from transposition of an entire 'realm.' Consider, for example, sound in the visual order. To speak of the sonority of a painting is no longer to move about an isolated predicate, but to bring about the incursion of an entire realm into alien territory. The well-worn notion of 'transporting' becomes a conceptual migration, if not an armed and luggage-laden overseas expedition. The interesting point is that the organization brought about in the adopted region is *guided by* the use of the entire network in the region of origin. (236)

Metaphor functions as a process with a meaningful direction or 'semantic bearing.' The 'predicative assimilation' of the world is accompanied by a 'self-assimilation' involving a sensing of our own perspective of the world: 'We feel *like* what we see *like*' (Ricoeur 1981b, 243). The function of the poetic feeling 'is to abolish the distance between knower and known without canceling the cognitive structure of thought and the intentional distance which it implies' (244). Poetic transpositions by means of metaphor are transpositions 'of feelings of the first-order, of emotions' allowing for feelings with '*ontological* bearing ... They are ways of "being-there," of "finding" ourselves within the world' (245). This bearing 'cannot be separated from the negative process' that suspends, or puts in '*epoché*,' the first-order bodily feelings that 'tie us to these first-order objects of reference' (246, 245). It is along this second plane of emotion that one finds direct access to both the discovery of self and the tradition or primary faith that is one's world. The bodily feelings are not cancelled but only suspended, allowing for a binocular or stereophonic perception of three dimensions: (1) self, (2) the world of the text, and (3) the self and text in the world. Merleau-Ponty had already stated: 'My body ... reverberates to all sounds, vibrates to all colours and provides words with their primordial significance through the way in which it receives them' (1962, 236). Paul Ricoeur extends the scope of this reverberation to include feeling, discourse, and imagination. He states that 'we may assume the Heideggerian thesis that it is mainly through feelings that we are attuned to reality. But this attunement is nothing else than the reverberation in terms of feelings of the split reference' of verbal and imaginative structure (1981b, 246).

The structure of this metaphoric process has a living, three-dimensional quality that can be understood as an interplay between the reader or listener centred in time, the world of the text, and the work in the world. Metaphor is the principle of dynamic production that generates the relations between the poles of this triangle. The process begins when the reader or listener encounters semantic impertinence between a word, as foreground, and its context, as background, within the sentence. When semantic impertinence calls into question the first-order sense of a word, the reader or listener opens herself or himself to the primary level of perception and recalls non-sense. This non-sense rises to form a crest of poetic feelings or 'negative, suspensive' feelings, on the one hand, and transfigured literal feelings, on the other (Ricoeur 1981b, 245). At this moment fear becomes terror and compassion becomes pity. Transfigured feelings 'insert us within the world in a nonobjectifying manner' (245). These transfigured literal feelings 'have ontological bearing' and fall into everyday literal emotions, thereby bringing about a metamorphosis of the listener's or reader's experience of being in the world (245). This moment of first-order feelings rises to a second crest that forms the horizon of poetic discourse on the one hand and ordinary discourse on the other (1976, 66–7). It is at this moment mediating poetic and ordinary discourse that the reader or listener must open to new semantic possibilities in order to resolve the non-sense called forth by the semantic impertinence. Between poetic discourse and ordinary discourse a combined effort of all discourse breaks forth with a new, creative sense and achieves a semantic bearing that reveals the metaphoric reference in the world of the text (1981b, 242). The world of the text is, of course, a metaphoric world, a world that both is and is not. By playing out the metaphoric process the reader or listener opens to a reverberation between the sense created and the non-sense called forth in the encounter with semantic impertinence. Poetic discourse is a means by which the reader or listener is invited to open himself or herself to the very core of perception.

The text as a work in the world is also brought into play. While the reader is open to the reverberation of sense and non-sense, he or she is also open to the body's reaction to words in the sentence. Words are also physical attitudes and first-order feelings that are intertwined with the work in the world. The metaphoric world does not cancel the first-order world. It continues to play a role in perception. Between the reference of the work in the first-order world and the metaphoric reference of the text's world, lies a semic field. A semic field is the name given to 'the collection of elementary constituents of a concept-entity' (Ricoeur 1977, 201). From this semic field emerges an idea or concept that distances the metaphor from the immediacy of lived experience and universalizes it. The concept lies within a region of abstraction and analysis from which to reflect upon the process. When the objective concept or idea is taken as a point of departure and the process is retraced back to its beginnings in non-sense, we can speak of an ironic perspective. When the dynamic process of sense creation is taken as the point of departure and directed towards the experience of appropriating a new world, we can speak of a metaphoric perspective.

The metaphoric process, then, begins in an encounter with semantic impertinence. While the referential dimension of this process lies between the sentences and the world they project, a self-reflexive dimension is to be found between the reader and his or her reading of the sentences. While the literal sense of the word is suspended in order for a new sense to be created, the body continues to adopt attitudes towards the words it encounters. If the semic field is found between the metaphor and the universal concept, then between the metaphor and each reader lie sensa, that is, sounds, images, and feelings 'that adhere to the "sense" ' (Ricoeur 1977, 238). Through the three modes of tension, that is, tension in the relational function of the copula, tension in the statement, and tension in the interpretation, the reader becomes part of a dynamic process of appropriation. His or her action to assimilate the metaphoric reference by creating a new sense can never be achieved in absolute terms because the movement of distanciation makes only one side of the text available from any given standpoint.

The resemblance mediating the character and structure of Gadamer's question, Merleau-Ponty's perception, and Ricoeur's metaphor permits a consideration of narrative perspective in terms of reading experience, perception, and tropes. Narrative, as a hermeneutical experience, takes its place in the hierarchy outlined by Gadamer: consciousness subject to 'the efficacy of history,' perception, hermeneutical experience, and concept (Ricoeur 1984, 2:164). The work of this resemblance permits a phenomenological 'questioning' into the nature and function of narrative perspective to stand by Ricoeur in his affirmation: 'Like a cube, or a volume in space, the text presents a "relief". Its different topics are not at the same altitude. Therefore the reconstruction of the whole has a perspectivist aspect similar to that of perception. It is always possible to relate the same sentence in different ways to this or that sentence considered as a cornerstone of the text. A specific kind of onesidedness is implied in the act of reading. This onesidedness confirms the guess character of interpretation.'[8] A cornerstone sentence will, therefore, have a structure and character that relate image, discourse with the world, and reader standpoint through a perspective that can be understood and explained in terms of 'figures' or tropes.

Time and the Experience of Narrative

The tension theory of metaphor and the key notion of appropriation open the way for Ricoeur to develop a theory of narrative that, in keeping with perception, proceeds not from an objective spatial criterion but from the temporal character of human experience. Faced with Aristotle's statement, 'Being good at making metaphors is equivalent to being perceptive of resemblances,' he asks, 'What is to be perceptive of resemblance if not to inaugurate the similarity by bringing together terms that at first seem "distant", then suddenly "close"?' (1984, 1:x). The relation between being, metaphor, and narrative suggests that ' "seeing-as", which sums up the power of metaphor, could be the revealer of a "being-as" on the deepest ontological level' (1:xi). He looks to the *Confessions* of St Augustine, 'in whose wake will follow Husserl, Hiedegger and Merleau-Ponty,' for an understanding upon which to construct an explanation of time related to the activity of story-telling (1:16).

Time, for St Augustine, is a dialectic of *intentio* and *distentio* of the soul. The *intentio* corresponds roughly to Merleau-Ponty's 'field of presence' that is much 'as the primary experience in which time and its dimensions make their appearance unalloyed, with no intervening distance and with absolute self-evidence. It is here that we see a future sliding into the present and on into the past' (M.M-P. 1962, 416). St Augustine calls it 'man's attentive mind, which is present, is relegating [*traicit*] the future to the past' (quoted in Ricoeur 1984, 1:19). This attentive mind of the present performs three functions 'expectation [*expectat*], attention [*adtendit*; this verb recalls the *intentio praesens*], and memory [*meminit*]' (St Augustine, quoted in 1984, 1:19). *Intentio* as the present time is therefore threefold: 'The present of past things is the memory; the present of present things is direct perception ... and the present of future things is expectation' (1:11). *Intentio* is, then, the concordance of all three functions (1:21). It is the inner fusion of man, that eternal 'inner *Verbum*' or language to which the steady mind 'listens' (1:27, 29). St Augustine, of course, does not explain *intentio* through analytical rationalization, but by way of a dialogue between the first and second person.

Distentio as a dialectical counterpart arises 'out of the *intentio* that has burst asunder' (Ricoeur 1984, 1:20). *Distentio*, like an 'event,' is the interruption of the field of presence by dividing it and distancing the expectation of the future and the memory of the past so as to allow for an interaction between them in the present. It is a non-coincidence of three modalities of action: 'the scope of the action which I am performing is divided [*distenditur*] between two faculties of memory and expectation, the one looking back to the part which I have already recited, the other looking forward to the part which I have still to recite' (St Augustine, quoted in Ricoeur 1984, 1:20). What is expressed in this one sentence is not only a fusion of horizons but also the act of reading. The active distanciation of the future from the past is what allows for the measurement of time not as a past or future thing but as an expectation or memory. Expectation and memory in turn present a 'spatiality of a unique kind' and 'these affections are like the reverse side' of the mind's continuity (1:21). This measurability in its extreme corresponds to the Nietzschean notion of monumental history or 'official time' of 'which chronological time is but the audible expression. To this monumental time belong the figures of authority and power that form the counterweight to the living times' (1984, 2:106). Clock time 'totally disassociates the notion of a "day" from that of celestial motion' (1:15). It draws us away from the eternal present into a measurement of 'how long has it been since' or 'how much time before ...' and is synonymous with a 'dispersal into the many' and a 'wandering' (1:27). St Augustine describes this measured time in spatial terms as 'the region of dissimilarity' that marks 'the difference that the soul discovers precisely in its movement of returning to its source and by its very effort to know its origin' (1:27). It is again important to note the priority and direction in this process. *Distentio* is a discordance that emerges from the concordance, and the movement from discordance to concordance is a return movement 'to know.'

Narrative extends the dialectic of the assimilating *intentio* and the distancing *distentio* by means of muthos. In narration the temporal understanding or *muthos* is explained by means of *mimesis*. Ricoeur's muthos and mimesis form a dialectic similar to that of noesis and noema. This dialectic makes narrative available as a product of work that says something meaningful about something to someone. The dialectic functions as a heuristic model, where muthos 'takes the form of a "story" ' or fable and mimesis 'is understood no longer in terms of "copy" but of redescription' of the world (Ricoeur 1977, 245). Mimesis is the noematic side from which the muthos or noesis can be approached.

The primary trait of muthos is 'metaphoricity,' which 'consists in describing a less known domain – human reality – in light of relationships within a fictitious but better known domain' (1977, 244). It is the synergetic sense or combined action of a co-ordinated understanding behind all of the events of a story. Muthos is the 'organization of the events' that constitutes a 'triumph of concordance over discordance' (1984, 1:33, 31). It is a 'grasping together,' a wholeness of beginning, middle, and end as well as an 'appropriate magnitude' (1:41, 38). Muthos is the starting point for a theory of narrative composition, not because it is the 'author's attitude' alone, but because it is an expression of 'narrative understanding' manifest in the text itself (1:36, 38).

Muthos is a fundamental notion behind Ricoeur's definition of the text in terms of a 'dynamic identity' (1985, 176). It is emplotment, that is, the mediating function that lies between the scattered events or incidents of a story. It shapes 'the fable' and gives it a sense (76). Emplotment brings together heterogeneous features. It is fundamentally concordant and assimilative.

In saying that muthos is a victory of concordance over discordance Ricoeur is stating that it is discordance as well. It is 'the play of discordance internal to concordance' that constitutes the 'internal dialectic of poetic composition' (1984, 1:38). The dialectic of discordant concordance that constitutes narrative understanding is itself an extension of time's *intentio* and *distentio*. Again, the notion of reversal is brought to the fore. As there is a movement of returning from the far region of *distentio*, so in tragic muthos there is a reversal, a recognition and a suffering. This is accompanied by a surprise at 'the height of the discordant' (1:43). Reversal, recognition, suffering, and surprise 'bring to their highest degree of tension the fusion of the "paradoxical" and the "causal" sequence ... It is these discordant incidents the plot tends to make necessary and probable. And in so doing, it purifies them, or, better, purges them' (1:43, 44).

Narrative understanding, emplotment, or muthos is not to be confused with analytical knowledge, 'theoretical reason,' or *theōria* (Ricoeur 1985, 177, 178). Ricoeur, like Gadamer, is interested in a narrative intelligibility that teaches '*practical wisdom or moral judgment*' (1985, 177, and Gadamer 1975, 431ff.). It is 'through our acquaintance with types of emplotment that we *learn* how to link excellence and happiness' (177). In all of Ricoeur's theory, the study of narrative as a rational scientific discipline takes second place to his more fundamental concern for experience, practical wisdom, or '*phronêsis*' (177). Phronesis, 'which is the intelligent use of action' is akin to common sense in that it is not analytical thought but a 'grasping together' or judging 'in the Kantian sense of judging, which consists not so much in joining a subject and a predicate as in placing some intuitive manifold under a rule' (178). It is the kind of '*subsumption* that emplotment executes by putting events under the rule of a story, one and complete' (178).

Mimesis is the 'denotative' dimension of muthos and forms its noematic counterpart in the dynamic identity of the text (Ricoeur 1977, 245). It is the imitation of an action through discourse rather than a reflection of things. It is directed more towards the coherence of muthos than at any particular part of the story (1984, 1:37, 41). It is an 'active process' directed at the reproduction of an event (1:33).

In keeping with his tension theory of metaphor, Ricoeur divides this active process into three interrelated moments of figuration: mimesis 1 or prefiguration, mimesis 2 or configuration, and mimesis 3 or refiguration. These three moments mediate the author and the reader, the text's production and its reception. In keeping with muthos, mimesis is also characterized by the same polarity of aggregative and disjunctive tendencies that interact and create the text. Prefiguration is the author's 'implicit categorization of the practical field in [her or his] cultural stock ... a first narrative organization [mise en forme] of this field' (1984, 1:47). The author is subject to 'the cultural constraints of acceptability' (1:47). Prefiguration, then, is the author's act of composition. Bearing in mind that the author works to create the imitation of an action, he or she must understand 'the world of action, its meaningful structures, its symbolic resources, and its temporal character' (54). This preliminary competence enables the author to represent (1) acts that function within the extension of a conceptual network; (2) acts that have symbolic importance; and (3) acts whose articulation bears a temporal character. This temporal character is marked by both an immediate here and now as well as by the concept of a past, present, and future.

Preliminary competence is accompanied by a linguistic competence. Linguistic competence functions in the paradigmatic order with rules of composition and innovative relations of intersignification, that is, 'between ends, means, agents, circumstances, and the rest [which] are perfectly reversible' (1:56). It also functions in the syntagmatic order of discourse, which 'implies the irreducibly diachronic character of every narrated story' (1:56). The prefiguration or preliminary competence of mimesis is therefore twofold. It demands an understanding of 'both the language of "doing something" and the cultural tradition from which proceeds the typology of plots' (1:57).

Configuration, or mimesis 2, is an 'operation constitutive of emplotment ... [that] draws its intelligibility from its faculty of mediation, which is to conduct us from the one side of the text to the other, transfiguring the one side into the other through its power of configuration' (1984, 1:53). Configuration 'opens the kingdom of the as if or of fiction (1:64). It is the pivot point of Ricoeur's theory, for it 'opens up the world of the plot and institutes ... the literariness of the work of literature' (1:53). The dynamic character of configuration as an emplotment or ordering is that of a mediation carried out in three ways: (1) it mediates the individual events or incidents and the story as a whole, that is, it draws a configuration out of a simple succession; (2) it brings together heterogeneous factors such as 'agents, goals, means, interactions, circumstances and unexpected results'; and (3) it brings together the discordance and the concordance of temporal *distentio* and *intentio* in what Ricoeur calls 'a synthesis of the heterogeneous' (1:65, 66). This dialect of *intentio* and *distentio* 'has a qualitative aspect of graduated tension' (1:85).

Mimesis 2 combines two temporal dimensions: the configurational dimension properly speaking and the episodic dimension. The configurational dimension draws or grasps the events into one temporal and meaningful whole. The conclusion of a story functions in order to provide 'the story [with] an "end point"', which, in turn, furnishes the point of view from which the story can be perceived as forming a whole' (1984, 1:66–7). Point of view, perception, and time come together in mimesis 2. Understanding a story 'is to understand how and why the successive episodes led to this conclusion' (1:67). The point of view, which grasps the story as one temporal whole, once again introduces a paradoxical reversal. It is this final point of view that permits a reversal in the flow of time from past towards the future. Through recollection and recapitulation, events can be traced backward, permitting a reading of the ending in the beginning and of the beginning in the ending.

The episodic dimension 'draws narrative time in the direction of the linear representation of time' by the consecutive presentation of different phases of action in external relation to one another (1:67). Each episode is also open in that it adds an 'and so forth' to the consecutive episodes and, finally, the episodic dimension follows 'the irreversible order of time common to physical and human events' (1:67).

Together with the temporal side, configuration is constituted by an actual side. The configurational act also has two characteristics that assure the continuity between the configuration and its refiguration by the reader. First, it is a 'schematism,' that is, an act of the productive imagination understood in the Kantian sense as a 'generative matrix of rules' (1:68). It is a synthesis of both the intellectual and the intuitive. This schematism of emplotment 'lends itself to a typology of the sort that Northrop Frye, for example, elaborates in his *Anatomy of Criticism*' (1:68). Emplotment, then, engenders a synthesis of the 'thought of a story, and the intuitive presentation of circumstances, characters, episodes, and changes of fortune' (1:68). The second characteristic of the configurational act is tradition, which accompanies the schematism that occurs in history. Tradition is not inert, but rather the 'living transmission of an innovation always capable of being reactivated by a return to the most creative moments of poetic activity' (1:68). It is also a dynamic unit in that it brings the stability of sedimentation, that is, 'the paradigms that constitute the typology of emplotment,' drawn from genre and individual works, together with innovation. Sedimentation rests on the formal feature of discordant concordance as well as on a cultural heritage. Innovation is never an absolute originality because the 'labor of imagination is not born from nothing ... [It is a] rule-governed deformation' (1:69). In its most radical form innovation contests not only a cultural heritage but also the formal principle of emplotment, which is discordant concordance.

If prefiguration is a 'passing from the paradigmatic order of action to the syntagmatic order of narrative,' then refiguration is its inverted counterpart. Mimesis 3 or refiguration is brought about by the act of reading. Here reading is understood as an act that takes up and 'fulfills the configurational act' and it is this action on the part of the reader that gives emplotment the 'capacity to model experience' (1984, 1:76). Reading is akin to both the grasping together of the temporal dimension of configuration and, particularly, to schematization and traditionality. It is 'a structuring activity' that transcends the spatial opposition of 'an "inside" and an "outside" ' (1:76). Schematization and traditionality 'are thus from the start categories of the interaction between the operations [*operativité*] of writing and reading' (1:76). These two aspects of both the configuration and the refiguration are therefore essential to any consideration of narrative perspective. The schematization consists of 'received paradigms [that] structure readers' expectations and aid them in recognizing the formal rule, the genre, or the type exemplified by the narrated story ... They govern the story's capacity to be followed ... To follow a story is to actualize it by reading it' (1:76). The formal structures recognized by the reader's intellect offer only part of the reading schematization. There is also the intuitive act that brings the essential role of sense once again to the fore: 'And if emplotment can be described as an act of judgment and of the productive imagination, it is so insofar as this act is the joint work of the text and reader, just as Aristotle said that sensation is the common work of sensing and what is sensed' (1:76). Finally, the act of reading is also an 'interplay of the innovation and sedimentation of paradigms that schematizes emplotment' (1:76–7). Although the text consists of holes and lacunae that 'challenge the reader's capacity to configure what the author seems to take malign delight in defiguring,' it is in 'reading [that] the *receiver* plays with narrative constraints, *brings about gaps*, takes part in the combat between the novel and the antinovel' (1:77;

emphasis added). There are 'gaps,' then, in mimesis 3 as well as in 2 and 1.

The narrative process, then, brings different elements into a productive dialectic. These elements do not lie in discrete opposition to one another but are distanced by degrees of tension. Muthos and mimesis form a nucleus for the process. Muthos brings together the principles of *distentio* and *intentio*, characterized by discordant concordance and concordance respectively. Varying degrees of emphasis placed on each of these poles can give rise to, say, a chronicle or a fable. While the '*histor*' of a chronicle's serial presentation derives his authority from a document read, the 'singer of tales' derives his authority from an inherited tradition (1984, 1:227, 229–89, and 1981a, 280). If muthos is a dialectic of *distentio* and *intentio*, discordant concordance and concordance, mimesis plays out three dialectic moments. First, prefiguration brings together preliminary competence and linguistic competence. Second, configuration is an interplay of time and action. Time is a dialectic of an episodic presentation and a configurational dimension. Action is an interplay between schematism and tradition. Schematism is a dialectic of productive imagination and formal rules, while tradition is an interplay of innovation and sedimentation. This traditional dimension is the fundamental sphere of interaction between the moment of configuration and the third moment of refiguration. Refiguration is the interplay between the act of reading and time. This act is a dialectic of tradition on the one hand and schematization on the other. The degree of similarity and difference between the tradition of configuration and that of refiguration will give rise to varying degrees of tension between these two moments of mimesis. Schematization is the interplay of imagination and the text's formal aspects. The temporal pole of refiguration is an interplay between the sequence of events and the reader's grasping the parts of the story as a whole. It is through this temporal act of listening or reading that a text comes to life.

Schematization, tradition, and time, in their formal and intuitive aspects as well as through their stable and innovative characteristics, constitute the sense of reading. The reference that lies beyond the 'sense of a work' is 'the world it projects and that constitutes its horizon' (Ricoeur 1984, 1:77). Here Ricoeur divides the receiver into two types. The first is that of the listener, suggesting an audio-oral dimension, and the second is that of the reader, suggesting a visual side of the mimetic process: 'In this sense, the listeners or readers receive [the world projected] according to their own receptive capacity, which itself is defined by a situation that is both limited and open to the world's horizon. Thus the term "horizon" and its correlative, "world", appeared twice in the definition of mimesis 3 suggested earlier: the intersection of the world of the text and that of the listener or reader. This definition, [is] close to H.-G. Gadamer's notion of a "fusion of horizons" ' (1:77). The reference of a narrative is 'the experience it brings to language and, in the last analysis, the world and the temporality it unfolds in the face of this experience' (1:79). This fusion of the horizon of a text and that of a receiver's world also functions in 'acts of discourse in general, literary works among these acts of discourse, and narratives among these literary works' (1:77). This is the order of specification that has been followed to this point.

Paul Ricoeur's Narrative Voice and Point of View

Emplotment brings about games with time that are played out between the text and the reader through discourse. In the same manner that discourse combines both sense and reference, so the system of verbal tenses brings together the time of narrating, or 'utterance,' and the time of things narrated, or 'statement.' When scrutinized, the utterance can impart a 'reflexivity' that leads back to the speaker (Ricoeur 1984, 2:5). The utterance makes a statement that refers to the time of the narrative world. Mediating utterance and statement is a relation of conjunction and disjunction. The play between these two dimensions of utterance and statement projects the meaningful world of a text that is an experience of time. A three-tired scheme emerges in which the reader's experience, the narrative voice's utterance, and the statement about the narrative world interact through concordance and discordance, conjunction and disjunction. The games with time are co-ordinated by a dialectic essential to all narrative art: point of view and narrative voice. For Ricoeur, these two dimensions form the means by which 'narrative is constituted [that is,] as the discourse of a narrator recounting the discourse of the characters' (2:88). The discourse of the narrator is centred on the utterance and the discourse of the characters, in the world of the text, on the statement. As Ricoeur's term suggests, point of view leans towards a spatial dimension and the sense of sight. It is directed towards the sphere of experience to which the characters belong, that is, the world narrated. Voice, by contrast, leans towards the time of narrating and the sense of hearing. It mediates the reading and listening audience on the one hand and the narrated world of characters on the other. It 'presents' the narrated world to the readers or listeners addressed. Characters are understood as beings who think and feel and are capable of talking about their thoughts, feelings, and actions. Ricoeur's notion of character, then, marks a shift from a mimesis of action to one of character's action and, finally of character's discourse about action.

As in much of his writing, Ricoeur begins his consideration of narrative perspective with a resumé and examination of positions based on 'abstraction' (1984, 2:92). In this way he sees one theory as grounded in the concept of narrative techniques and another in that of narrative strategies. In the former two 'major techniques,' that of psycho-narration and that of narrated monologue, form a point of departure (2:88ff). The first, psycho-narration, is a technique involving the 'direct narration' of thoughts and feelings attributed by the voice either to another or to itself. What has been termed 'omniscience' is most characteristic of this form. A second form of this same technique is that of the 'quoted monologue,' that is, the internal monologue of another or a self-quoted monologue. Here also omniscience presupposes a transparency of the mind. The second technique does not involve quoted monologues but a 'narrated' or recounted monologue.' The narrative voice reports the discourse of the characters 'in the past tense and in the third person,' but 'no boundary remains to separate the narrator's discourse from that of the characters' (2:90).

The concept of narrative strategies may also provide a ground for abstract approaches. These depart from 'a typology capable of accounting for the two great dichotomies,' first, that of third- and first-person narrative, and, second, the predominance or not of the narrator's discourse over that of the characters (2:91). In the first dichotomy there are 'two kinds of fiction ... fiction that recounts the lives of characters taken as third parties ... third-person narrative [and,] on the other hand, we also find fictional narratives that attribute the grammatical person of the narrator to their characters ... first-person narratives' (2:91). Through this first dichotomy runs the second dichotomy, that is, that of predominance. This second dichotomy is easier to identify in third-person narratives than in first-person narratives because in the former 'the difference between the narrator and the character [is] marked by the distinction of personal pronouns' (2:91). This double system of dichotomies based on difference intends 'to cover all possible narrative situations, (1984, 2:91). Ricoeur notes that a vital mediating dimension is left out of abstract points of departure, namely, 'the aptitude readers have for organizing and summing up plots and for grouping similar plots together' (2:92). He therefore proposes 'to adopt the rule of following closely the experience of the reader in the process of organizing step-by-step the elements of the told story in order to put a plot together [and to] ... encounter the notions of perspective and voice less as categories defined by their place in a taxonomy than as a distinctive feature, taken from an unlimited constellation of other features and defined by its role in the composition of the literary work' (2:92–3).

Ricoeur brings together the notions of time, subjectivity, hearing, and question under one consideration, that of narrative voice. In keeping with the subjective quality of time voice cannot 'be freed of all personalizing metaphor' to the same extent as point of view (2:96). His 'constellation' of features begins with a question and the auditive sense of perception:

Voice answers the question, 'Who is speaking here?' If we do not want to be misled by the metaphor of vision when we consider a narrative in which everything is recounted, and in which making something visible through the eyes of a character is, according to Aristotle's analysis of *lexis* (elocution, diction), 'placing before our eyes,' that is, extending understanding to quasi-intuition, then vision must be held to be a concretization of understanding, hence, paradoxically, an appendix to hearing ... The narrative voice is the silent speech that presents the world of the text to the reader. (2:99)

Voice is the pivot of interaction between configuration and refiguration. It is for this reason that Ricoeur says a narrator 'speaks to the reader with a keen ear' (2:136). The narrative voice also bears the intentionality of the text 'which is actualized only in the intersubjective relationship that unfolds between the solicitations coming from the narrative voice and the response of reading.'[9] Voice is therefore personal in nature. While in some novels there is one voice that establishes itself above the other voices, other novels present a polyphony of voices, each distinct yet posited in relation to every other (2:96). Ricoeur privileges voice 'precisely because of its important temporal connotations' (2:98). Apart from being the 'speaker of the narrative voice,' the narrator is that part of the emplotment that 'in fact determines a present – the present of narration' in the fiction (2:96, 98). This present of narration 'is understood by the reader as *posterior* to the narrated story, hence that the told story is the *past of the narrative voice*' (2:98). Characters in the narrated world unfold a different time. Their time ranges over the past, future, and present while the narrative voice is always present.

Point of view, although inseparable from voice, is governed by a different question: 'From where do we perceive what is shown to us by the fact of being narrated? Hence, from where is one speaking?' (2:99). It can be understood as 'a place of origin, an orientation or as the aperture of a light source, which at one and the same time illuminates its subject and captures its features' (2:95-6). The spatial quality of point of view is evident in the interrogative pronoun 'where.' This strategy of emplotment is linked to perception through space: 'It is first of all the spatial perspective, taken literally, that serves as a metaphor for all other expressions of point of view. The development of a narrative always involves a combination of purely perceptual perspectives, implying position, angle of aperture and depth of field (as is the case in film)' (2:94). Centred in the world of the text, then, point of view designates the attitudes between narrator and characters and 'governs the conceptual vision of the world in all or part of a work' (2:93). Strategic shifts in point of view help structure the text and help give primacy to both particular characters or the narrator. It is also within point of view that external and internal points of view are strategically opposed.

Point of view falls 'within the gravitational field of the narrative *configuration*' (2:95). This might give it the appearance of being more objective and therefore more attractive to a study carried out in terms of rational categories. It is intimately related to strategies of composition and reveals a work's style. Nevertheless, style presupposes the structure of question and answer. In this way, Ricoeur states that 'style, here, does not designate anything ornamental but the singular entity resulting from the union, in a unique work of art, of the questions from which it proceeds and the solutions it gives' (2:148). A unique 'historical style' is what Ricoeur calls 'traditionality' (2:14). Through the use of temporal nucleus of voice and the spatial field of point of view, Ricoeur brings the reader's literary competence and aptitude into play in the question-and-answer process.

Point of view and voice are, then, considered as a single function mediating mimesis 2 and mimesis 3. If voice is 'silent speech' heard by the keen ear of a reader, point of view is 'the invitation addressed to readers to direct their gaze in the same direction as the author or the characters' (2:99). This invitation is one that the reader's aptitude and competence may or may not want or be able to accept. The creative potential of Paul Ricoeur's experiential approach to narrative and its value for the study of literature is a great as it is complex. Of the many questions it opens some of the most pressing concern the interaction between the perspective of the text, that is, point of view and voice, and the perspective of the reader, that is, his standpoint in the world and his questioning voice. This global understanding of perspective is what I call 'narrative perspective.' If sense is the medium of world configuration for both perception and discourse, how does a shift in sense affect narrative in general and narrative perspective in particular? Will a shift in emphasis from ear to eye be reflected in the techniques of voice and the strategies of point of view constituting the 'sense' of the text? Would discordance and concordance, *distentio* and *intentio*, distanciation and assimilation enter into different degrees of productive dynamism accordingly? If schema and sedimentation (which co-ordinate the configuring and refiguring act) lend themselves to a typology like that of Northrop Frye, can the 'sense' of narrative perspective also offer a typology? How do changes in 'sense' change the 'shape' of a text? If there is a progressive relation between the perception of discourse, the epistemological dimension, and the critical dimension, then how would these changes affect the perspective of a literary criticism that substitutes spoken circumstance with textual circumscription (Valdés 1987, 55)? What can be said of a critical methodology that finds its standpoint in the notion of 'reversal'? If the reference of the text is an experience of both time and the world it unfolds, can the perspective or sense shift the narrative towards the pole of space or towards that of time in order to create narrations 'about space' as well as 'about time' (Ricoeur 1984, 2: chap. 4)? Can the technological individuality of a reading public be linked, through discourse, to the epistemological activity of 'grasping together' that characterizes perception and reading and, if so, can this individuality be explained in terms of the medium of discourse? What method of investigation into the character and structure of narrative perspective will allow these questions to find answers in the reader-text encounter? These are but a few of the questions that must be dealt with if literature is to be understood not as a discrete cultural phenomenon within a selected linguistic community but as a universal and trans-temporal quality of human culture. In the never-ending search for answers, the essential role played by narrative perspective may offer insight into the process of man becoming humanity through literature.

4

The Concept of Narrative Perspective

Paul Ricoeur's phenomenological hermeneutics brings together the ontological premise of phenomenology and the historical premise of hermeneutics in a new and productive relationship (Iser 1979, 5). From the standpoint of hermeneutics, his theory of language as discourse and narrative as the experience of time intimately relates the first and the third moments of consciousness exposed to the effects of history. This process of language, perception, and experience gives rise to a fourth moment when the 'universality of experience' unites the 'various individual perceptions' under the 'true universality of the concept' and achieves the 'universality of science' (Gadamer 1975, 314). From the standpoint of phenomenology, Ricoeur's theory opens the strata of perception to reveal the metaphorical process as it brings discourse, feeling, and the dialectic of non-sense and sense into the creation of meaning.

The notion of perspective has played a key role in the dialectic of question and answer at the level of language, in the body-world dialectic at the level of perception, and in the interaction between reader and text in the experience of narrative. It is marked by a fundamental direction proceeding from the question to an answer that ultimately reflects the question. This notion also proceeds primarily from a non-sense through a sense to an object, the 'ultimate truth' of which reflects the perceiver (M.M-P. 1968, 155). Finally, the notion of perspective proceeds primarily from sense to a first- and second-order referent. These, in turn, reflect back upon the very process of making sense that is the human experience of time. Sense itself becomes an 'ultimate referent' (Ricoeur, quoted in White 1985, 292).

The concept of narrative perspective cannot be divorced from these more general notions of language, perception, and experience. To the degree that 'narrative' is language, it is consciousness subject to historical effects. To the degree that 'perspective' is sense, it is perception. To the degree that 'narrative perspective' is essential to literature, it is vital to the interaction between reader and text in the human experience of time through narrative. As narrative, it is a configuration that the reader takes up and puts into play (Ricoeur 1984, 1:53). The hermeneutical experience, that is, the listening to, the questioning and answering the text, makes narrative perspective a virtual relationship between the text and the reader in the dialectic of realization. If narrative perspective is a channeled view that sets out 'the specific mode of access to the object intended,' two channels are involved; one historical, the other textual (Iser 1978a, 113). A virtual narrative perspective in its 'stereoscopic' character cannot down-play either direction (Ricoeur 1977, 256, and 1984, 2:149–50).

This has been, I believe, a major issue underlying different approaches to narrative perspective. Henry James, both in his rejection of 'the romantic privilege of the "first-person" ' and in his emphasis 'of employing but one centre,' as well as Percy Lubbock, who sees point of view as a 'question of method ... deciding the look that the story is to wear as a whole,' recognize but play down the subjective role in favour of objective form (James 317, 320 and Lubbock 251, 265). E.M. Forster, in his celebrated response to Lubbock, stresses the author's ability 'to bounce' the reader around as well as the author's personal relation to the characters (78). He places the subjective role 'plumb in the centre' of his considerations (79). He sees the author's 'power to expand and contract perception' underlying point of view as having 'a parallel in our perception of life' (81). Norman Friedman also considers point of view to be 'the aesthetic relationship between the author and his work' (109). M.H. Abrams turns to a more 'objective,' formal criterion and 'establishes a broad division between third-person and first-person narratives' (134). Against the form of 'person,' Wayne C. Booth counters with 'To say that a story is told in the first or the third person will tell us nothing of importance unless we become more precise and describe how the particular qualities of the narrators relate to specific effects' (150). The pendulum has swung back to the subjective pole only now this subjectivity is brought into play in terms of the reader.

The advent of formalism and structuralism brought with it an 'objective' perspective. Jurij Lotman outlines 'artistic point of view' as the relation of a system (that is, a hierarchy of relations and their orientations creating a world) to a subject or a consciousness capable of engendering a similar structure (265, 268). He sees the whole text ' "shot" in one depth, [where] the depth as such is not perceived,' eliminating in one phrase the living subject who may be 'deeply' moved in multiple ways by a text (265). Lotman's adherence to formalist binary oppositions leads him to either a 'correct and true' reading, which coincides with the point of view of the text as a whole, or to an 'incorrect' reading, which opposes it. This two-dimensional character of height and width gives way to a consideration of narrative perspective in spatial terms, that is, of objective relationships between parts. The concept of person reflects the same tendency. Rather than being an upsurge of time, the temporal dimension of the subjective field is reduced to a route between two points on a flat map (239). Lotman quite literally takes the map for the being-there, ignoring the ontological dimension of present, past, and future. Recent developments in the field of narratology have sustained a similar point of departure in the objective space of the text. Narratology's point of view can now be explored in terms of perception's time-and-space dialectic.

Narratology

The objective study of narrative from a spatially oriented standpoint has found recent expression in the work of Gerard Genette, Shlomith Rimmon-Kenan, and Mieke Bal. A certain irony is felt in that their spatial *perspectiva artificialis* often leads to contradiction in its enthusiastic search for objectivity. The resulting 'exact construction' can be both confusing and beyond practical use for the common reader. Genette's study of narrative as controlled information divides the text (understood as the signifier independent of the story, or signified) into mood and voice. Mood is, in turn, divided according to the 'common and convenient spatial metaphor' of distance and perspective: ' "Distance" and "perspective," ... are the two chief modalities of that *regulation of narrative information* ... as the view I have of a picture depends for precision on the distance separating me from it, and for breadth on my position with respect to whatever partial obstruction is more or less blocking it' (Genette 1980, 162). Percy Lubbock's study of 'point of view' is, in Genette's view, exemplary. He feels, however, that it has the shortcoming of not exploring adequately the difference between the narrator and the character who orients the point of view. He proposes the important questions of 'Who sees?' and 'Who speaks?' as cornerstones for developing a typology of the relation between the narrator and his story, as well as for determining his position within that story (186). In order to distance himself from the 'too specifically visual connotations of the terms *vision, field* and *point of view*,' Genette does not suggest a term with an audio-oral connotation, but proposes the 'more abstract term *focalization*' (189). While Genette limits his study to narrative as 'signifier,' he also calls upon an 'informed reader' to give an '*interpretation*' that 'we should not confuse [with] the *information* given by a focalized narrative' (197). Again, although the reader does not play a part in the text, narrative 'always says less than it knows, but it often makes known more than it says' (198).

Voice is considered with some reluctance by Genette. He proposes to consider voice 'for its own sake, after having met it so often without wanting to' (211). Voice is a mode of action related to the subjectivity of person. Person is understood here as 'all those people who partic-ipate, even though passively, in this narrating activity,' but the reader of a work is not included in this category (213). In dealing with fictive entities one must not confuse the fictive recipient, which is within its domain, and the reader himself. Genette feels that a critical reading of narrative voice is an inevitable attack on the narrative's integrity. The narrative situation presented by the voice involves two protagonists: the narrator and narratee. This situation is 'like any other, a complex whole within which analysis, or simply description, cannot *differentiate* except by ripping apart a tight web of connections among the narrating act, its protagonists, its spatio-temporal determinations, its relationship to other narrating situations involved in the same narrative, etc. The demands of exposition constrain us to this unavoidable violence' (215).

Genette rejects the grammatical pronouns as a criterion for estab-lishing a relationship between narrator and story. Because all narrators can narrate their story '*only* in the "first-person," ' he states that the 'real question is whether or not the narrator can use the first-person to designate *one of his characters*' (244). Two types of narrative emerge: *heterodiegetic*, with the narrator absent from the story he tells, and *homodiegetic*, with the narrator present as a character. Modern literature is exemplified by the 'Borgesian fantastic ... [which] does *not accept person*,' but 'violates' the levels of first-person and third-person het-erodiegetic and homodiegetic narration (247).

Five functions correspond to the narrative voice. The 'narrating' func-tion is the telling of the story as such. The 'directing' function is a metalinguistic, internal organization of the narrative. The function of 'communication' corresponds to Roman Jakobson's phatic and conative functions.[1] It operates in the narrating situation from the narrator to 'the narratee – present, absent or implied' (Genette 1980, 255). Genette emphasizes that 'we, the readers, cannot identify ourselves with those fictive narratees anymore than those intradiegetic narrators can address themselves to us or even assume our existence' (260). The fourth, or 'testimonial,' function is 'very homologous with the one Jakobson names, a little unfortunately, the "emotive" function' (256). The 'ideological' function is 'a vehicle of realistic motivation' and a 'didactic form of an authorized commentary on the action' (257, 256).

Time also plays a role in the typologies of voice. It comes to bear on the types of narrating: 'subsequent' or past-tense narrative; 'prior' or future-tense narrative (although it can be conjugated in the present); simultaneous or 'contemporary' narrative, and 'interpolated' narrative located between moments of action.

Genette also abstracts different levels of narrative: the extradiegetic, the intradiegetic or diegetic, and the metadiegetic levels. The extradiegetic level is the '(literary) act' carried out at a first level, 'outside' the narrative so to speak, while the diegetic level presents a narrator inside the narrative (228). The metadiegetic level is found 'inside' another narrative. It is framed by or contained within the diegetic level and involves a narrator who is already a character in the framing intradiegetic level.

A final aspect of the narrative levels is that of *narrative metalepsis*. Metalepsis is not a level but an 'additional detour' to the narrative levels (237). It is an 'intrusion by the extradiegetic narrator or narratee into the diegetic universe' (234). It is a term extended to all 'transgressions' of the 'sacred' boundary that separates the text from the world of reality:

All these games [of transgression], by the intensity of their effects, demonstrate the importance of the boundary they tax their ingenuity to overstep, in defiance of verisimilitude – a boundary *that is precisely the narrating (or the performance) itself*: a shifting but sacred frontier between two worlds, the world in which one tells, the world of which one tells. Whence the uneasiness Borges so well put his finger on: 'Such inversions suggest that if the characters in a story can be readers or spectators, then we, their readers or spectators, can be fictitious'. The most troubling thing about metalepsis indeed lies in this unacceptable and insistent hypothesis, that the extradiegetic is perhaps always diegetic and that the narrator and his narratees – you and I – perhaps belong to some narrative. (235–6)

Metalepsis is unacceptable to Genette because of the fundamentally visual and spatial nature of his understanding of narrative. He is concerned with closed borders, and the historical experience of time does not receive his attention. His narrative understanding seeks to restrict interpersonal experience as a criterion for the study of narrative. While, on the one hand, he appeals to 'common sense' ('*We* know that ... ,' 'It is *obviously* with respect to ... ,' '*common* usage,' '*common* and convenient'), on the other he proposes an abstract analysis founded on *distentio* and distanciation (200, 25, 162; emphasis added). In characterizing the boundary between text and the world of reader as one surpassed only by 'violence,' 'transgression,' and analytical tearing apart, little room, if any, is left for mediation, 'transcendence,' and the narrative understanding that precedes any involvement with narrative (Ricoeur 1984, 2:5). Genette's recent *Palimpsestes* of course does explore '*transtextualité* ou transcendance textuelle du texte' (1982, 7). This transcendence, however, concentrates on the relations between a text or *hypertexte* and an antecedent *hypotexte*, not on potential or ' "(as yet) untold" stories' that readers 'see in a given sequence of the episodes of our lives' (Ricoeur 1984, 1:74). These different types of narrative understanding, anchored in 'everyday experiences,' do not find room in his study (1:74). The 'familiarity with literary works' as transmitted through different cultures' 'unique historical style ... called "traditionality" ' is intertwined with everyday understanding (Ricoeur 1984, 2:14). Transtextuality cannot replace narrative understanding.

Genette's unacceptance of mediation, in favour of a 'frontier,' limits the potential of his insight in other ways as well. While he invokes Jakobson's emotive, conative, phatic, and metalinguistic functions to describe the narrator, the all-important *poetic* function and *referential* function are noticeably missing. This absence inhibits him from developing the full impact of his questions 'Who sees?' and 'Who speaks?' on precisely the most important level, that of the reader in the world. What is more, the 'tremendous cultural achievement' signalled by writing cannot be explored, if the relations of the *message* to the *medium*, the *speaker*, the *hearer*, the *code*, and the *reference* are ignored (Ricoeur 1976, chap. 2). The questions 'Who sees?' and 'Who speaks?' cannot be enclosed within the text. It is not simply a matter of rephrasing the issue in equally visual terms such as 'focalization.' The equally important questions 'To whom does the voice speak?', 'Who hears in the text?', and 'Who *listens* beyond its frontiers?' must also be asked. As Gadamer has stated, 'all writing, if it is to be understood, requires a sort of heightening of the inward ear ... A sharpening of the ear is demanded' (1975, 496). The narrator may well direct his words to the narratee, yet it is difficult to accept the notion of them not being equally intended for the reader (the '-you and I-' Genette invokes), albeit '*off to the side*' (Genette 1980, 236, 262). It is after all a reader who asks these questions and it is often the reader who must provide the answers. These questions point not only to the text, but also to the self-referential function of reading and to the standpoint of the reader in the world from where the questions are voiced.

When Genette outlines the variable relationships of time that arise between the narrating and the story, he again appeals to the dimension of 'you and I' lying outside that sacred frontier marking the limit of his proposed field of study: 'When I read *Gambara* or *Le Chef-d'oeuvre inconnu*, I am interested in a story, and care little to know who tells it, where, and when; if I read *Facino Cane*, at no time can I overlook the presence of the narrator in the story he tells; if it is *La Maison Nucingen*, the author makes it his business to draw my attention to the person of the talker Bixiou and the group of listeners he addresses; if it is *L'Auberge rouge*, I will undoubtedly give less attention to the foreseeable unfolding of the story Herman tells than to the reactions of a listener named Taillefer, for the narrative is on two levels, and the second – *where someone narrates* – is where most of the drama's excitement is' (1980, 236, 212–13). While the reader's perception of the story is definitely given an important role in the narrating instance, Genette insists that the recipient of the narrative not be confused with the reader outside the text and therefore beyond the realm of narratology (213). On the one hand, he abstracts the text as signifier independent of the story; on the other, he calls upon the story as an important point of reference. On the one hand, he argues against entangling the reader in the story; on the other, he appeals to the reader's perception of the story. Again, while he admits that the story and the narrating can become entangled, he does not admit the same of the reader's narrative understanding (217).

Genette's effort to exclude the reader standpoint or 'narrative understanding' from his theory comes to bear on the typology of narrating as well. While the narrating instance is a relationship between narrator and story, stories have meaning, and meaning does not depend on grammatical structures alone. Time cannot be reduced to tense. The notion of prior narrating is to the point here. Prior narrating is also 'subsequent' to a narrative understanding both inside and outside the sacred frontier mediating worlds. The notion of future is very much a projection of a past, including a reader's past, ahead of the present. Thus, an apocalyptic or prophetic narrative told in the present or future tense may be to different degrees both prior and subsequent depending on the when, where, and by whom of the reading, as well the when, where, and by whom of the telling. The relationship between the narrating and the story may also become highly ironic. A community of readers also plays a role in coming to terms with the time of the story told and the temporal relations possible between the narrator and the events they share. Narrating may be prior and again not be prior. Once the story becomes a point of reference for a typology of temporal relations, grammatical tense alone is not adequate. A reader also stands at the centre of a story's temporal relations and here, as Ricoeur puts it, 'we *see* some images only to the extent that we first *hear* them' (1979, 134).

Despite Genette's claim that the distance between episodes and narrating location 'lies neither in time nor in space' but in a difference of relations, he necessarily employs both a temporal and spatial criterion to create the narrative levels of the text (1980, 227). The admittedly inadequate way he chooses to distinguish these relations between episodes is, nevertheless, one that privileges a spatial criterion of inside or outside, above or below. Again, temporal intervals between events are considered in terms of an objective 'distance.' Diegetic or narrative levels are not created by a voice mediating the reader and the world of the text, but rather by the voice's relationship to the characters in that world. Although the here and now of narrating is always accompanied by a 'here' and 'now' of reading, the different relationships that develop between the voice and the reader are ignored.

Genette binds point of view to this spatial criterion as well. While he intends to move away from the visual implications of the 'Who sees?' question and proposes to 'rechristen' perspective as 'focalization,' his three focalization types are primarily visual and spatial: *nonfocalized* narrative or 'vision from behind'; *internal* focalization, that is, a 'narrative with "point of view"' after Lubbock'; and *external* focalization or 'vision from without' (189). Genette's concepts of distance, breadth, and obstructions blocking the view of focalization do not rest upon the essential factor of depth both preceding and relating each of these notions. While he refers to his spatial metaphor as both common and convenient, it appears to be neither. On the contrary, his analysis is both artificial and abstract. It is based on the principles of difference and abstract precision through an objective, spatial focalization (189).

This near-ironic appeal to common sense by means of a highly abstract, or artificial sense becomes more apparent in the study of narrative by Shlomith Rimmon-Kenan. If Genette appeals to common sense but argues artificial sense, Rimmon-Kenan reverses the procedure. She appeals to the objective, abstract criterion of a spatial sense only to argue the common sense of reading processes.

Rimmon-Kenan's 'post-Genettian theory' also divides the text into focalization, on the one hand, and narration or voice, on the other (1983, 85). Focalization is a 'textual factor relating to both story and narration.'[2] It is then subdivided into a subject focalizer, 'the agent whose perception orients the presentation,' and an object focalized, or 'what the focalizer perceives' (74). Types of focalization are decided by its position, external or internal, to the story and the degree of persistence on one predominant focalizer.

The facets of focalization are divided into two co-ordinates. Rimmon-Kenan makes the important observation that the highly visual sense of focalization proposed by Genette is too narrow. She notes that 'perception (sight, hearing, smell, etc.) is determined by two main coordinates: space and time' (77). Here a reversal has taken place, for space and time do not *determine* perception. As argued above, perception cannot be reduced to an impingement of 'pure' sense data on the senses.[3] On the contrary, perception realizes space and we *are* time. Her objective, spatial criterion intends 'to show how the external/internal criterion manifests itself in each' (77). Unfortunately, the potential of her insight into the sense spectrum is not fulfilled. The relation of these senses to the two co-ordinates of space and time is reduced to a dichotomy of inside/outside.

Rimmon-Kenan's psychological facet of focalization deals with the cognitive and emotive orientation of the focalizer. Again, a spatial dichotomy of 'either from without or from within' is used to restrict not only knowledge and conjecture but also belief and memory (80). The ideological facet is understood as 'a general system of viewing the world conceptually' (81). Her 'concept,' however, does not proceed from experience, perception, and language as a historical mode of being in the world. She does point out, albeit confusingly, that 'focalization is non-verbal; however, like everything else in the text it is expressed by language' (82).

The levels and voices that constitute Rimmon-Kenan's situation of narrative communication follow Genette's categories closely. Of Seymour Chatman's participants in communication, that is, 'Real author – Implied author – (Narrator) – (Narratee) – Implied reader – Real reader,' the first and the last are initially rejected (S.R-K. 86). This initial exclusion of the real author and reader is then extended to the implied author and reader as well. Her criterion is focused on the text, narrator, and narratee: 'I propose ... the exclusion of the implied author and reader from a description of the communication situation, my second suggestion calls for the inclusion of the narrator and the narratee as constitutive ... factors in narrative communication' (88). The exclusion of the implied author and reader is somewhat relative, for she goes on to say that the 'implied author and reader will be mentioned when relevant' (89). Of the remaining participants, 'the empirical process of communication between author and reader is less relevant ... than its counterpart in the text' (89). To add to the confusion, the reader is not 'real.' He or she is not a person perceiving and experiencing a text through an intersubjective encounter with the narrative voice, nor does a *metaphorical*, narrative understanding play a part in the narrative process. She rejects as 'extreme the concept ... of a real reader, whether a specific individual or the collective readership of a period' (119). Having thus rejected the implied author as a notion that 'must be de-personified' and the implied reader, as well as the real reader, she makes her position clear by quoting Menakhem Perry and Christine Brooke-Rose: 'It should be clear from my declared focus that the "reader" is seen in this book [*Narrative Fiction: Contemporary Poetics*] as a construct, a "metonymic characterization of the text" ... an "it" rather than a personified "he" or "she" ... Such a reader is "implied" or "encoded" in the text "in the very rhetoric through which he is required to "make sense of the content" or reconstruct it "as a world." ' (88, 119). The text, then, makes the sense not the reader. He or she is not required to make sense metaphorically, but is himself or herself metonymically constructed.[4] Perception is again explained as an impingement upon the senses for the 'linear figuration of signs ... imposes upon the reader a successive perception of bits of information' (119). Rimmon-Kenan affirms that the 'text can direct and control the reader's comprehension and attitudes' through the position of items of infor-

mation in the text (120). By defining the reader as a metonymical construct in the text she does not take into account what Paul Ricoeur calls
the shift 'from the sphere of perception to that of language' made
possible through the 'semantic innovation characteristic of the metaphorical usage of language' (1979, 129). This shift from perception back
to language is only made possible through the reverberation of non-
sense becoming sense at the time of assimilation. Ricoeur warns, however, that 'to understand this procedure, one must first admit that the
reverberation proceeds not from things *seen*, but from things *said*' (130).

In her attempt to integrate perception into the consideration of narrative perspective (at the cost of a reader), Rimmon-Kenan relies on
Menakhem Perry's psychological concept of 'primary effect': 'Information and attitudes presented at an early stage of the text tend to
encourage the reader to interpret everything in their light. The reader
is prone to preserve such meanings and attitudes for as long as possible'
(120). Unfortunately, the primary effect is enclosed within the text and
therefore leaves certain pressing questions unanswered. Would not a
'real' reader's linguistically constituted standpoint in the world, his
narrative understanding in itself, constitute a 'primary effect'? Would
not his or her previous understanding of the world play a part at least
in the first step of a narrative encounter, that is, the selection of a
specific text by reading its title and its author's name? Some kind of
'understanding' appears to be at work from the outset for, she claims,
'the reader ... does not wait until the end to understand the text' (121).

This 'paradoxical position of the text *vis-à-vis* its reader' comes to the
fore when Rimmon-Kenan states that 'literature models do not involve
a mediation through some concept of the world' (122, 124). She explains
that making 'sense of a text requires an integration of its elements with
each other, an integration which involves an appeal to various familiar
models of coherence ... "Models of coherence" can derive either from
"reality" or from literature' (123, 124). The reader (understood as a
metonymical construct of the text) must, nevertheless, find reality models
in both chronology and 'causality' as well as through contiguity 'in
space' (124). Literature models also come to bear on the reader, for he
or she must rely on specifically literary exigencies or institutions and
play a part in the essential end that a text must achieve: 'in order to
be read it must make itself understood' (122). Both genre and text
appear in Rimmon-Kenan's study as self-contained units 'making
themselves' understood. She proposes that the former permits the
latter to be understood before it is read. Strange occurrences in a text

'can be made intelligible and acceptable if the text belongs to the genre of the Marvelous' (125). Thus, it is the institution that permits meaning to exist, not the reader. Little if any attempt is made to mediate literary models and notions of reality. Genre precedes the text rather than proceeding from an epistemology. It is 'some concept (or structure) which governs our perception of the world' (124). The process of language-perception-experience-concept is reversed. This reversal is only possible from a spatial standpoint in the 'object' of the text. It, needless to say, presupposes the very process it reverses.

This reversal permits Rimmon-Kenan to base her concept of representation on Genette's paradoxical claim that 'language can only imitate language' and to dismiss mimesis as an imitation of action in favour of 'mimetic illusion' (S.R-K. 108). As with 'perspective' in history, I find it difficult to conceive of language stepping outside itself in order to imitate itself. Mimesis poses a 'problem' that she proposes to solve by dealing with 'the illusion of imitation of events' (108). This 'illusion of mimesis' is achieved by reducing intersubjective or personal considerations, in favour of objective data: 'Thus the illusion of an imitation of events is achieved by supplying the maximum of information and the minimum of informant' (108). In attempting to discard 'the very notion of "showing" ' Rimmon-Kenan's 'mimetic illusion' moves the theory of narrative and perspective one degree closer to hallucination and another degree farther from perception itself (108).

The narrator is defined 'minimally, as the agent which at the very least narrates or engages in some activity serving the needs of narration,' and she proposes to distinguish 'degrees of perceptibility of the narrator in the text' (88, 89). The same criterion is proposed for the narratee, who is explained as the 'agent which is at the very least implicitly addressed by the narrator ... even when the narrator becomes his own narratee' (89). The function of person in narration is thus brought to a minimum.

Having rejected the reader and mimesis in favour of the text and illusion, Rimmon-Kenan goes on to make a singularly important observation: 'The narrative level to which the narrator belongs, the extent of his participation in the story, the degree of perceptibility of his role, and finally his reliability are crucial factors in the reader's understanding of and attitude to the story' (94). If this 'reader' does not appear to be confined to the text, Rimmon-Kenan's 'dynamics of reading' appears to be even less so (119ff.). Again, following Menakhem Perry, she states that 'reading can be seen as a continuous process of forming hypotheses, reinforcing them, developing them, modifying them, and sometimes replacing them by others or dropping them altogether. It should be noted, however, that even rejected hypotheses may continue exercising some influence on the reader's comprehension. By the end of the reading process, the reader usually will have reached a "finalized hypothesis", an overall meaning which *makes sense of the text* as a whole' (121; emphasis added). This is not the text making itself understood but the reader making sense of the text. Such sense-making depends on conventions that 'establish a kind of contract *between* the text and the reader, so that some expectations are rendered plausible, others ruled out" (125; emphasis added). Reading is further explained as 'filling gaps' with information rather than with meaning (128).

Rimmon-Kenan's final consideration of reading moves to include hermeneutics and the concept of reading as a process. She does not understand hermeneutics as a meaningful activity but rather as an absence of information: 'the most typical gap in narrative fiction is hermeneutic (also called "information gap")' (128). She also rejects the 'more far-reaching "revisionism" of some reader-oriented studies, because that is often at odds with the very project of narrative poetics' (118). While she refuses to discuss 'problems like reader's response or the formation of attitudes,' she ends her consideration of the text and its reading with an interesting analogy of the reader's role in constructing the text: 'How to make a bagel? First you take a hole.... And how to make a narrative text? In exactly the same way. Holes or gaps are so central in narrative fiction because the materials the text provides for the reconstruction of a world (or story) are insufficient for saturation. No matter how detailed the presentation is, further questions can always be asked; gaps always remain open' (118, 127). Her final argument emphasizes the 'centrality of literary structures to the organization of experience' and the 'kind of spiralling movement' that keeps literary 'exploration' on the move (132).

Shlomith Rimmon-Kenan's theory of narrative fiction as contemporary poetics constitutes an important moment in post-Genettian theory, because it moves from a spatial criterion to end in a hermeneutical standpoint. On the one hand, she holds that 'the text is the only observable and object-like aspect of verbal narrative' and that it must be 'the anchoring-point for any discussion of the other aspects' (6). The depth provided by metaphor is set aside in favour of a 'view' from which 'story and narration may be seen as two metonymies of the text' (4). To this is added the concept of a reader as a metonymical 'it' that processes information or data upon command from the text. The notions of point of view and voice are not mediated by a tertium quid of 'narrative perspective' but are treated as discrete units. The predominantly visual and spatial formulation of focalization introduces other senses, but does not develop the co-relation between the sense and the perspective beyond an inside vs. outside dichotomy. Perception is formulated as a dichotomy of presence vs. absence (rather than as a dialectic of visible and invisible) and is explained in terms of an impingement upon the senses, that is, as radiating from the objective text and then seen by the reader. Her fundamental mode of operation is a formal logic implying a univocal criterion of cause and effect.

On the other hand, her theory also attempts to introduce a reader who questions, who fills in gaps and realizes the text through a spiralling hermeneutic activity. It approaches an equivocal, transcendental logic by proposing a study of the function of literature in organizing experience, but does not consider the function of a linguistically constituted perception in organizing the experience of the text through an intersubjective fusion of perspectives. On the one hand her theory stands in a formal logic, on the other it directs itself towards but does not reach a transcendental logic. Hermeneutics *is not* the providing of information to fill gaps but, as developed by Gadamer and Ricoeur, the realization of meaning within a tradition. Ricoeur helps point out the difficulty of Rimmon-Kenan's position:

It is in this sense that the logic of the double meaning proper to hermeneutics can be called transcendental. If the debate is not carried to this level, one will be quickly driven into an untenable situation; in vain will one attempt to maintain the debate at a purely semantic level and attempt to make room for equivocal meanings alongside univocal meanings, for the theoretical distinction between the two kinds of equivocalness – equivocalness through a surplus of meaning, found in the exegetic sciences, and equivocalness through the confusion of meanings, which logic chases away – cannot be justified at the level of semantics alone. Two logics cannot exist at the same level. (1974, 19)

It appears that in approaching the limits of a spatially defined standpoint in the object of the written text, Rimmon-Kenan's alternating current of thought directs itself now towards the hermeneutical experience, now towards the stable, formal concept. As in figure 1 on page 27 above, the refiguration vacillates with the perspective. On the one hand it reverses the direction of hallucination and perception; on the other it directs the reader to fill the gaps that 'he' or 'she' may or may not perceive (S.R-K. 129). This alternating sense is most evident in her consideration of voice and the reader.

The untenable position that Rimmon-Kenan sustains must reconsider focalization and voice in one of two senses. On the one hand, it can objectify its position totally. It can make the written text absolute and primordial. It can claim *to be* the answer and therefore not have to respond to intersubjective questioning. Such an answer would be both alienated and artificial. It can invert the hallucination-perception process completely and claim that all perspectives are forever distanced from the text, for meaning 'is' non-sense. On the other hand, it can further explore the insight into perception as a reaching out to the world rather than an impingement, and sense as a mediation of language and experience. It can take up 'the reader's dynamic participation' as a dialectic of question and answer with the text within a community of experience (S.R-K. 129). It can hear the reverberation of sense emerging from non-sense as the intersubjective dialogue between text and reader is played out. I believe this to be the direction Rimmon-Kenan finally takes, for she ends her *Narrative Fiction* with an understanding of the reading process as a 'guessing game, an attempt to solve a riddle or puzzle,' and reminds the 'real' reader that 'further questions can always be asked; gaps always remain open' (126, 127).

Mieke Bal represents a further step in this latter direction. Her *Narratology* (1985) intends to provide a tool with which 'to formulate a textual description in such a way that it is accessible to others' (4). Her theory is also based on difference. She differentiates between (a) the *text* as a manifestation of a story; (b) a *fabula* as a sequence of events that are grammatically formulated like the 'deep structure' of the sentence and that constitute the deep structure of the narrative text; (c) a *story* as 'the *way in which* these events are presented'; (d) *event* as the transition from one state to another; (e) *actors* as agents not necessarily human; and (f) *act*, defined 'as to cause or to experience an event' (5).

Three observations can be made at this initial point. First, while experience as an act replaces effect in a cause/effect dichotomy, it is restricted to an actor *interior* to the story. It is not an event between the text and the reader. It is not an act of reading that is being considered, for such an act always involves a human reader who cannot be reduced to a structure in the story alone.

A second observation is that the 'deep structure' of the fabula is proposed as a substitute for the standpoint of the reader as a perceiving subject and for his or her narrative understanding. The way in which the reader's perspective orders the events in his or her experience of the text is considered extraneous to the narrative process. He or she does not refigure the text through a dialogue with the narrative voice.[5] This notion of deep structure, which Bal draws from Greimas's semiotic square, cannot provide the primary condition for grasping any meaning whatsoever because the relations obtained in the square presuppose the subjective, *personal* relations already at work in the realization of discourse as a dialogue (13 and 47, and Ricoeur 1984, 2:48–9). Again, the visual argument that white exists because of (a) contradiction (white vs. not-white), (b) contrariety (white vs. black), and (c) presupposition (not-white vs. black) itself presupposes the ontological quality that is inherent in the personal relations at work within the verb at the heart of discourse. Thus, Emile Benveniste has pointed out that the structural relations of person in discourse can be understood as (a) 'I' exist because I am a 'subjective person' and 'you' are a non-subjective person; (b) 'I' am a subjective person and therefore not a 'he, she,' and 'it', or non-person; and (c) 'you' are a non-subjective person and therefore not a non-person.[6] These structural *'corrélations de personnalité*,' however, re-late ' "figurations" ' of human beings and therefore presuppose 'la réalité humaine du dialogue' (Benveniste 1:235, 225, 232). When parting from the living *experience* of language as discourse, the same transcend-ent quality that characterizes perception as an opening and reaching out to the world comes to the fore: ' "je" est toujours *transcendant* par raport à "tu". Quand je sors de "moi" pour établir une relation vivante avec un être, je rencontre ou je pose nécessairement un "tu", qui est, hors de moi, la seule "personne" imaginable. Ces qualités d'intériorité et de transcendance appartiennent en propre au "je" et s'inversent en "tu" ' (Benveniste 1:232).

Greimas's visual criterion, then, recalls what is already at work in meaningful discourse, and here transcendence as well as contrast is at work. The ontological level of being an 'I' capable of recognizing a 'you' as well as a 'he, she, it' in language precedes the abstract, visual op-position of discrete, objective units such as Greimas's white vs. black. The definition of event and the way in which events are presented must be extended to include what 'figures' as an event for a reader not only in the appropriation of a text with which he or she enters into dialogue, but also what 'figures' as an event in the appropriation of his or her language and tradition upon doing so: 'Le langage est ainsi organisé qu'il permet à chaque locuteur de *s'approprier* la langue entière en se désignant comme *je'* (Benveniste 1:262). The role played by the reader's perspective in his or her value-ridden selection and ordering of events in her or his dialogue with the text rests firmly on his or her perception in language and tradition.

Finally, Bal explores any text as a variation of some presupposed, finite, and atemporal narrative system that can be described (3). This absolute system is available because 'it is in principle possible to give a complete description of a text, that is an account of all the narrative characteristics of the text in question. However, such a description would consume a great amount of time and paper, and would, in the end, be rather uninteresting' (9). It is neither a matter of paper nor of boredom. In accordance with the principles of perception it is impossible to know any object completely. Bal's argument leans towards a closed circle because the fixed narrative system must be derived from variable texts and the variable texts are understood in terms of the fixed system. If the 'logic of events' underlying the description of the text is to be understood as 'a course of events that is experienced by the reader as natural and in accordance with the world,' then this logic is incompatible with any absolute understanding and description (12). A complete description of the entire text is not possible if 'everything that can be said about the structure of fabulas also bears on extra-literary facts' (13).

It is on the basis of these three observations that Mieke Bal's concept of narrative perspective can be considered. Narrative is characterized by two types of spokesmen, 'the narrator and the actor' (Bal 8). The notion of voice is split in two. The narrator is understood as 'a function and not a person,' as an 'it' located at the level of text rather than of the story (119). Closely related to the narrator and at the level of the story is found a focalizing agent. The focalizor is essential because it is located between the linguistic text and the material fabula. It is spatially defined as 'the point from which the elements are viewed' (104). This point can lie with a character, that is, as *'internal* focalization,' or with an anonymous agent or *'external* focalization' (105). For Bal these actor-spokesmen 'are, in theory, disconnected from the embodiment in a person. This is implied in our structural approach' (27). She admits, however, that reality does not obey her theory because 'the practical result is that the subject is usually a person or a personified animal (in animal fables) or an object' (27).

This divergence of theory from practice is widened further by her teleological classification of actors in groups of 'actants.' It is based on the logical presupposition 'that human thinking and action is directed towards an aim' (26). While it is difficult to understand how any 'object' spokesman would necessarily obey this 'human' criterion, the aim to which a spokesman aspires is 'the achievement of something agreeable or favourable, or the evasion of something disagreeable or unfavourable' (26). Thus Bal co-ordinates past and future action, not through a will in the present but by means of a hedonistic aim founded on a logic of desire. This aim does not account for such 'illogical' acts of the will as self-sacrifice that are also encountered in narrative through the voices of narrative spokesmen.

Bal introduces a logical grammar based on sentence structure as a universal model through which narrative actants are filtered. The distance between Bal's theoretical principle and her pragmatic necessities once again hinders the relation between the reader, the logic of narrative, and the cause-effect logic of grammar. The universality of the grammatical model imposed on the text supplants the reader's perspective that perceives the elements and brings them into a whole. This substitution affects all three levels involved in narrative perspective. *Langue* and 'structural logic' replace 'language' and narrative logic; a universal model is substituted for perception and reader perspective; a teleology substitutes the experience of an event in the present that co-ordinates past tradition and future action. The fabula, as a universal model, substitutes plot, and perception becomes predetermined by that 'one model' (Bal 18). The dilemma created by her definition of fable as 'a series of *logically* and chronologically related events' is that it cannot claim both the 'natural logic of events' and the 'universal logic of grammar' (18; emphasis added). Paul Ricoeur's argument is to the point here: '[Plot] is an act of judgement, one arising from an act of 'grasping together.' Or to put it another way, plot stems from a *praxis* of narrating, hence from a pragmatics of speaking, not from a grammar of *langue* ... "Conceptual necessities immanent in the development of roles" stem more from a semantics and a logic of action than from a true logic of narrative' (1984, 2:44).

Perspective is also explained by Bal in terms of focalization. Focalization, which is closely related to the narrator, is the 'specific angle' from which the material is 'looked at' (49–50, 120–1). It constitutes a crucial axis in her narratology and is defined as 'the technical aspect, the placing of the point of view in a specific agent' (50). It is the 'prime means of manipulation,' understood as 'treatment,' whereby the 'fabula is "treated", and the reader is being manipulated by this treatment'

(50). Again, her absolute criterion excludes the reader's perspective and 'treatment' of the story: 'Any treatment can be reduced to the *point of view* from which the image of the fabula and the (fictitious) world where it takes place are constructed' (50).

Before translating perspective into focalization, Bal first translates point of *view* into 'point of *perception*' and again confines perception to space and vision (93; emphasis added). Where 'place' is the 'physical, mathematically measurable shape of spatial dimensions,' 'space' is these places 'seen *in relations to their perception* [sic]' (93). The point of perception, which replaces point of view, is 'situated in a space, observes it and reacts to it' (93). The point of perception, be it anonymous or a character, 'can result in a typology of spatial presentation,' and this general question of 'points of perception ... lies at the root of every presentation' (93). While this is undoubtedly true, only part of perception is spatial in character and therefore this notion of point of perception cannot cover every presentation. Spatial aspects are determined, according to Bal, by three senses: '*sight, hearing* and *touch*,' in a descending order of relevance (94). Visual aspects contribute most to space. Sounds contribute by determining a certain 'distance' or 'proximity,' and touch indicates 'adjacency' and therefore has 'little spatial significance' (94). These three senses combine in Bal's narrative to create a frame around a character through a dichotomy of inner/outer space.

Perception plays an important role in this mathematically measurable concept of place and space. It is important and encouraging that Bal brings both hearing and touch into play, albeit only at the level of space and playing only a minor role. It is unfortunate that the potential of these senses is not further developed. No sooner is focalization introduced than both hearing and touch are dispensed with in order that sight may answer the question concerning 'various points of perception' (93). Perception is not explained as proceeding *from* proximity *to* distance. Distance is not explored in depth as the grasp the subject has of an object, but only as a measured difference in position. Bal claims to deal with a cause/experience dichotomy, yet the essential role of perception does not reach experience itself. Perception is considered only as 'a psychological process strongly dependent on the position of the perceiving body' (100). It must be recalled that position itself depends not on objective space but on a body in action (M.M-P. 1962, 249–50). Position cannot constitute the fundamental criterion for even the psychological processes without reducing subjective action to objective motion. By eliminating the reading experience, Bal ignores the fact that, with perception, what 'makes part of the field count as an object in motion, and another as the background, is the way in which we establish our relations with them by the act of looking' (M.M-P. 1962, 278). She avoids the notion of perception in the primary onto-logical sense of time and reaching out to the world. This subjective notion presents Bal with 'difficulties' because perception 'depends on so many factors that striving for objectivity is pointless' (100). While the term 'perspective seems clear enough' in that it 'covers both the physical and psychological points of perception,' Bal rejects it because of the role the term has played in 'the tradition of narrative theory' (101). The terms 'point of view' and 'narrative perspective' are dis-missed for the same reason (100, 101).

Focalization intends to eliminate the subjective pole of perception all together. It is not the relation between a person and that which he or she perceives. It does not proceed from an active understanding in language that helps constitute a 'position' in both time and space. It is an objective term denoting 'the relation between the vision and that which is "seen", perceived' *within* the story of the text (100). Thus, narrative perspective is again reduced to point of view and again con-ceptualized as a standpoint without an understanding in tradition. Once again the terms are rechristened in order to 'make a distinction between *those who see* and *those who speak*,' but only within the sacred frontier of the story (101). For Bal *focalization* has the added 'advantages' of effectively reducing any interference from the personal side of perception: 'It is a term that looks technical. It is derived from pho-tography and film; its technical nature is thus emphasized. As any "vision" presented can have a strongly manipulative effect, and is, consequently, very difficult to extract from the emotions, not only from those attributed to the focalizor and the character, but also from those of the reader, a technical term will help us keep our attention on the technical side of such a means of manipulation' (102). This restricted visual definition treats the term 'technical' as 'mechanical.' It is not concerned with the generation of individuals but with their manip-ulation (Ricoeur 1976, 77). Being confined to a strictly formal criterion, *technê* is not an intersection of codes and structures generating, to quote Ricoeur, a 'location and individualization of the unique text [which] is also a guess' (1976, 77). Without guesswork this translation of percep-tion and perspective into a technical term marks a theoretical standpoint solidly located in distanciation rather than assimilation. By attributing its origin to photography and film, Bal dissociates 'perspective' from one of its more traditional uses in the art of painting and sculpture. Perspective in art and focalization in photography involve different modes of perception and are not interchangeable without significant loss on the part of the perceiving subject. If perception is to play a part in focalization, then it is impossible to manipulate or reduce the reader to a 'focalizor ... compared to a camera' (Bal 114). Merleau-Ponty emphasizes the difference between art and photography:

Le tableau fournirait à mes yeux à peu pres ce que les mouvements réels leur fournissent: des vues instantanées en série, convenablement brouillées, avec, s'il s'agit d'un vivant, des attitudes instables en suspens entre un avant et un après, bref les dehors du changement de lieu que le spectateur lirait dans sa trace. C'est ici que la fameuse remarque de Rodin prend son importance: les vues instantanées, les attitudes instables pétrifient le mouvement – comme le montrent tant de photographies où l'athlète est à jamais figé. On ne le dégèlerait pas en multipliant les vues. Les photographies de Marey, les analyses cubistes, la *Mariée* de Duchamp ne bougent pas: elles donnent une rêverie zénonienne sur le mouvement ... Ces prises sur l'espace sont aussi des prises sur la durée. Rodin a ici un mot profond: 'C'est l'artiste qui est véridique et c'est la photo qui est menteuse, car, dans la réalité, le temps ne s'arrête pas.' La photographie maintient ouverts les instants que la poussée du temps referme aussitôt, elle détruit le dépassement, l'empiétement, la 'métamorphose' du temps, que la peinture rend visible au contraire. (1964a, 77–8, 80)

If, as Bal states, focalization is 'the most important, most penetrating and most subtle means of manipulation,' then there must be very good reason why this 'so often neglected aspect' has not been reduced to one unambiguous, and universal 'single distinction' (116, 117). I feel that there must be some reason why so many theorists have been reluctant 'to break with tradition,' such as that established, as she puts it, in the 'philosophically and psychoanalytically tinted *Poetics of Space* by Bachelard' (117).

The narrator in *Narratology* is 'a function and not a person' (119). Bal declares: 'I shall refer to the narrator as *it*' and this '*it*' is not a storyteller but rather 'that agent which utters the linguistic signs which constitute the text' (119, 120). Nevertheless, the narrator 'is *always* a "first-person" ' from a grammatical point of view and constitutes 'the most central concept in the analysis of narrative texts' because it 'narrates, i.e., utters language which may be termed narrative since it represents a *story*' (122, 120). While focalization functions at the level of story, narrative technique describes the relation between the narrator and the story. By dividing the text into narrator and narrative technique, focalizor and focalization, actor and functional desire, Bal hopes that 'one will inevitably arrive at the conclusion that *seeing*, taken in the widest sense, constitutes the object of *narrating*' (121). Again, the notion of 'narrator' does not take into account the understanding or substance supporting the point of perception. The narrator is reduced to one spatially inclined sense. In his consideration of voice and point of view Ricoeur has already warned: 'If we do not want to be misled by the metaphor of vision when we consider a narrative ... then vision must be held to be a concretization of understanding, hence paradoxically, an appendix to hearing' (1984, 2:99). However 'tinted' with Aristotelian and Augustinian philosophy this warning may be, the issue remains: Who or what helps one see what one sees if not the inner voices of tradition?

The rich potential of Mieke Bal's investigation into the 'space' of narrative situations is never fully realized because of her reluctance to take 'side trips to other disciplines' and because she 'views' the reader as a 'problem' (150, 152). The function of personal pronouns is limited to 'the status of the narrative agent and its relationship to what is narrated' (149). *Personal* language is relegated to a *dramatic* situation among actors and characters at the intermediary level of story. When 'the narrator addresses itself, explicitly or implicitly, to the reader' at the level of text, this is called '*text interference*' (138–9). The 'real' question, that is, what *personal* relation is established between the narrating person and the person reading by the use of first, second, or third person, is never addressed. Nowhere does this *real* question become more crucial than in the function of Bal's 'mirror text' (146). Here the function of the reader is to 'predict the end of the primary fabula' by capturing 'the partial resemblance through abstraction.' The reader's role is to realize this relatively insignificant 'indication' (146). The most significant and central issue of critical theory, however, is relegated to the actor or character 'within' the story:

Because he has the insight that double meanings should be taken seriously, the actor is able to interpret the embedded fabula as a mirror of what is to happen. That is why he can save himself ... The actor's realization that double meanings should be taken seriously is itself a sign. It is a 'prescription' for the reading of literature ... Just as for the actor-witness the right interpretation of the doubleness of the meaning of the embedded text was a matter of life or death, so the double interpretation of the relationship between primary and embedded text is a matter of life and death, to be or not to be, for literature. (147–8)

I feel that this all-important question of metaphorical meaning cannot be relegated to the actor-witness, for it is within the relationship between the reader and the text, that is, within the *narrative perspective*, that it is posited. Meaning also lies with the reader, the 'I' that listens. The reading of literature must still be carried out by a reader. The question of 'to be or not to be' is an ontological one that cannot alienate the reader. I believe that literature ultimately *is* for readers. The reader both *is and is not* the narrative perspective where and when meanings are decided. All of Bal's *Narratology* tends towards this one final question of meaning. She is quite right in stating, 'It is, therefore, impossible to just suppose that, as a general rule, the assertions of an actor carry the meaning of the whole text' (149). Thus, narratology's effort to achieve objectivity eventually leads it back to certain central questions of meaning shared with phenomenological hermeneutics, and these must be addressed regardless of however problematic the responsibility of the reader may be. To the degree that both Mieke Bal and Shlomith Rimmon-Kenan recommend Menakhem Perry's psychological study of focalization, they must address the concluding words of his investigation: 'I have read "A Rose for Emily" dozens of times, and I must confess that with each new reading I have to remind myself once more that Emily is *not* the representative of the past and marshal once again the evidence against such a view of her. During the reading the thought always manages to steal its way into my mind: perhaps she *is* that after all' (357).

My understanding of Genette and of post-Genettian structuralist narratology is that of a progressive movement towards the question of perception and the reader. This movement is brought on by the tension that results from an alternating appeal first to an 'objective' standpoint in a spatially defined text and second to the common sense of a reader marginalized by the universal grammar of narratology's spatial model.

I must stress that my explanation of narratology has not intended to disprove any position because of its internal contradiction, and I must also stress that I am not challenging the legitimacy of the text's formal dimension as an object of inquiry. I fully agree with Mario J. Valdés when he states that each approach to the study of literary texts (including the present inquiry) 'consciously or unconsciously maps out the terrain of its undertaking' (1987, 39). Nevertheless, it is not insignificant that narratology vacillates between marginalizing if not excluding the reader, on the one hand, and then drawing support from his or her perception of spatial aspects, on the other. I believe the contradictory stance of narratology is in keeping with a standpoint firmly established in the objective spatial pole of perception. It is the view of a thinking subject, of 'mental inspection,' that is exemplified by the diaeretic phenomenon of figure 1 on page 27 above. It brings to the fore those very characteristics of visual perception functioning in 'outer space': distanciation, paradox, reversal of order, illusion, and ultimately concordant 'discordance' not discordant 'concordance.' Again, I agree that each theory of literature is about 'certain features that have been selected as being the ones that matter ... For example, a structuralist theory of criticism describes specific formal relationships *as they are perceived* to occur in the linguistic organization of a text' (Valdés 1987, 40; emphasis added).[7] The issue is not only that the narratologist marginalizes or excludes the reader from his or her considerations, but that in doing so he or she denies his or her own status as a reader who is perceptive of a particular spatial dimension of the text. To the degree that narrative is language and perspective is perception, a consideration of narrative perspective must come to terms with the narratologist's position as part of a process shared with other members of a community of readers whose standpoint is grounded in history. Keeping in mind that autonomy does not necessarily imply frontiers to be transgressed, I feel that 'a sort of hesitation, no doubt an unconscious one, to recognise and respect the autonomy of that instance [of narrating]' could be overcome, if the reader's perception of the text were also fully recognized and respected (Genette 1980, 213). It is towards this fruitful recognition and respect that narratology has undoubtedly moved.

Thus, it is not so much that the narratologists' object of study must be challenged, but rather that their particular point of departure within the process of perception must be elucidated. As I have tried to show above, the reader's perception is an important matter, and narratology shares the importance of this matter with other approaches such as phenomenological hermeneutics. It is also to a community of readers and a tradition of commentary that a narratologist appeals for validation of the structures he or she perceives in the text's configuration. Precisely because both phenomenologist and narratologist must come to terms not only with the continuity in time of a particular sequence of words but also with a common process of perception (which does not exclude different degrees of emphasis), *some* agreement concerning the text is possible and an enriching exchange of ideas can take place. Again, while it may be argued that narratology's concern for the text as spatial form stands at odds with phenomenological hermeneutic's concern for the text as temporal 'figuration,' I do not believe this to be the case. I understand them as complementary because they share a common process.

With this complementarity in mind, I can agree with Mieke Bal that certain geometrical configurations are valuable in understanding literature, but they can only be understood as heuristic devices that help explain the world of the text, especially within a highly analytical and abstract community of criticism. I can also agree fully with Bal's belief that in many cases the text's 'space is "thematized": it becomes an object of presentation itself, for its own sake' (95). Nevertheless, I must also agree with Paul Ricoeur that there are ' "tales about time" inasmuch as in them it is the very experience of time that is at stake in these structural transformations' (1984, 2:101). No *one*, absolute, universal model can be imposed on both of these narrative types. Narrative perspective, however it may be rechristened, can mediate both of these narratives if language, perception, and experience are not reduced to one *visual* sense. Language is always more than system and *langue*. Perception is always more than sight. Experience cannot be reduced to one universal structural model.

Deconstruction

I have mentioned above two directions or senses made possible by such alternating currents of thought as those noted in Rimmon-Kenan's perspective. Mieke Bal marks a development towards a perspective of common sense. Deconstruction *moves* to the other standpoint and conceives an abstract, artificial reversal of sense. The narrative 'understanding' that is inseparable from our everyday experiences becomes a 'subscription' to a literary perspective of the world. As Terence Hawkes explains, 'we tend to "literarize" all our experience, reduce it to a kind of "book": a process that, it has been argued, has been continuous with us since the renaissance and the concomitant development of the book-industry' (145). Deconstruction does not subscribe to a theory of the text manipulating the reader nor to one whereby the reader helps constitute the text. The reader is replaced by the text. Thus, as Georges Poulet puts it, 'the work lives its own life within me; in a certain sense it thinks itself, and it even gives itself a meaning within me' (quoted in Hawkes 149). In other words, the direction is totally reversed in order that 'the work reads *us* as much as we read it' (Hawkes 149). The cause-effect relation between a text that manipulates a reader who is handled is set forward as a paradox in which the former replaces the latter. The point of departure is not a level of primary faith in language but a conceptual sign.

This post-structuralist movement recognizes and shares the hermeneutical dimensions of metaphorical perspective, but the function of perspective is run contrary to itself. The essence of deconstruction is its direction. A mirror is placed, as it were, in conceptual space behind the object and, reaching out to the world, is reflected back. An abstract exploration proceeds from passion to action. Its 'movement' centres on a 'black hole,' distancing or *'spacing'* two perspectives that show 'the error of the other' in an irresolvable dichotomy (Culler 164–5). The mirroring does not admit mediation and assimilation, but nothingness or identity. Deconstruction does not admit an appeal in terms other than those mirrored structures exemplified by the sentence 'That necessary violence responds to a violence that was no less necessary' (Derrida 18).

Christopher Norris has noted that deconstructionists select texts precisely because of the 'ironic' distance between two perspectives at work:

George Eliot's *Daniel Deronda* is a favoured example, inviting such treatment [of cause as effect] for several reasons. First, it stages a virtual confrontation between the realist mode of the 'Gwendolen Harleth' chapters (the parts Leavis signally approved of) and the visionary strain of the mysteries surrounding Deronda's Jewish identity and sense of mission. From this point of view it can be said to 'deconstruct' the commonsense [sic] assumptions linking the ideology of nineteenth-century realism to the judgements of modern conservative critics like Leavis. Moreover, it throws into sharp relief the paradoxes about cause-and-effect which deconstruction is resolved to uncover. (133)

This 'black hole' at the core of deconstruction is not, I believe, the locus of primordial faith and the upsurge of metaphor. In linking paradox with cause and effect the constructive dynamo of metaphor is thrown into reverse, creating what Hayden White has called an 'absurdist moment' (1978, 261ff.). Whether deconstruction is an absurd moment or whether metaphoric perspective is but another product of 'the narrower epoch of Christian creationism and infinitism' is not the issue (Derrida 13). The issue is one of mediation between action and passion, voice and letter, time and space. The question is whether a pneumatological understanding can meet a grammatological comprehension *in sense*.

I shall retrace the steps of language, perception, and experience that are directed towards the world, not in order to debase deconstruction's important insight into the phenomenon of reversal, but in order to report a balanced mediation (Derrida 12). My understanding of metaphoric perspective as outlined above undergoes a 'profound reversal' (10). The proposed standpoint in conceptual outer space looks back through the tense difference in the relational function of the copula through the space between the elements in the semic field, highlights the movement of distanciation, makes absolute the signifier, and comes to rest on the outer frontier of space and time. Derrida is concerned not with inner time or Subject but with '*Spacing*,' which is always the 'unperceived,' 'nonpresent,' and 'nonconscious' (68). This standpoint in the conceptual structures of the intellect can conceive the unperceived through the linguistic sign defined as a dichotomy of positive signifier and negative signified. Derrida bases his concept on the discrete signifier or form because, borrowing from Saussure, 'in language there are only differences' (68). For Derrida, this difference is writing, that is, a 'hinge [brisure]' (69). This hinge, however, only opens in one direction, from the signifier to another signifier (69). While he mediates time as becoming space and space as becoming time, he is not willing to extend the mediation to the concept of a hinge. I understand a *brisure* as also being *a mean* and as *such* it also *means* the signified. The sign is thus presented in antagonistic terms that resist mediation and favour opening up the signified in order to liberate the signifier.

The issue cannot be so easily reduced to this dichotomy. A more profound issue is that of sense itself. Saussure's insight into difference does not stand alone. It is not just differences that are displayed, but also perspectives that are played: '*Résumé le plus général*: Voici le sens le plus général de ce que nous avons cherché à établir: Il nous est interdit en linguistique ‹quoique nous ne cessions de le faire› de parler "*d'une chose*" à différents points de vue, ‹ou d'une chose en général›, parce que **c'est le point de vue qui** FAIT la chose ... Je n'hésite pas à dire que chaque fois qu'on introduit une distinction ‹soi-disant› de "point de vue", la question vraie est de savoir si nous sommes en face des mêmes "choses", et que ‹si› c'est le cas, c'est par le plus complet et le plus ‹inespéré› des hasards' (1:26, col. 3). The real issue, then, is not the introduction of distinction or difference but the role that perspective plays in the creation of a world. At the most profound level of this issue lies Ricoeur's question of appropriation: 'These paradoxes, in turn, lead back to a much more fundamental question: in expressing itself, how can life objectify itself, and, in objectifying itself, how does it bring to light meanings capable of being taken up and understood by another historical being who overcomes his own historical situation?' (1974, 5). Again, if it is not a chance opening and a chance closing of the hinge of a signifier, then what *does permit* an agreement on what is to constitute the object under consideration. This 'agreement concerning the object' as a fundamental prerequisite for the character of experience as discourse to be realized is eliminated (Gadamer 1975, 341).

Derrida's reversal of the question-answer dialectic has profound implications as well. It is by objectifying his standpoint to the alienated spatial pole that Derrida can then move to question the question. This he does visually 'by challenging the very form of the question and beginning to think that the sign ⋈ that ill-named t̶h̶i̶n̶g̶, the only one that escapes the instituting question of philosophy: "what is ... ?" ' [*sic*] (19). The 'is and is not' of metaphoric language as well as the 'thing and no thing' of perception are 'disfigured' or 'defaced' by crossing them out and are thus made available only by way of reading. This questioning the question also presupposes a standpoint subscribed as *the* answer. Derrida's position, by implication, makes no lesser a claim than 'to be' the 'answer' that Western philosophy has avoided. This in itself may or may not be the case but there are further implications affecting language and communication at the root of perspective. Deconstruction is not concerned with the action of language but with a 'movement of language' (Derrida 7). In being the answer, deconstruction escapes the necessity to respond. It justifies textual supplementation in itself, alienated from a community of critical dialogue because it is the answer. It becomes irresponsible, that is, not entering into the community's questions and answers. For this reason the 'crucial question still remains unanswered: For whom do the deconstructionist critics write and for what purpose?' (Valdés 1987, 54). By 'being' the answer deconstruction does not respond to 'the insatiable need to engage in dialogue and gain for ourselves the wisdom of personal insight' (55). This irresponsibility cannot be limited to a dialectic of '*past significance in present meaning*' alone, but must be extended to include the projection of the past beyond the present to its future consequence.[8] It is no accident that Vincent Leitch ends his study of deconstructive criticism with 'Reflections on the Responsibilities of the Literary Critic' (264–7). Responsibility becomes problematic when it is no longer an integral part of the question-answer dialectic, that is, when it is objectified as a 'fear especially [of] blame or punishment, moral or legal sanctions,' and when it is founded on a 'desire or [appreciation of] praise and reward' (266). There is more to responsibility than fear and desire. It may be that the 'deconstructive man' shuns dialogue because he 'neither pesters the world for truth nor indulges the dream of origins' (38). It may also be that to 'hustle is more compelling and more captivating than to pester' (267). Nevertheless, if this constitutes the deconstructive response, then I still find it difficult to relate the urgent demands of Gadamer, Merleau-Ponty, and Ricoeur, not to mention those of my colleagues, to the answer of either a hustler or a pest.

I have stated that the issue lies not so much in difference as in perspective or sense itself. This is made clear by the spatial configuration of perception. The *spacing* of deconstruction does not present perception as sense emerging from non-sense or the visible from the invisible. It reverses a dichotomy of being/nothing and conceives an 'unperception' rather than a non-sense (Derrida 24). Here a 'profound reversal' takes place in the hierarchy of perception, representation, illusion, and hallucination (10). In the same way that Derrida conceives of language as a conceptual movement, so also *sense* is reduced to an abstract and intellectual 'thought sense' opposing the spoken word (15, 8, 13, 21). 'Thought sense' itself proceeds not from experience but from an 'unperceived mediation' (24). In this way the deconstructionist signifier does not proceed from non-sense to sense but follows a program of sense always directed towards an intellectually posited unperception. Language is here no longer a mystery or a miracle but an intellectual '*problem*' (6). The substitution of unperception for non-sense and the priority it is given create a field of inquiry preoccupied with diaeretic or disjunctive distanciation in Western philosophy and culture. Its preoccupation lies with an *opposition* to writing 'in the common sense' and 'writing in the metaphoric sense' (17). It is concerned with discrete dichotomies of life vs. death, good vs. bad. As Merleau-Ponty has shown, the field of synaesthetic communication and the horizon of primary perception do not divide and discriminate dichotomies. These primary levels of perception mediate and intertwine. I feel that this substitution of a conceptual 'unperception' for non-sense, negates the meaning of stillness, of silence, and of emptiness that mediates and that does not go unperceived. It is very much perceived in 'the still center of the order of words' and in the 'criticism which is compelled to keep on talking about the subject [and] recognizes the fact that there *is* a center of the order of words' (Frye 117–18).

The danger of a position that negates both common sense and metaphorical sense in order to liberate and sublimate 'space and sight' as well as the 'unperceived' and 'ill-named,' is that it may find its standpoint in hallucination (Derrida 24–5, 19). It might then be said of deconstruction that it 'no longer inhabits the common property world, but a private world, and no longer gets as far as a geographical space ... [It] dwells in "the landscape space", and the landscape itself, once cut off from the common property world is considerably impoverished ... Everything is amazing, absurd, or unreal, because the impulse of existence towards things has lost its energy, because it appears to itself in all its contingency and because the world can no longer be taken for granted' (M.M-P. 1962, 287). The reality of such brilliant hallucination is, from its standpoint, indistinguishable from perception. Deconstruction is preoccupied not with representation but with 'illusion' (Derrida 20).

Within the field of illusion deconstruction is also selective. It is not concerned with voice as 'merely one illusion among many,' but with the 'illusion' of voice that deludes itself with 'the history of truth' (Derrida 20). The reversal of language to a conceptual problem and the reversal of perception to an illusive unperception is followed by a reversal on the experiential level as well. Derrida points out that the issue of being in itself has never been the object of ontological studies. The issue is that of the *'sense* of being' (21; emphasis added). Nevertheless, to recall Gadamer's words, 'sense involves direction' (1975, 326). Derrida correctly states that sense 'is nothing outside of language,' but he ties language 'to a particular system' (21). In this way language and being do not and cannot interpenetrate *through* sense unless being is reduced to the systems of 'modern linguistics' (21). Thus, the field of intersensory synaesthetic communication in being would have to be contradicted and reversed into a system. Even if such a reversal were possible without contradicting the notion of an intersensory synaesthetic field, the resulting system would only expand our knowledge of being. It could not come to terms with the level of understanding that has preoccupied Gadamer, Merleau-Ponty, Ricoeur, and Valdés. This level is not concerned with knowledge as such but with 'the wisdom of personal insight' referred to above as phronesis (Valdés 1987, 55). Ultimately it is the wisdom of personal insight that mediates past significance, present meaning, and future consequence for sensible beings. The mediating function of wisdom is inseparable from the notion of advent that is shared by both Merleau-Ponty and Ricoeur (M.M-P. 1962, 69).

Once reversed, experience becomes the product of thought. Lived experience is comprehended as the very dogmatic opinion that hermeneutics deconstructs. The 'unique experience of the signified' is explained as an 'experience of the *effacement* of the signifier,' but never as its *configuration* (Derrida 20; emphasis added). Yet even here experience cannot differentiate interpenetrating signifier and signified. Derrida's standpoint in the answer is what allows him to presuppose that 'I do what others fail to do, I give my dreams as dreams' (316). This knowledge of dream as dream vs. wakefulness runs a greater risk than any violence against signifier or against word might imply. The risk is greater because 'he who thinks that he knows better cannot even ask the right questions. In order to be able to ask, one must want to know, which involves knowing that one does not know' (Gadamer 1975, 326). Western philosophy does not begin with the knowledgeable question 'What is ... ?' (Derrida 19). It begins with a humble confession that 'I do not know.' The questions that proceed from this do not point to non-sense alone, because it is 'of the essence of the question to have sense' (Gadamer 1975, 326). The direction involved in deconstruction's 'mental experiences' runs from the answer to the question, from the sense to the non-sense, from the concept to experience (Derrida 11). I have tried to include the phenomenon of reversibility on all three levels of investigation. With the reduction of experience to a modern linguistic dichotomy of signifier/vacuum, it is essential to bear in mind Paul Ricoeur's notion of direction: 'But in the movement of going and coming ... the return is not equivalent to going ... The upsurge of saying into our speaking is the very mystery of language. Saying is what I call the openness or better the opening out of language' (1974, 96). Nor do I believe that phenomenological hermeneutics can be drawn into a false dichotomy of a Western philosophy of the spoken word vs. an Eastern 'spiritual culture' of 'hieroglyphic script' (Derrida 25). Eastern spiritual culture has not been limited to an exegetic exercise 'reserved for a very small section of a people [possessing] ... the exclusive domain of spiritual culture' (25–6). It has also concentrated on 'those unities of breath' that deconstruction refuses to mediate (26). Both the paradox and error that are created by an alienation of the spoken word's understanding from script's comprehension appear to be the subject of the following eighth-century Chinese spiritual text in which both speaking and writing figure:

If you cling to forms, you will increase heterodox views (and) if you grasp the void you will increase ignorance.

Those who cling to the void, vilify the sutras by saying that they do not use written words (Scriptures). (If they were correct in) saying that written words should not be used, it would not be right even to speak because the spoken word is also an aspect of the written word. They also say: 'The direct way establishes not written words' (but they forget that) the two words 'establishes not' are also words ...

Those clinging to externals while performing ceremonies in their quest for the truth, or while setting up spacious Bodhimandalas where they expose the error and falsehood (of the notions) of existence and non-existence will not for many aeons perceive their own nature ...

If someone puts a question to you and asks about the existing, mention the non-existent in your answer. If you are asked about the non-existent mention the existing in your answer ... (Thus) the mutual dependence of the two extremes will bring to light the significance of the 'mean'.[9]

This text suggests that Chinese spiritual culture *is* founded on the written hieroglyph and again it *is not*. It *is* founded on the voice and again it *is not*. Only a meaningful standpoint can provide the depth essential for even a deconstructionist 'movement' to be a 'signifier.' Phenomenological hermeneutics, as I understand it, does not intend to repress the profound reversal it fully recognizes, but it does intend to recognize it *'as such'* (Derrida 68).

Perspectives of Figuration: Prefiguration

The question of the reader has undoubtedly proven problematic for narratology. The question that has proven challenging for reader reception theory has been the identity of the literary text. It is no accident that a text addressing this issue found its genesis in Wolfgang Iser's idea of critical dialogue.[10] As Owen Miller has pointed out, Robert Weimann's historical overview of critical activity up to 1982 brings to light the 'historically determined "subtext" which makes the question of a textual identity a problem both as an object of communication and as a vehicle of cultural and critical endeavour' (1985, viii). The central role played by narrative perspective in this issue is underscored by Weimann. In his view, it 'assumes a central role for both the writer and the reader' because it is *the means* of fictional and historical world 'appropriation' and 'must be seen as being at the heart of the narrator's method' (1976, 265, 236). Narrative perspective also lies at the heart of Weimann, Iser, and Jauss's standpoints in the prefiguration, configuration, and refiguration, respectively, of the text.

Robert Weimann is primarily interested in the role played by a novelist's 'poetic perception' in prefiguring the text (1976, 235). As Genette is undoubtedly indebted to Percy Lubbock, Weimann is, by contrast, indebted to Wayne C. Booth. Using a similar formulation of the problem, he affirms, 'If today point of view is to be more than the strategy of first- or third-person narration, it must involve the structural correlation of these two basic functions. Both are part of the specific "practical-spiritual" achievement of art: *one* (representation) relates the novel to the objective nature of the world; the *other* (evaluation) to the subjective nature of the viewer' (235–6). Narrative perspective is then 'a connecting medium between representation and evaluation' as well as 'a means of achieving and communicating their unity' (236). The 'most essential aspect' of narrative perspective is its correlative function between an author's actual point of view or his standpoint and his technical point of view or medium (240, 242). The author's actual point of view is understood by Weimann not as a writer's expressed opinions or intentions but, quoting Arnold Kettle, as 'the artistic sense ... his sensibility' (242). Narrative perspective can be understood only as 'the sum total of the author-narrator's achieved attitudes to both the world (which includes his readers) and the story as a generalized image of what the novelist wishes to say about the world through his art' (244). The reader, although not central to Weimann's concern, plays an important role in the literary process. It is the reader's most basic task 'to resolve the irony in the meaning of perspective and to recover that element of wholeness to which point of view is the counterpart' (266). To this end the reader 'has to appropriate the world of the novel just as the novelist has to appropriate the world through the novel' (266). This appropriation by both the reader and the author is realized through language. Appropriation takes place only to the degree that the reader or the author 'comprehends (or achieves) the relatedness of the narrating consciousness of form to the narrated form of consciousness, the scene to the sense, focus to perspective' (266). An important result of Weimann's coordinating literary origins or genesis (*Entstehungsges-chichte*) and literary impact (*Wirkungsgeschichte*) is its effects on the qual-ity of point of view (144). Thus he affirms, 'Once the quality of point of view is defined in terms of both the narrative modes of representation as evaluation *and* the rhetorical as the communicative achievement of the novel, the writer's perspectives and the reader's attitudes can be related' (263).

Despite the importance given to the role of the reader, Weimann concentrates his consideration of point of view primarily on the socio-economical and political conditions of the text's production (251ff.). In keeping with Marx's belief that production is determined by 'natural laws,' Weimann argues in terms of cause-effect relations.[11] The author's standpoint, as revealed in the structures of the text, is determined by socio-economical laws of appropriation. Weimann's fourfold process of (1) literary genesis or origin, (2) aesthetics of representation or struc-ture, (3) aesthetics of reception, and (4) literary impact [that is, (1) *Entstehungsgeschichte*, (2) *Darstellungsästhetik*, (3) *Rezeptionsästhetik*, and (4) *Wirkungsgeschichte*] parallels Marx's economic process of 'produc-tion, distribution, exchange and consumption' (Marx 89; Weimann 1976, 12–13). That Weimann's primary interest lies with the author's prefi-guration of the text is in keeping with the priority Marx gives to pro-duction over consumption. The 'mediating movement' runs directly from the former to the latter: 'Thus production produces consumption (1) by creating the material for it; (2) by determining the manner of consumption; and (3) by creating the products initially posited by it as objects, in the form of a need felt by the consumer. It thus produces the object of consumption, the manner of consumption and the motive of consumption' (Marx 91, 92).

The absolute nature of a 'production that produces' on level (1) and (2) is debatable, as is the need being created by the product and not by the 'consumer.' Reading as a form of consumption thus becomes 'mediated as a drive by the object' (92). The need felt by a 'consumer' of the text proceeds *from* the product *to* the reader. Again perception is directed from the text to the reader without due consideration of the role different manners of perception, that is, narrative perspective, play in creating the object of art: 'The need which consumption feels for the object is created by the perception of it. The object of art – like every other product – creates a public which is sensitive to art and enjoys beauty' (92). Weimann creates an analogy between 'the pro-duction and the perception of textual identity,' 'the production and consumption of cultural artefacts,' and 'the production and reception,' in which perception, consumption, and reception all follow one direction: from the product to the consumer (1985, 287, 276). The result is a false dialectic in which perception and reception oppose production. His critique of Hans Robert Jauss's 'bourgeois' standpoint is based on this notion of perception as an impingement on the senses (1975, 11). Only such a one-directional notion would give production by the author an indisputable priority. While accusing Jauss of 'making absolute, the sphere of literary "consumption," ' he affirms, 'As far as these basic terms of economic analysis can be made to apply to the study of literature, the analogy is valid in the sense that it suggests that, no matter how justified the increase of attention to literary "consumption," it is production which in the last resort is the predominant factor which mediates the mode and content of the reception' (1975, 21, 20). From his 'productive' standpoint Weimann affirms that if the process of appropriation or *Aneignung*, that is, 'making things one's own' (1983, 466), 'does not primarily depend on what the text means but on what the text does to the reader, then ... the reader's *response to the text* cannot be quite independent of the *writer's response to the world*' (1982, 32).

Weimann's understanding of *Aneignung* or appropriation as assimilation *rather than* distanciation and his understanding of perception as a non-productive impingement on the senses comes to bear on his notion of narrative perspective. It is explained primarily as 'the writer's wholeness of perception,' which takes on 'a major social function ... one that a Marxist approach (which is hostile to any apology of alienation in whatever form it appears) will consider as a supreme criterion of value' (1976, 235). Distanciation in its productive role is overlooked. Weimann encounters a problem in conceptually reconciling Ricoeur's notion of the text as 'a whole, a totality' and as 'a cumulative, holistic process' without recourse to some 'ideological *subtext*' (1985, 287, 275). If, as Weimann affirms, 'common-sense' does not enter into the notion of subtext, it is because he sees socio-economic or political factors rather than perception as playing the major role in the text's production (275). The 'whole' of the text is not just some conceptually 'presumed' condition but a unity that proceeds from 'the mediation of bodily experience' (Weimann 287 and M.M-P. 1962, 203). As with the undeniable role of aseity in the perception of any object, the role of distanciation is essential for the production of any concept: 'the successive stages of this experience [of a cube] are for me merely the opportunity of conceiving the whole cube with its six equal and simultaneous faces, the intelligible structure which provides an explanation of it' (M.M-P. 1962, 203). It is in this sense that Ricoeur proposes *Aneignung* or appropriation not only as making things one's own but as ' "to make one's" own *what was initially "alien"* ' (1981a, 185; emphasis added). For Ricoeur the cumulative process that gives birth to the conflict of interpretations is a 'reconstruction of the whole [which] has a perspectivist aspect similar to that of perception' (212). Without making any apology for distanciation, Weimann must also consider it in a positive light. Appropriation is not just assimilation but also essentially a *distanciation from* or 'dispossession of the narcissitic *ego*' in order that the self may be unveiled (Ricoeur 1981a, 192). It is in this way that Ricoeur can speak of a 'Productive Distanciation' that ensures 'the absence of absolute knowledge' (1976, 43–4).

The productive potential of Robert Weimann's relating literary genesis (*Entstehungsgeschichte*) with the impact of literature (*Wirkungsgeschichte*) through narrative perspective (*Erzählperspektive*) comes to the fore with the questions it gives rise to (1976, 241). If the author's point of view is to be understood as an artistic sense and sensibility then would it not be more productive to consider it in terms of perception rather than ideological subtext, in terms of a common-sense reality rather than its economical or political standpoint? Again, if appropriation or *Aneignung* takes place to the degree of relating consciousness, would it not be more appropriate to relate the 'form of consciousness' to mediums of perception rather than to socio-political or economical factors (1976, 11)? If 'rhetorical' is understood as the 'communicative achievement' that relates the perspectives of prefiguration and refiguration, then would it not be appropriate to correlate rhetorical configurations with the mediums of sense perception as distinct modes of communication through discourse (263)? This correlation of sense, narrative perspective, rhetoric, and fabulous configuration appears central to Weimann's study of literary prefiguration:

The aural culture may retain its value in the transcribed energies of speech, direct address, exclamation, and the sonic quality of rhetoric associated with town criers, carnival societies, and the premodern element in an older, public type of author function. But in the historiographic *fabula* of the Renaissance, the utopian echoes from the carnival world of oral discourse must surrender

to the ascendancy of an alphabetized culture in which the problem of signification is a 'hieroglyphic' one in the sense that it emerges *ante oculos*, thus
allowing for all the splendor and deceit ... of illusion and the gesture of verification. (1983, 476–7)

How could a writer's audio-oral perspective and a reader's ocular perspective be mediated? Can this audio-oral perspective be limited to a
European Middle Ages or a European Renaissance when, as Hans
Robert Jauss has clearly stated, 'whoever is interested in the aesthetic
experience of the overwhelming majority of humanity which is not yet,
or no longer, reading, must reach through the realms of listening,
watching and playing the manifestations of which have scarcely en-
tered the history of writing' (1978, 139). More specifically, what can be
said of, say, a Latin American perspective, where 'the distinction between the two types of discourse,' that is *fabula* and *historia, did not
suffer a radical break between 'the need to appropriate the particular
world of history in the universal terms of poetry,' on the one hand,
and narrative, which 'tends to be appropriated in, and by particular
standards of, the ordinary world of history,' on the other (Weimann
1983, 476)?[12] Again, what sense is to be made of a perspective whose
ordinary world of history extends from the 'queendom' of Califa, called
California, to El Dorado, to Las Amazonas, and to La Fuente de la
Eterna Juventud?[13] What might be the meaning for literary history
'today' of this narrative understanding that finds its beginnings in the
production of Alfonso de Ercilla y Zúñiga's major *epic* poem *La Araucana*, fifteen to thirty-five years *after* 'the patronage-seeking Lazarillo'
marked a new form of appropriation in Europe (Weimann 1976, 263)?[14]
If the subjective nature of narrative perspective plays an important role
in the selection and evolution of narrative material and strategies, is
this subjectivity a wandering innovation or does sedimentation play a
role? Finally, if point of view is the medium and the means of both
unity and tension between the evaluation and representation, would
not a consideration of the means of communication be more appropriate
for narrative perspective in a study of literary history than socio-economic categories of *Aneignung*? If literary theory intends to speak for
'Western' literary expression, 'literature' in general, or narrative perspective in specific, then the distance between a Latin American perspective and a modern European perspective must be mediated.

Perspectives of Figuration: Configuration

One of the most significant contributions to modern European literary theory has undoubtedly been Wolfgang Iser's *The Act of Reading*. Despite the text's title, Iser's interests do not lie exclusively with a consideration of the techniques of refiguration and interpretation. As Robert Weimann has pointed out, Iser 'presents the most cogent arguments *against* interpretation [because] interpretation constrains the text through the continuing application of a norm ... which seeks to restore the universal claims which art has in fact abandoned' (1985, 282, emphasis added; and Iser 1978a, 12). Iser's consideration of prefiguration and refiguration proceeds *from* the *schema* of the configuration *to* the traditions of the writer and reader. The act of reading lies primarily in the textual strategies that cause the reader to react *against* traditional norms (Iser 1985, 220). The principle of distanciation dominates Iser's standpoint. His stress is on literature's fictional quality in opposition to 'reality.' Thus, for Iser, a text must 'by its very nature ... call into question the validity of familiar norms' and '[after] all, the ultimate function of the strategies is to defamiliarize the familiar' and, again, 'the comprehension and representation of a special reality can only take place by way of negating the familiar elements of a schema' (1978b, 103, 106). Comprehension replaces understanding and the focus of attention is on immanent structures 'underlying that process of rearrangement *within* the text which ultimately prestructures the aesthetic object the reader *is given* to produce' (1978b, 100; emphasis added).

It can be said that while Robert Weimann is concerned with mediating the temporal distance between past significance and present meaning, Wolfgang Iser is concerned with the spatial gaps and horizons that help provoke a distance between a reader and his inherited views. Iser's interest in the abnormal proceeds from a far more abstract standpoint than that of either Jauss or Weimann. It presupposes a revision of perception in terms of space that distances it from perspective. Iser presupposes that all 'literary texts are by nature fictional' and conceptualizes the literary process by means of a 'triad [of] the real, the fictional, and ... imaginary' (1985, 205–5). His process has an implicit direction from the former to the latter.

Perception, for Iser, does not necessarily mediate language and experience. In his view it structures an imagination that *opposes* the fictional to the real (1985, 205). In order to achieve an objective standpoint in the levels of configuration itself he conceptualizes perception in principally spatial terms of gestalt analysis and perspective in primarily visual terms of form. His optical and spatial criterion for perception is based on the 'ideas of the perception of pictorial art' that link art to illusion in Ernst H. Gombrich's *Art and Illusion* (Iser 1978b, 105). The essential attribute that Iser ascribes to fiction is a development of illusion's potential to disclose itself as such. The 'self-disclosing fictional text' has the potential to reveal its own fictionality and when that does not occur it is the task of philosophical discourse to unmask it (1985, 216). The literary text 'as fictionalizing ... is not identical to that which *it* represents' (216). Within Merleau-Ponty's hierarchy of hallucination, illusion, representation, and perception, Iser's interests lie between the second and third terms. He is concerned with perception primarily as a reception of structures. Meaning proceeds from experience, but experience here is not so much the result of perception as a response 'to a given amount of information' (1978a, 90). Perception here is not founded on an experiential process of reaching out from a tradition through sense to the world.

Gombrich's idea of perception develops the 'concepts of "schema" and "correction" that are based on gestalt psychology' (1978b, 105). The schema 'functions as a filter' and is governed by the economy principle (105). This principle includes the 'reduction' and '*exclusion* of perceptual data' (105; emphasis added). Iser takes the principle of economy from Rudolf Arnheim's *Art and Visual Perception: A Psychology of the Creative Eye* and applies it to Gombrich's schema (105). The filter is a structure, that is, 'some basic scaffolding or armature that determines the "essence" of things' (105). This structure cannot lie on the level of primary faith, nor on the level of intersensory synaesthetic communication, and therefore would appear to begin on the primordial level of space. Correction constantly modifies the structure but it does not appear to allow for an expanding schema. The balance achieved between the world's increasing complexity and the economy solidifies into 'reliable stereotypes' and these are what are corrected (105). Iser makes of correction a 'normative principle that regulates the perception and representation of the world' (106). Thus, 'comprehension and representation of a special reality can *only* take place by way of negating the familiar elements of the schema,' and what is important to Iser 'is the *fact* that the correction violates a norm of expectation contained *within* the picture itself' (106: emphasis added). For Iser, then, only a distanciation from 'traditional schemata' is valid as a criterion for art (1976b, 106). He is concerned more with the formal rules and productive imagination constituting the action of configuration than with the interaction of sedimentation and innovation constituting the act of refiguration. Iser's concern lies with comprehension rather than understanding, with *'significance* in the schemata' rather than meaning (1978b, 107).

Perception plays a key role on the prefigurative side of configuration as well. Iser moves his attention from psychological dichotomies of schema and correction to the abstract, spatial dichotomies of foreground/background, figure/ground, and innovation/redundancy that comprehend a particular 'thought system or social system' (107). The foreground, figure, or innovation are set against background, ground, or redundancy. A text's new background becomes comprehensible only to the extent that it is set against the original background or repertoire from which the textual strategies were first selected. The ground is unformulated and variable as opposed to a figure, which is invariable and formulated.

Iser draws on Edgar Rubin's studies in the psychology of visual perception to explain the role of figure and ground in creating ' "the fields" of perception' (1978b, 108–9). Selection reduces sense data to the form of a figure and excludes the diffuse data as background. Here the figure and ground are not mediated by the experiential depth of the observer. They are opposed to one another within the text by a 'contour, which may be defined as the borderline common to the two fields' (Rubin, quoted in Iser 109). This visual phenomenon allows an inversion within the selection to take place whereby the foreground becomes background and the background becomes foreground, much in the way outlined in figure 1 on page 27 above.

Iser explains that the literary figure/ground relationship differs from the psychological relationship in three ways. In literature 'the background and foreground are not given, but are dependent on selections made prior to "perception" ' (1978b, 110). What Iser places prior to perception, however, is not a preliminary competence constituted by language as a mode of being in the world. He privileges that competence within a linguistic system that selects certain particular aspects from a paradigmatic order and reduces them to a structure of strategies that break the ties to the norm of the paradigm and then work to undermine it. The strategies of selection in Iser's explanation function only against the excluded norms: 'Every literary text inevitably contains a *selection* from a variety of social, historical, cultural and literary systems that exist as referential fields outside the text. This very selection is itself a step beyond the boundary, in that the elements of reality are lifted out of the respective system in which they fulfil their specific function ... The act of selection, however, deconstructs their given order, thereby turning them into an object for observation' (1985, 207). A mediation between the paradigmatic and the syntagmatic orders is not Iser's concern. The movement from ground to figure does not presuppose a primary level of language that transcends the dualism of foreground/background oppositions. It presupposes 'acts of boundary-crossing' – a 'negating act' that produces 'the imaginary by transgressing language itself' (223–5).

Another difference between literary and psychological foreground/ background dichotomies lies in the concept of reversals. Iser states that reversals in gestalt psychology are occasioned 'by outside influences' and 'in literature the reversal is manipulated by structures within the text' (1978b, 110). I feel that this difference between psychology and literature based on an inside/outside dichotomy does not come to terms with reversibility within the essential dimension of question and answer, where the relationship between the reader and text also becomes reversed. Once again, the tenet that the phenomenon of reversibility is encountered at the most objective pole of perception is in keeping with Merleau-Ponty's position. Nevertheless, it will be recalled that in perception the structures do not 'manipulate' the reversal so much as 'indicate' and 'recommend' it (M.M-P. 1962, 263). What they indicate is a reversal whereby the questioning role natural to the reader moves 'outside' to reflect back from the now-distanced 'object' of the text, and to look back to the reader for a reply. When understood in paradigmatic terms of understanding as well as in Iser's syntagmatic terms of comprehension, the role of reversal takes on new dimensions. His exploration of reversibility must also take into account the paradigmatic depth it presupposes in order to run against and undercut norms. This Iser of course does, but he reduces that depth of tradition and sedimentation to a superficial category of dogmatic opinion and stereotypes that his idea of reversal corrects.

Gadamer's notion of experience also runs against dogma and opinion, but it admits 'a curiously productive meaning' for traditional experience, and the knowledge of tradition 'is not simply a deception that we see through and hence make a correction, but a comprehensive knowledge that we acquire' (1975, 317, 329). The effect of moving the questioning function from the centre of the reader to a role of the text cannot be experienced by the reader in terms of Iser's 'surprise effect' alone (Iser 1978b, 110). This movement will also be experienced as a suppression of his or her questioning nature and as an urgent invitation to respond. In that reversal suppresses the questioning nature of the reader, he or she may well feel that it is akin to the very opinion Iser claims it negates. As Gadamer notes: 'It is opinion that suppresses questions' (1975, 329). The reader's reply to a reversal can also bring about that 'art of reading' that is the process of questioning. Again, Gadamer stresses that a 'person who possesses the "art" of questioning is a person who is able to prevent the suppression of questions by the dominant opinion' (330).

One final distinction between foreground/background, inside/outside in literature and psychology is explained by Iser. While psychology involves a 'straightforward switch from "formed thing" to "unformed material," ' literature presents the switch of textual strategies in order to produce a tension and set off 'different actions and interactions' (1978b, 110). In literature this switch is not in and for itself, but is a means to an end. It must be added, however, that not only does the direction of the switch takes place from 'formed' thing to 'unformed' material, but also the action it sets off will be a response that returns from the unformed non-sense to form a new sense. Again, the direction is not just from formed to unformed but also from unformed to formed. A switch produces tension that catapults difference into the exploration of new meaning 'underlying' action and interaction. This new meaning, if it is to be meaning, must be then reported through similarity to the depth of the paradigm in which the switch takes place. The productive tension of metaphor broadens the horizon of both 'self' and tradition through this dynamic elasticity of language.

Iser divides the textual strategies into a dichotomy of theme and horizon. The textual strategies 'organize the *internal* network of references' and pre-structure the shape of what is to be produced by the reader (1978b, 110). Distanciation is again Iser's point of departure. Perspective 'rather than' perception is the organizing principle behind the text's internal system of references. Unlike the text's repertoire (that is, the 'existing norms in a state of suspended validity'), Iser does not relate perspective to perception through sense (1978a, 70). The 'system of perspectives' is assembled in order to build up the aesthetic object (96). While perception is allowed to dominate the axis of selection and correction, perspective is moved to another axis altogether. Each takes up a different position within Roman Jakobson's famous definition of the poetic function: '*poetic function projects the principle of equiv-*

alence from the axis of selection into the axis of combination' (quoted in Iser 1978a, 96). Perception functions on the paradigmatic axis and perspective is distanced to the syntagmatic axis. This distanciation in itself might be mediated by assimilation, but Iser consistently opposes any underlying principle of equivalence, even along the paradigmatic axis. It is precisely the non-equivalence of the axis of combination that he projects onto the paradigmatic order so as to negate existing norms and privilege innovation. Iser states that 'the novel ... is a system of perspectives designed to transmit the *individuality* of the author's vision,' while narrative is not just the author's view of the world, it is 'an assembly of *different* perspectives' (1978a, 35, and 1978b, 111; emphasis added). The function of equivalent or similar perspectives is not considered. Iser seeks to avoid the fact that 'the most audacious blows to our paradigmatic expectations do not get beyond the interplay of "rule-governed deformations" by means of which innovation has always been a reply to sedimentation' (Ricoeur 1984, 2:25).

Iser borrows the notion of theme and horizon from Gadamer, but Gadamer's understanding of tradition is excluded (1978a, 97). Theme and horizon parallel foreground and background, figure and ground in a spatial dichotomy that is not quite the same as Gadamer's hermeneutical situation. In Iser, the 'hermeneutical' is sacrificed to an act of reading whereby the reader must 'assemble for himself that *which is to be accepted'* and the 'manner in which he assembles it *is dictated* by the continual switching of perspectives' (1978a, 97; emphasis added). The standpoint does not rest upon a historically pregiven understanding but in a 'gap' and a suspension of the norm's validity (97). Iser's act of reading is an assimilation of the author's world, but only 'on the terms laid down by the author' (97). It does not propose a 'triumph of concordance over discordance' through the correlation of the aesthetic object of art with the perceiving subject's familiar world (Ricoeur 1984, 2:23). It will be recalled that Merleau-Ponty presents the perceiving subject as having a character similar to that of a work of art. Iser's immanent strategies reverse the direction of transformation in the reader. Ricoeur's apocalyptic mode of transformation, whereby 'from being imminent, it has become immanent,' is reversed (1984, 2:23). For Iser, immanence lies in the text's strategies, not through the reader's transformation.

The gap that provides the standpoint, or rather 'viewpoint,' is not conditioned, according to Iser, by the reader's narrative understanding, or historical substance (1978a, 112). Much like Menakhem Perry's primary effect, Iser's dialectic of protention or expectation and retention or memory is not founded on 'the "steady" mind of one who listens' (St Augustine, in Ricoeur 1984, 1:29). His gap is realized by a 'wandering viewpoint [that] carves its passage' through the present (1978a, 112). As Ricoeur points out, St Augustine has shown that the temporal condition of reading puts 'an end to wandering, the fallen form of *distentio animi* ... [in which] thoughts still twist and turn' (1984, 1:29).

Iser proposes four perspectives: 'that of the narrator, that of the characters, that of the plot, and that marked out for the reader' (1978b, 111). Each constitutes 'a channeled view' and these inner perspectives bring out the aesthetic object (1978a, 113). Because all perspectives cannot be embraced by the reader at once, the theme is that particular view with which he or she is involved at any moment. Iser's horizon is built up by previous themes in the text. His theme/horizon structure, however, shows little interest in the reader's narrative understanding and tradition-oriented perspective, either before or after the text. Thus, 'the structure of theme and horizon *organizes the attitudes of the reader*' (1978b, 112; emphasis added). The 'ultimate function of the aesthetic object' set up by the perspectives is not to bring about an appropriation of another mode of being in the world nor a self-understanding in the reader (113). The ultimate function is to create a 'transcendental viewpoint' suspended above and 'reflecting' all of the interacting perspectives (1978a, 98). I feel that such a suspended point of view is closer to the 'true universality of the concept' than to the experience and perception of the text through perspectives (Gadamer 1975, 314). The aesthetic object, comprehended as 'the ultimate meaning of the text,' is then located upon a platform suspended in space from which the reader 'may *react* to the "world" incorporated into the text' (Iser 1978a, 98). In turn, the 'literary text represents a reaction to the world' (98). Iser's 'act' of reading then becomes a 'reaction' of reading. While his theme/horizon structure reflects in part the structure of experience, the character of experience, that is, the tradition-laden dialectic of question and answer between reader and text, does not receive its due.

Iser does not choose the vital narrating function to illustrate variations of the theme-horizon structure. He opts for the 'perspective of the characters' in the world of the text to illustrate four basic types of perspective arrangement (1978b, 114). The communicative function is moved from the interpersonal level of reader and voice to the spatial pole where 'a stance ... causes attitudes to be adopted by the recipient, who is made to react to what he is given to observe' (1985, 220). The

four perspective types form a hierarchy based on their degree of opposition to traditional norms. The 'counterbalance, opposition, echelon
and serial' arrangements move from integration with the norm to disintegration (1978b, 115). The counterbalancing arrangement is found
in 'devotional, didactic and propagandist literature' and its function is
to compensate for 'deficiencies in specific thought systems' (115). Iser
does not view this aesthetic object as a celebration through language
of a mode of being in the world, but primarily as a compensation for
a lack (Ricoeur 1974, 96). If the criterion for the aesthetic object is one
that involves a reaction against the norms of a world, this counterbalancing arrangement would appear to imply a minimal aesthetic value.
The oppositional arrangement 'sets norms against one another by
showing up the deficiencies of each norm when viewed from the standpoint of the others ... [and thereby producing] a kind of reciprocal
negation' (Iser 1978a, 101). A balanced affirmation of shared or assimilated views is not considered. The 'continual conflict' causes the reader
'to understand the influence the norms have on him in real life' (1978b,
116).

From this cause-effect character of opposition Iser moves to the echelon arrangement. An echelon arrangement denies the reader a grasp
of any reliable guidelines. This 'denial of orientation' robs the reader
of any sense of a 'referential element' (1978a, 102). The perspective
evokes 'a multiplicity of referential systems in order to bring out the
problematic nature of the norms selected' (1978b, 116). The reader's
attitude is stimulated in order to incorporate the multiplicity within
the structure of his or her own disposition. What appears to be functioning here is an effort to unite many 'parts' under a consistent 'whole.'
The final serial arrangement takes precedence over the others in that
it brings about a production of 'the very conditions under which reality
is perceived and comprehended' (117). These conditions, however, no
longer involve the integration into a consistent whole. On the contrary,
the reader 'must constantly abandon the connections he had established or had hoped to establish,' even from one sentence to the next
(117). With 'no clearly discernible trace of any hierarchy,' the reader is
faced with an accelerated 'alternation of theme and horizon' that disintegrates or *scatters* any norms (117).

Iser's negative current of thought, and particularly his use of perception and perspective, privileges the pole of distanciation in the
dialectic of appropriation. While opposing interpretation because it
imposes universal norms, he is also forced to impose a norm of dis-

tanciation in his treatment of a configuration directed towards the reader. Iser bases his theory on his experience with English literature. Upon this criterion he dictates the universal function of all literature. This universal function is *not* 'to represent reality – it is a pointer to something which it is not, although its function is to make that something *conceivable*' (1985, 217; emphasis added). Iser's literature is 'fiction' understood as a reality-negating function rather than as a way of shaping reality (Ricoeur 1979). This reality-negating 'function has been the characteristic of literature at least since the Renaissance ... [and] this process has remained common to *all* fiction ever since' (Iser 1985, 217; emphasis added). Needless to say, this 'artificial' view dispenses not only with the literary status of pre-Renaissance texts but also with today's literary production realized from an audio-oral *perspectiva communis*. Iser does admit that the 'repertoires of the text as sender and the reader as recipient will also overlap,' but this overlapping of horizons is proposed only as a 'precondition for the "circulation" ' of the text within a community, and therefore does not constitute a major factor in the composition of the aesthetic object (1978a, 83).

Wolfgang Iser's configuration concerns itself primarily with the question of how 'figurative language ... permits and conditions conceivability' (1985, 213). His explanation of the 'act' of reading at the level of configuration is, unquestionably, one of the most valuable contributions to our understanding of the structures and strategies involved in configuration. Nevertheless a 'gap' remains in Iser's own theory as to the character of preliminary competence and time. I do not believe that the reader's mode of being in the world and its assimilative function can be so easily dismissed. The value of this chiasm in Iser's theory does not lie in its carving a passage along which to wander. Its value lies in providing the time and space in which to explore and report some of the potential questions and answers that the reader of Iser may find generated between his or her assimilated understanding and his or her distanced comprehension. These questions may not intend to negate or invalidate any of Iser's insights, but they might very well attempt to create a more balanced dialectic. Some of these questions are posited not only in the gaps but also 'around' what *is* there as well. If space cannot exist in perception without a 'sense' of direction, and if direction emerges with the body poised to carry out an action within a setting of figure and background thrown around the spectacle, then is it really all that 'clear that we must and do suspend *all* natural attitudes as adopted towards the "real" world once we are confronted with the represented world' (Iser 1985, 217; emphasis added)? While perception of the reader's immediate, first-order environment is certainly suspended, does this suspension in itself not allow the reader's perspective to come to the fore as it acts to meet the world of the text? If attitude, sense, and direction are inextricably intertwined in perspective, is it not possible that the sense of the reader's narrative understanding as well as the emotional and even physical attitudes he or she adopts in realizing a text will *all* come into play as the 'sense of it all' is 'figured out'? If so, what senses indicate what direction?

If distance is measured by the perceiver's grasp of things then must not the reader's narrative understanding and tradition play an essential role even in a theory that finds its standpoint closer to distanciation than assimilation? To what degree does the reader's tradition prefigure his expectations beyond the scope of the text's strategies? Is the negation of tradition also a negation of time and the personal pole of the dialectic? If motion is the modulation of a familiar setting then can it be equated to the more radical 'negation' of a familiar setting, and if so is it motion or action that interests Iser? Is not the vital dimension of depth provided by the 'here' and 'now' of the reader's narrative understanding, a tertium quid that mediates rather than transgresses borders of space and tension of time?

If this understanding is correlated to the reader's sense and attitude towards the world, then what triad might emerge from a common perspective closer to the assimilative pole of appropriation? Can the character of a reader's perspective meet the strategies of the text's perspectives? Again, can a typology of reader perspectives provide a counterpart to Iser's four textual perspectives? What variations in the dialectic of question and answer emerge from a dialogue between similar and different perspectives? How would these perspectives select and arrange strategies in both conflicting and associated aesthetic objects? To the degree that the sense of hearing and the sense of sight are intimately involved in the communication processes, would these senses help organize the textual strategies in different ways? Again, if 'the strategies organize both the material of the text and the conditions under which that material is to be communicated,' would the different senses, attitudes, and modes of perceiving the world also play a role in varying the conditions of communication (Iser 1978b, 101). If Iser is to speak for *all* literature since the Renaissance what is to be said of the aesthetic experience of a text, oral or written, in Jauss's 'over-whelming majority of humanity?' These questions spill over into the field of refiguration.

Perspectives of Figuration: Refiguration

Hans Robert Jauss's theory of aesthetic reception attempts to move away from any 'aesthetics of negativity' with a 'modernist bias' (1985, 165). He proposes a hermeneutical project 'to recuperate the text which has become alien through temporal distance and reinsert it "in the living presence of dialogue, constituted originally as question and answer" ' (154). He seeks to co-ordinate the past's refiguration of poetic texts with that of the present. Jauss 'poses the problem of understanding what is alien by insisting on the distinctness of the horizons not only of past and present experience, but also of familiar and culturally different worlds' (147). His attention falls on culturally different worlds, with different perspectives to meet the text, that lie primarily on a diachronic level. While Jauss's standpoint appears to be firmly grounded in Hans-Georg Gadamer's notion of consciousness subject to history's effects, he gives particular attention to the concept of aesthetic cultivation (Gadamer 1975, 73).

In order to explain the refiguration of poetic texts, Jauss's methodology also employs a triad. Reading is not explained as a spatial switching of foreground and background, but as a temporal accumulation of three moments: 'understanding (*intelligere*), interpretation (*interpretare*), and application (*applicare*)' (Jauss 1982, 139). The first moment or *poiesis* occurs during a first reading and involves an 'immediate understanding within *aesthetic* perception' (1982, 141; emphasis added). This 'perceptual reading' is followed by subsequent readings and a second moment of *aisthesis* or interpretation (142). The reflective interpretation of a poetic text '*always* presupposes *aesthetic* perception as its pre-understanding' (142; emphasis added). A third moment of application, or *katharsis*, proceeds from the first, thematic moment of *poiesis* and the second, reflective moment of *aisthesis* (1985, 168). The moment of application is realized when 'a text from the past is of interest not only in reference to its primary context, but ... [when it] is also interpreted to disclose a possible significance for the contemporary situation' (1982, 143).

Jauss's methodology rests on a principle of aesthetic perception. It is ultimately an *aesthetic* 'act of *perceptual* understanding that introduces and constitutes the aesthetic experience of the poetic text' (1982, 142). This priority of aesthetic perception within the triad of literary hermeneutics presupposes a substantial *difference* and 'contrast [between] everyday perception that degenerates into a norm [and] a mode of perception at once more complex and more meaningful, which as aesthetic pleasure is able to rejuvenate cognitive vision or visual recognition (*aisthesis*)' (142). This aesthetic perception based on 'cognitive vision' and opposed to a 'degenerating' everyday perception does not develop the 'priority of hearing over sight' or the importance Gadamer gives to everyday hermeneutical experience (1975, 420). Jauss's reliance on an 'aesthetic character' as the 'regulative principle' behind the text runs the danger of alienating a 'literary' hermeneutics from a 'historical' hermeneutics (1982, 148). This aesthetic character is similar to Gadamer's concept of 'aesthetic differentiation,' that is, a 'process of abstraction' by which a work of art 'becomes *visible*' (1975, 76; emphasis added). Unlike Gadamer, however, Jauss describes the specific function of literature in social existence as a 'disappointment of expectations' (1982, 45). This viewpoint does not coincide with Gadamer's understanding of aesthetic experience, which, as opposed to illusion, *does not* bring about an 'experience of disappointment' (1975, 75).

Jauss does not develop the notions of everyday perception *and* aesthetic perception in a manner that stresses both difference and *similarity*. He tends to ignore 'the very idea of traditionality ... that identity and difference are inextricably mixed together in it' (Ricoeur 1984, 2:20). The result, as Robert Weimann puts it, is that 'one of the rudimentary questions in the history of literary reception remains unanswered – a question which was many years ago raised by Levin L. Schücking when he remarked that the "primary question of literary history should be – what is read by various segments of the people at a specific time and why?" ' (1975, 24). Despite his insistence on a point of departure from an aesthetic experience of differentiation, Jauss paradoxically warns that there can be no universal application of one code of understanding and interpretation because aesthetic perception – 'like all aesthetic experience – is intertwined with historical experience ... [and] is subject to historical change' (1982, 148). If his 'historical' experience is related to Gadamer's historically conditioned experience (as appears to be the case), then aesthetic experience is inseparable from everyday language as a mode of being in the world and from the everyday process of perception. Thus, Robert Weimann opens his critique of Jauss's 'reception aesthetics' by pointing 'to a major bias in Jauss's own approach to literary history: it involves the paradox of a method which while claiming to explicate literature according to its historical function, places itself beyond this very aspect of function by orienting itself according to a principle of mere self-definition' (1975, 15). Weimann goes on to point out that Jauss's horizon of expectations 'is not established in terms of ... the actual business of living, but rather, it is deduced from purely literary criteria' (1975, 22). For Jauss, then, the work of art is received and judged more as an aesthetic object over and against the 'everyday experience of life' than as a dialectic of similarity and difference (Jauss 1982, 41). Jauss's differentiation between an aesthetic and an everyday perception does not allow for what Ricoeur has termed the 'anchorage points for narrative' in the 'everyday experience ... of the episodes of our lives,' nor does it acknowledge the undeniably 'literary' quality of perception in general as understood by Merleau-Ponty (1984, 1:74).

For Jauss, the moment of interpretation or *aisthesis* is built upon the moment of aesthetic perception or understanding. It involves 'the reflective reduction on the part of the interpretation that would understand the text as an answer' to an implicit or explicit question (1982, 142). This explanation built on an aesthetic understanding allows Jauss to claim that 'literary hermeneutics has as its real point of departure the understanding of the aesthetic experience ... [and it] does not therefore require agreement about an object' (1985, 155). This dismissal of the need for agreement concerning the object at the level of interpretation poses several problems. First, to the degree that his *aisthesis* works with Gadamer's notion of a 'hermeneutical phenomenon,' Jauss would have to consider Gadamer's understanding of interpretation in terms of an interpersonal conversation that underscores the importance of agreement: 'Just as one person seeks to reach agreement with his partner concerning an object, so the interpreter understands the object of which the text speaks ... Something is placed in the centre, as the Greeks said, which the partners to the dialogue both share, and concerning which they can exchange ideas with one another. Hence agreement concerning the object' (1975, 341). If aesthetic experience is to include all three moments and if interpretation is to mediate understanding and application, then some degree of agreement concerning the object is needed. Ultimately interpretation must share some 'common ground' whereby interpretations can become part of a dialogue among the 'members of a community' (Valdés 1987, 55).

A second problem is that, without an agreement concerning the object, the possibility of the aesthetics of perception becoming an aesthetics of illusion or hallucination is decidedly enhanced. While such interpretations might make claim to validity within their own right, they would not be in keeping with Jauss's standpoint or with Gadamer's claim that the 'aesthetic is different' from 'illusion, magic, [and] dream' (1975, 75).

A third problem presents itself because the interpretation of a literary text helps provide a literary object that 'is not an idea that somebody has in mind,' but a noematic object that 'can be identified and reidentified by different individuals at different times as being one and the same' (Ricoeur 1976, 90). Thus, as Ricoeur points out, 'the notion of an ideal *Sinn* borrowed from Frege was extended in that way by Husserl to all psychic achievements, not only to logical acts but also to perceptual, volitional, and emotional acts. For an objective phenomenology, every intentional act without exception must be described from its noematic sides as the correlate of a corresponding noetic act' (90). A reflective interpretation of the noematic side, or 'answer,' must seek agreement concerning the identity of the object before the noetic act, or 'question,' can be decided upon. Again, an interpretation must *figure* out the *sense* by starting from an understanding of the text that *at least* has the potential of being recognized and agreed upon as such by other members of a community. Finally, by dispensing with the need for agreement concerning the object, Jauss does not make allowance for the universality of the concept that proceeds from the hermeneutical experience.

Jauss's moment of application or motivation concerns itself with the 'specific issue [of] how a classic work may be decanonized, how it may be introduced into the horizon of contemporary experience ... in such a way that the link between past and present experience is not broken' (1985, 169). His application of aesthetic perception and explanation is therefore concerned primarily with maintaining a classical canon alive and does not deal fully with the equally important application of giving contemporary production life by stimulating its careful reception. If Iser's interest lies primarily with all literature from the Renaissance to modern production, Jauss's interest lies heavily with the reception of 'medieval literature in the vernacular' and how it 'might serve as an example for contemporary research' (1985, 159). It is within this final moment of application or *katharsis* that Jauss introduces the primary notion of voice. At this final level the reader can make the text 'speak to him' and that 'voice of an unknown "I" speaks into the space' of ·

an expectation (1978, 141, and 1982, 151). Despite his point of departure in an aesthetic perception, Jauss goes on to suggest applying the rather disappointing variations-on-a-basic-pattern, or *'plurale tantum,'* structure of 'today's irresistible television series' to the serial structure of reception found in the *chanson de geste* and old Romance epic of an 'oral tradition' (1978, 144, 145). Now, the technological means or medium of communication (which must be explored) undoubtedly plays an essential role in reception. Jauss's distanciation of an 'aesthetic' perception from a 'degenerating' everyday perception, however, does not appear to provide an assimilative potential whereby the techniques of literary communication can be reconciled with those of everyday communication. On the one hand, his notion of today's televised *plurale tantum* bypasses the mediating tertium quid of everyday perception in order to explain late medieval literary reception. On the other hand, Jauss's notion of application leaves today's reader with such questionable tools as 'a medieval perspective' with which to introduce (not revive) any major literary contribution proceeding from today's oral traditions.

Several questions are provoked by Jauss's understanding and explanation of aesthetic reception. Does not the immediate understanding of aesthetic perception presuppose an everyday perception and a process of guesswork upon which everyday language comes to bear? If a similarity in structure and character mediates the dialectics of question-answer and perception-world, then how can direction, sense, perspective, and medium in communication contribute to an appropriate understanding, explanation, comprehension, and validation of texts both 'classical' and of contemporary innovation? Again, how can perception and sense, language and means of communication provide an appropriate link not only between past and present production and reception but also between prefiguration and refiguration within today's different traditions? Would the interpretation of a twentieth-century text in terms of a 'medieval' reception be appropriate? In other words, if medieval perception was predominantly audio-oral in its perspective, are today's audio-oral traditions to be called medieval? Again, would the application of one's own understanding of one's own medieval perspective to another's twentieth-century text not 'overlook his claim' to contemporaneity and would it be able 'to listen to what he has to say to us' (Gadamer 1975, 324)? Would this 'form of self-relatedness' not be 'something that is directed ultimately towards oneself and [therefore] contradicts the moral definition of man' (322)? How can the everyday means of communication intertwine with the meaning communicated by literature? How can this meaning, in turn, be related to noematic structures of the text's reference, and what noetic sense or medium of questioning do they reveal? Can the media of communication, sense, and narrative perspective come together in such a manner as to mediate Robert Weimann's concern for rhetorical, communicative achievement, Wolfgang Iser's interest in typologies of perspective, and Jauss's own preoccupation with culturally different worlds? After all, do they not share a common tradition ... figuratively speaking?

5

Figuring out Narrative Perspective: Facets of Structure

In keeping with the abstract and analytical nature of concepts, the preceding theoretical explanations of narrative perspective have been divided into varying degrees of difference and distance. These different positions can be different only to the degree that they belong to a community founded on a shared tradition and bound together by a common purpose.[1] In keeping with the circular nature of phenomenological hermeneutics, it is now necessary to propose an understanding of narrative perspective that hearkens to the voice of this tradition and its collective enterprise. My inquiry has concentrated on presenting an understanding and an explanation of the fundamental issues underlying narrative perspective, that is, language, perception, experience, and concept. This understanding and explanation aims at the more balanced relationship of assimilation and distanciation, voice and sign, ear and eye, temporal tradition and structural space. Of equal importance has been the direction and sense mediating the terms. This process of understanding and explanation leads to an interpretation of narrative perspective that cannot rely on a steadfast and closed definition of the term. Unlike the post-Genettian, metonymic approach I do not seek to define its terms 'minimally' (Rimmon-Kenan 88). I interpret the function of narrative perspective in the communication process using heuristic devices understood in their *maximum* dimension. The challenge of such an interpretation, given the complexity of language, perception, experience, and the concept of narrative perspective, is to keep these devices as simple and applicable as possible. I share Shlomith Rimmon-Kenan's frustration with the complexity of today's notion of 'reader,' that is, as 'the "Actual Reader" (Van Dijk, Jauss), the "Superreader" (Riffaterre), the "Informed Reader" (Fish), the "Ideal Reader" (Culler), the "Model Reader" (Eco), the "Implied Reader" (Booth, Iser, Chatman, Perry), or the "Encoded Reader" (Brooke-Rose)' (118). While each of these terms differs from the others, all seek an engagement with, or are mediated by, a 'first-person' situated in a world constituted by language and perception who experiences the world of the text through a dialogue with the narrative voice. Each and every reader is ultimately an 'experiencing I' that enters into a relationship with a narrating voice or 'you' and a narrated world – an 'it,' 'she,' and 'he.' While the reader's standpoint in this interpersonal relationship can be implied by the text, the personal perspective that perceives the text cannot be dictated by the text's strategies alone.

The text, unlike a work, is a virtual phenomenon. By this I mean that it (a) is a synthesis of the heterogeneous in the narrative field, (b) is a configuration act of intelligibility, (c) is constituted by history and tradition as well as by individual innovation, and (d) emerges at the intersection 'between the world of the text and the world of the reader' (Ricoeur 1985, 183, 175–86). The text lies in a symbolic dimension of life where symbol, to quote Ricoeur, 'hesitates on the dividing line between bios and logos. It testifies to the primordial rootedness of Discourse in Life. It is born where force and form coincide' (1976, 59). The symbolic dimension in which perception meets a text reflects the primordial level where the upsurge of time and language meet sense. Symbol, like metaphor, is 'a two dimensional phenomenon' in that it points to a sense of the world and back to the non-sense from which it proceeds.[2] The world of sign and reference that is transformed by texts and in which the work circulates has no exclusive jurisdiction over what is real. In keeping with Merleau-Ponty, each level has the 'value' of reality (1962, 342). It is the standpoint and the sense, the point of departure and the direction taken that will vary. Any particular proposal as to the nature of narrative perspective must dismiss all claim to absolute knowledge of the issue. Taking into account the polysemantic value and the etymology of figure and facet, each interpretation, including the present one, is only a grasping of multiple facets together, in order to figure it out (Ricoeur 1981b, 229). What can be offered are certain general guidelines that may help to achieve an appropriate 'sense' of narrative perspective.

I would like to consider narrative perspective as a virtual relationship that is realized between the techniques and strategies of configuration, on the one hand, and the traditional (as well as individual) perspectives of the implied author and the reader in the prefiguration and refiguration, on the other. Narrative perspective is subjective to the degree that it is 'the temporal character of human experience,' and it is objective to the degree that it structures the 'activity of narrating a story' (Ricoeur 1984, 1:52). To the extent that narrative is language and perspective is perception, narrative perspective will be achieved by a vital, dynamic process generated between three dimensions: the subjective dimension of time, the objective dimension of spatial relations, and the phenomenological dimension of perception. This dynamic process functions on an appropriate principle of assimilation and distanciation in productive generation. These abstractions are, of course, only a conceptualization of a vital process and serve only as heuristic devices. Perspective cannot be limited to any one pole precisely because it is a mediating process. At the core of experience, sense/non-sense, object/subject, life/death, illusion/actuality, external/internal, and perception/hallucination intertwine, for these remain categories of the intellect. If, as Hans Robert Jauss puts it, the process of perception is like reading a 'score' of music, then the instruments of the orchestra cannot be taken for the symphony played (Jauss 1982, 141). The facets of narrative perspective underlying textual configuration will constitute my point of departure. This 'noematic' side can be divided into considerations of voice on the one hand and narrative world on the other. Narrative voice can be understood as both 'person,' essential to any dialogue, and 'dramatization,' or the degree to which the voice participates in the events that it relates. Narrative voice also includes 'scope,' or the degree of privilege the voice has to perceive a world. Finally, 'reliability' is the attitude characterizing the relation between the two interlocutors in the textual dialogue.

To say 'voice' is to say so symbolically for there is no 'sound' involved, except for the body's reaction to the perceived words. In this I agree with Gadamer's reassertion of the 'ancient insight into the priority of hearing over sight' (1975, 420). As has already been made clear by Merleau-Ponty, one perceives written or oral language with the whole body. In the synaesthetic field of the senses the communication between one sense and another 'is the rule' not the exception (M.M-P. 1962, 229). Voice is personal in the temporal dimension of memory and the ever-present now. It is not limited by flat surfaces and has inherent depth. If the senses can be arranged in a hierarchy of 'Touch – taste – smell – hearing – sight,' the movement from 'intimacy' to 'precision' is from the former to the latter (Ong 1977, 136). There are, of course, voices that appeal to the sense of sight, sound, smell, taste, or touch and this quality is a fundamental technique in the strategy of the voice. In terms of intimate contact with one's linguistically defined milieu, hearing takes priority over sight. In the words of Walter J. Ong, voice 'represents another world of dynamism, action, and being-in-time' (1977, 136). It must be emphasized that narrative perspective is the result of the questions and answers of the reader's perspective as well as of the strategies of the voice that rhetorically offer the reader implied positions.

Narrative voice brings together person, dramatization, scope, and reliability. The time spent on each facet and the direction the voice takes in moving from one to another will help determine the character and the structure of the narrative perspective. The duration and sequence of the reader's questions will in the same way help establish the character and the structure of his experience. This movement on the part of the reader is not a 'wandering point' to use Iser's expression. It wanders only in accordance with the individuality of the reader. It is 'directed' by the strategies of the voice, on the one hand, and by his or her own tradition, into which he or she was born and to which he or she belongs, on the other. Narrative voice can be represented as the act of moving among these six facets:

A. person   D. reliability   E. sequence
B. dramatization   C. scope   F. duration

It is temporal both in the experience of the reader (the time spent searching for an answer to questions surging from his or her individuality and tradition) as well as in the voice as it narrates from within the chronological system of the text. Again, as movement it may wander but as an action it is also directed. The direction a perspective takes is open to intersubjective debate within a tradition, and here the individual wandering must draw support from intersubjective agreement on the character of the directing structure (Gadamer 1975, 341).

Because of the nature of dialogue, which characterizes both the hermeneutical experience and the relation between humanity and world in perception, the matter of person cannot be ignored. 'Person,' considered at the level of the sentence in discourse, is not to be confused with the technical use of the term in drama. I understand person as 'figuration' in the etymological sense offered by Benveniste: 'Cette classification est notoirement héritée de la grammaire grecque, où les formes verbales fléchies constituent des πρόσωπα, des *personae*, des "figurations" sous lesquelles se réalise la notion verbale' (1:225). Person can be subdivided into a dialectical opposition, that of person (I-You) and that of 'non-person' (he, she, it) (Benveniste 2:99). Both 'I' and 'You' are empty and interchangeably filled by different people taking part in a dialogue. 'You' and 'I' are rooted in the presence of dialogue (1:253, 263). 'I' is the transcendent key to discourse and is related to the adverbs 'here' and 'now.' It is unique and mobile. 'It,' like the other pronominal forms, does not refer to objective positions but to the enunciation itself, each time unique and reflexive of its own use. 'I' is the centre of subjectivity from which 'You,' as not-'I' subjectivity, is established (1:232). The first- and second-person pronouns are the subjective poles of person and, as Benveniste points out, 'l'installation de la "subjectivité" dans le langage crée ... la catégorie de la personne ... [et le] changement de perspective que la "subjectivité" peut introduire' (1:263). The third person, or rather 'non' person, 'a pour caractéristique et pour fonction constantes de représenter sous le rapport de la forme même, un invariant non-personnel, et rien que cela' (1:231). It is the person through which 'things' are predicated and constitutes the objective character of discourse. If the word 'person' or 'personal' proceeds from the Greek notion of figuration, it follows that the third-, non-person standpoint would be related to an 'objective' observation of facets. The passive voice, for example, seeks to eliminate person by inverting the subject-object order, and claims authority through an objectivity that, nevertheless, presupposes 'person' in dialogue. As the non-person proceeds from the polarity of 'persons' in communication, it possesses a reflective quality: 'Le langage n'est possible que parce que chaque locuteur se pose comme *sujet*, en renvoyant à lui-même comme *je* dans son discours. De ce fait, *je* pose une autre personne, celle qui, tout extérieure qu'elle est à "moi" devient mon écho auquel je dis *tu* et qui me dit *tu*. La polarité des personnes, telle est dans le langage la condition fondamentale, dont le procès de communication, dont nous sommes parti, n'est qu'une conséquence toute pragmatique' (1:260).

The choice of pronoun in narrative voice cannot help but establish a relationship in two directions, that of the narrative world and that of the reader. The use of first person or first 'figuration' (in the broad sense) tends to create a 'you' in the reader. The use of 'you' helps create the standpoint of the 'I.' The use of an 'it' helps create a common standpoint of 'You and I,' that is, we. The choice of pronoun is a choice of figuration that will affect the narrative perspective on all levels. From the empty core at the centre of 'I' emerge the figurations of the narrator's voice and the reader's questioning and answering voice. The use of a highly impersonal pronoun such as 'one' or 'no one' can create an abstract, reflexive, and highly analytical 'artificial' standpoint. Mario Valdés has noted a fine example of this artificial use by Jorge Luis Borges in his opening to 'Las ruinas circulares': 'Nadie lo vio desembarcar en la unánime noche, nadie vio la canoa de bambú sumiéndose en el fango sagrado, pero a los pocos días nadie ignoraba que el hombre taciturno venía del Sur y que su patria era una de las infinitas aldeas que están aguas arriba.'[3]

Dramatization can be understood as the degree to which the voice enters into the cause-effect relations of the story's action. As each facet of voice is related with all others, dramatization is related to person, scope, and reliability. Thus, as Valdés puts it, the voice 'may be situated in the extreme position of first-person participant or he may be at the other pole as hidden source of revelation, or at any point in between the extremes' (1982, 26). In any case, the degree of involvement is an important factor in establishing the value structure of the narrative text.

The scope can be understood as the degree of synthesis within the power of the narrating voice, that is, what potential parts of the temporal and spatial dimensions can be brought into a consistent whole. The substance or understanding from which material is selected and 'figured' includes the foreground and background, inside and outside dimensions of space, as well as the past and future possibilities drawn into the presentation. The reader's activity of creating a conceptual whole from his experience when he or she finds a gap is a dimension of the reader's scope. The greatest gap in any text is that found between its end and its beginning. The conclusion 'gives the story an "end point," which, in turn, furnishes the point of view from which the story can be perceived as forming a whole' (Ricoeur 1984, 1:67).

The reliability of the voice stands separate from its other facets in that it is not so much a different category as a direction of movement. The voice may act constructively in a cause-effect sequence or reverse the act and move to de-construct or undermine itself with the paradox of effect-cause. This reversal highlights the facets themselves, leaving the figuration they presuppose in the dark. Both hyperbole and understatement are strategies that reflect back on the voice, reversing the sense of perspective.

Time, through sequence and duration, is fundamental to narrative structure. It is a direct result of the subjective personality of the narrating voice. All of the text's facets cannot be present to the reader all at once. The reader will contribute to the construction of sequence through memory and to duration through the time spent pondering different moments of the text. Although the text's facets cannot be totally present at any one moment, the figure of its past, present, and future not only can, but must be, totally present in the present of the reading experience. Any one moment is an event in a history of moments and an advent of future moments of revealed meaning. The past and the future are available through the present. Each perspective of a present event is also a future prospection and a past retrospection (Ricoeur 1984, 1:13).

Paul Ricoeur appropriately suggests a figure that mediates the geometry of space and the figures of speech to explain his understanding of a *'tale about time'* (1984, 2:132). A tale about time creates a relation between two foci 'in the form of an ellipse' (2:132). This heuristic device can also help explain the temporal configuration of a 'common' perspective. The oval-shaped ellipse, understood as the locus of a point (P) such that the sum of its distances from two fixed points (F', F) is a constant, describes an assimilative, aggregative relationship. The two foci, F' and F, suggest standpoints of a reading-listening person and a narrating person in the shared, personal, 'Now' of the relating situation. The oval points (P) surrounding the two standpoints can be understood as the story's succession of narrated events. While the utterance of the narrating activity can be explained using the systematic structures of *langue* (L), and the reader's questions and answers can be understood in terms of the dialogical situation of *parole* (L'), both are preceded by *langage* and it is the sum of the two that realizes the text through discourse.

Throughout history and throughout the world 'today,' the distance and the mediation between the reporting narrative voice at F and the reading listener at F' will vary, yet both will remain within language as discourse and in the fixed present of the reading-listening and reporting situation.[4] As a figure of speech, ellipse is a meaningful 'leaving out.' The omission is meaningful to the extent that the past sequence of events is related to the reader's present understanding and constitutes a directed advent of future possibilities. The meaning does not depend on the reader's perspective (F' – P) alone, but upon the relation of his or her perspective to that of the voice (F – P) and what the reader 'figures' the voice means. The ellipse may be a 'leaving out' but it is not a vacuum. It is full of personal and intersubjective meaning. Ellipse does not represent an accelerated duration or 'maximum speed' alone

(Rimmon-Kenan 53). The reader's experience of the omission also comes into play. The reader may spend long hours, days, or even years pondering the meaning of an omission. In this way the four sentences and the resounding ellipse of eight days that are the fourth chapter of the picaresque *Lazarillo de Tormes* give Harry Sieber reason to develop fourteen pages of in-depth interpretation (45–59).

Again I would like to mention the importance of not imposing this figure of geometry and speech like some conceptual schema or filter upon the text to make it psychologically accessible. Ellipse is a heuristic device that can help explain a series of temporal relationships that emerge with the refiguration of the text and through the interplay of perspectives in narrative. It is a heuristic device that proceeds from the temporal experience of the text, and it is this experience that takes priority.

The subjective quality of voice and time is by no means separate from the objective quality of world and space. Facets E and F above already begin to fuse with spatial relations. Narrative perspective, like perception, brings time and space together in a transitional dimension that is the imaginary world of the text. Narrative world emerges from the narrative voice and reader perspective. It deals with the phenomenal world of spatial relations. Relations of Space can be understood as relations between objects in a foreground as scene of action and a setting as background to the scene. The relation between objects of symbolic significance to either the narrating voice or the questioning and answering reader will modify the character and structure of the narrative perspective. The narrative perspective of H.G. Wells's *War of the Worlds* is not the same for an English reader as it is for a Mexican. To the former it is science fiction; for the latter, who has inherited a *Visión de los vencidos* (León-Portilla), it is, in part at least, history.

Spatial relations between objects are seconded by relations between characters to create a social structure. Again, it is the reader's perspective that will move to meet the strategies of type, reliability, role, and privilege of the characters. Narrative World is the space mediating and separating the objects in foreground-background presentation, as well as the relation between the characters in a social hierarchy:

1. foreground   2. type   3. reliability
4. background   5. role   6. privilege

The character type can be understood in terms of his or her relation to the narrating voice and the reader's questioning voice. Hero or villain depends on when and where the character is located in the world of the text. A character developed as a hero yet found in a bank, after hours, putting money into his pockets may subsequently be seen from a different perspective. Hero or villain depends on the reader's tradition as well because 'ethical qualifications come from the real world' and not from textual strategies alone (Ricoeur 1984, 1:47). Character type is also decided by 'the social structure of the narrative world' and by the perception of a reader who understands through the perspective of a linguistically 'in-formed' social tradition (Valdés 1982, 33). Whether the character is a common archetype or individualized prototype will depend upon the interaction of distance and mediation between the character and his or her world, on the one hand, and the reader's understanding of the world, on the other.

The relation between narrating voice, questioning reader, and character type is inseparable from the role the character plays within the cause-effect relations of the story's action and events. Characters are 'experiencing' figures in the narrative world. It is through their experiences in this world that the voice, as Jean Pouillon puts it, 'tries to give the reader the same understanding of the characters as the reader has of himself' (quoted in Ricoeur 1984, 2:183–4). This degree of involvement in the cause-effect relation of the story's action will affect the reader's experience of the narrative world. In turn, the reader's experience of the world will undoubtedly come to bear upon the manner and degree of questioning applied to a role.

The character role is not limited to the narrative world alone, for it also provides a standpoint and participates in 'the stream of narration' (Valdés 1982, 33). According to Pouillon, the difference 'between the narrator's point of view and that of the character, which is taken directly from novelistic technique, remains closely related to the distinction ... between prereflective and reflective consciousness' (quoted in Ricoeur 1984, 2:184). The greater the narrating role of the characters the greater the reflection in the sense figured below. As Paul Ricoeur notes, the greatest degree would be 'a pure novel of multiple voices – Virginia Woolf's The Waves – [which] is no longer a novel at all but a sort of oratorio offered for reading' (1984, 2:97).

The privilege of a character is what E.M. Forster deals with by suggesting 'flat' and 'round' characters (67). A character is round if the narrating voice brings together parts from all spatial and temporal dimensions into a whole with height, width, and depth. She or he is flat if the voice cannot or chooses not to deal with a third dimension.

A privileged character is one who has been fully developed and fore-grounded. This part-whole relationship cannot be enclosed in textual strategies either. The roundest character may still fall flat and not achieve a concrete universality in the reader's experience.

Reliability in terms of character is established by the character's alienation from the events in the narrative world and by the degree of paradox he or she introduces into their cause-effect structure. An unreliable character stands distant from the events and appears to undermine their direction of movement. A stereotype character participates in the cause-effect structure in a reliable manner and is dependent on the sense of the text's action. An alienated character has a greater degree of independence from the sense of action presented by the narrating person. He or she has a greater freedom to speak and is often privileged with a greater capacity to know. The paradox an unreliable character introduces moves from sense to non-sense. It moves from the action of the story to invite a participatory act on the part of the reader. Once again, hyperbole often plays a strategic role in reversing the sense of perspective.

The sequence and duration creating a chronological order is fundamental to structure and is the direct result of the narrating voice. Like sequence and duration, foreground and background are related to modes of perceiving the world and are directly related to the standpoint of the voice. These facets have constituted the point of departure for many of the theoretical approaches discussed above. All foreground and background relations are mediated by a 'Here' of the voice and a 'Here' of the reader. The distance and mediation between the two points will vary. While an ever-present 'Now' can be readily shared through a common experience of time, the 'Here' of standpoint already involves two separate points that will tend to be shared artificially through abstract analysis and reflection.

If ellipse can be helpful as a heuristic device for a text about time, then I would like to suggest that a parabolic perspective can help understand a text about space. The concave or 'cave-like' parabola, according to the *New Webster's Dictionary*, is a 'plane curve produced by the intersection of a cone with a plane parallel to one of its sides,' and a cone is 'a geometrical solid ... having an ellipse or the like for a base.' The temporal ellipse from which it is drawn therefore precedes the spatial parabola. A parabola (like figure 3 on page 221 below) can be described as the locus of a point (P) whose distance from a fixed line (L) always equals its distance from a fixed point (F) not on L. This configuration defined by distance places the reader (F′) out of the picture, behind the narrative voice (F). The ellipsis is cut in half and the reader alloted a passive role. The voice directs itself away from the reader into its world of narrated events (P). This world emerges between the standpoint of the voice and the fixed structures of *langue* (L) that the voice explores in order to structure space. Much like Frye's lyrical poet, the voice, 'so to speak, turns his back on his listeners, though he may speak for them, and though they may repeat some of his words after him' (250). The voice then reflects or rather rebounds off the cave-like world of the text through the characters in a polyphonic 'echo' that the reader-audience hears and is invited to repeat. Rather than a circular succession the reader might encounter an alternating, zig-zag pattern as the perspective moves in a dichotomy from left to right and right to left. This alternating, pendular swing reveals a tension between what Ricoeur has called 'clock time' or 'monumental time' and the mortal time of experience (1984, 2:101–12, 190). The apparent objectivity of voices that seem to come from the text itself highlights the parabolic inversion or phenomenon of reversibility and leaves the reader with little personal reliability. The temporal relation of ellipse invites the reader perspective to participate in the action through refiguration. The spatial relation of parabola reflects back upon the process of perception and back upon perspective in particular, as well as back upon the reader's will to act and 'play' a part in the 'display' of narrating. If the elliptical sense of succession emerges from a text about time, the non-sense of reversibility emerges from the foregrounded paradox of parabolic texts about space.

In contrast to a text about space there is, of course, the claim that a text *is* space. When difference is added to distanciation and made absolute, then the oval ellipse is cut in half and the resulting two parabolas are placed back to back and separated by a vacuum. From this postulated absence, writing (L) could claim to reflect everything. Deconstruction appears to subscribe to this conceptual view. Such an arrangement that turns the ellipse inside out mirrors a hyperbola. A hyperbola is the locus of a point (P) such that the *difference* of its *distances* from two fixed points (F′, F) is a constant. Between a point of view (F), the text's facets (P) and writing (L), on the one hand, and the reader (F′), a deconstruction of the text (P′), and an infinite supplement (L′) to writing, on the other, lies an unmediated difference (C). The reader's perspective does not participate in refiguring the text but is undone by it. The reader's perspective can only deconstruct the text's *facettes* (P) along its own line of interpretation (P') by exploring infinite, distancing supplements to writing (L) along L'. This abstract, analytical concept is twice removed from ellipse. It does not emerge from an experience with the text but from a conceptual standpoint adopted before analysis.

The Character of Figures

The facets of the noematic side of a text help reveal figurations on the noetic side. It may be impossible to develop a typology of innovation and imagination, but it is possible to understand the traditional forms of sedimentation. A heuristic typology can be developed for the rule-governed behaviour from which innovation springs. While Wolfgang Iser's typology of perspectives is founded on a psychology of perception that highlights the opposition to and distance from norms, a standpoint within the phenomenology of language, perception, and experience must work with a typology that is not at odds with traditional modes of understanding. As Robert Weimann has pointed out, such a typology cannot ignore the historical consciousness 'in-forming' the prefiguration of the text, nor, as Jauss has insisted, can it ignore the different modes of reception involved in the refiguration of the text (Weimann 1985, 276). Finally, it must also interact with the facets on the noematic side of narrative perspective. Typologies bring various parts into a consistent whole and, in their effort to achieve consistency, often appear to claim that they are exhaustive or absolute. A hermeneutical and phenomenological standpoint, by the very nature of perception, dismisses any such claim. In the words of Paul Ricoeur: 'This is a typology but not a taxonomy, inasmuch as it does not claim to be exhaustive or closed. Point of view is only one of the ways to reach the articulation of the structure of a work of art' (Ricoeur 1984, 2:185).

Having taken narrative voice and narrative world into account, there remains to develop the reader's vital standpoint in a world figured by language. If narrative perspective provides the channel or medium through which the reader enters into a process of creation with the text, on the one hand, and through which the very process of perception, refiguration, and self-appropriation are revealed, on the other, then it is through the very 'figures' of language that a typology of understanding may be 'figured out.' Gadamer stands with Von Humboldt in stating that 'language maintains a kind of independent life over against the individual member of a linguistic community and

introduces him, as he grows into it, to a particular attitude and relationship to the world as well' (1975, 401). He affirms that 'to have a
"world" means to have an attitude toward it' (1975, 402), and this
noetic sense of language differs from the noematic or objective side of
perception:

In the same way as with perception we can speak of the 'linguistic nuances'
that the world undergoes in different linguistic worlds. But it remains a characteristic difference that every 'nuance' of the object of perception is exclusively
different from every other one and that the 'thing-in-itself' helps to constitute
the continuum of these nuances whereas, with the nuances of the linguistic
views of the world, each one contains potentially within it every other one,
ie. every one is able to be extended into every other one. It is able to understand,
from within itself, the 'view' of the world that is presented in another language.
(1975, 406)

In order to create a vital third dimension, narrative perspective must
deal with the question of linguistic nuances 'in-forming' the standpoint
of the reader as he speaks to the text with his questions and answers.
To the degree that 'we are thinking from the center of language,' I
would like to propose a typology of reader perspectives based on tropes
in keeping with the figurative nature of metaphor and person (Gadamer
1975, 418). Each trope in this 'tropology' is a nuance, an attitude, a
way of figuring out the world and the text, a way of making sense, a
perspective or outlook that helps perceive and create the text as well
as reveal the reader's self. This vital dimension experiences language
first and foremost through discourse with the text and secondly as an
analysis of abstract form through a concept of *langue*.
    It is here that I feel Hayden White's tropics of discourse can be of
assistance. White understands 'tropic' in both the classical Greek mode
of 'turn,' way, or manner and the classical Latin mode of 'metaphor'
or figure of speech (1978, 2). Discourse, by contrast, is understood as
a 'mediative enterprise' moving back and forth like a shuttle weaving
a texture between 'received encodations of experience and the clutter
of phenomena' as well as 'between alternative ways' of encoding a
reality that are in some way 'provided by the traditions of discourse'
(1978, 4). White offers a mediative typology of discourse functioning
between the reader and the world, that is, between the 'poetic figurations of reality' and the 'noetic comprehension of it' (14). For a typology of 'modes of understanding' he proposes a fourfold schema

beginning with the dialectic tension within the copula and leading to a 'self-reflexivity on the constructivist nature of the ordering principle itself' (22, 6). White's fourfold schema follows Kenneth Burke's 'master tropes' in order and direction from metaphor to metonym, to synecdoche, and on to irony (5). Unlike the master tropes, as presented in Burke's *Grammar of Motives*, however, White's schema does not constitute a closed schema. In his search for 'a typology of the modes of discourse [that] would provide entry into a typology of the modes of understanding ... [and that] might permit us to mediate between contending ideologues,' White proposes an open development of the schema along the dialectical lines of Giambattista Vico's *New Science* (22, 197–217). The unfolding develops in a never-closing but spiralling circle that permits different and similar perspectives to be functioning in different degrees of similarity at the same time. White's schema resembles the hermeneutical circle described by Ricoeur when he speaks of 'an endless spiral that would carry the meditation past the same point a number of times but at different altitudes' (1984, 1:72).

The metaphorical characterization of a domain of experience is one that 'whatever else it does, explicitly asserts a similarity in a difference and, at least implicitly, a difference in a similarity' (White 1978, 72). This is the fundamental mode of poetic apprehension in general and is essentially mediative (10). It can be associated with early childhood development in an ontogenetic field of inquiry and to a 'supposedly' more primitive social order.[5] Tradition at this level is obvious to the extent of being unimpeachable. Time here is an ever-present 'Now' and space is that of the immediate 'Here.' A natural order prevails over chaos and the individual is subordinated to the totality of the world. I understand White's primary level as a consciousness of identity, in which such discrete conceptual dichotomies as signifier vs. signified, life vs. death, good vs. bad, and right vs. wrong tend to intermingle in the immediate and symbolic experience of a natural order. A natural order is not only biological and physical but also an order of language, natural to a being that can understand and be understood. This primary level appears similar to the notion of consciousness that Benjamin Lee Whorf uses to bring 'Standard Average European' and Hopi temporal verb forms together: 'Everything is in consciousness, and everything in consciousness is, and is together. There is in it a sensuous and a nonsensuous.'[6]

Metonymic consciousness, by contrast, is reductive and mechanistic in its operations. It reduces the world to 'part – part relationships and ...

[comprehends a] field in terms of the laws that bind one phenomenon to another as a cause to an effect (White 1978, 73). A greater diversity is achieved at this level. The shift in modality from that of metaphor to that of metonym is not 'logical' but tropological. White emphasizes the linguistic importance of this shift: 'Once the world of phenomena is separated into two orders of being (agents and causes on the one hand, acts and effects on the other), the primitive consciousness is endowed, *by purely linguistic means alone*, with the conceptual categories (agents, causes, spirits, essences) necessary for the theology, science and philosophy of civilized reflection' (1973, 35). Thus, the 'essentially *representational*' transforms into a '*reductionist*' metonymy (34). This mode of consciousness is, then, 'essentially *Extrinsic*' (35).

The shift from a metonymic mode of figuration to a synecdochic mode is a move 'in the opposite direction' from the essentially extrinsic relations of the former to an intrinsic relation of qualities in the latter (White 1978, 73). This return to the intrinsic is 'an integration within a whole that is *qualitatively* different from the sum of the parts and of which the parts are but *microcosmic* replications' (1973, 35). It establishes relations between superficial attributes and a presumed essence. It also sanctions a movement 'towards integration of all apparently particular phenomena into a whole, the quality of which is such as to justify belief in the possibility of understanding the particular as a microcosm of a macrocosmic totality' (1978, 73). This, then, is a consciousness of intrinsicality.

In contrast to Metaphor (which 'sanctions the prefiguration of the world of experience in object-object terms'), Metonymy (in part-part terms), and Synecdoche (in part-whole terms), Irony is in a sense 'metatropological' (White 1973, 36, 37, and 1978, 73-4). It 'represents a stage of consciousness in which the problematic nature of language itself has become recognized ... [and points] to the absurdity of the beliefs it parodies' (1973, 37). Its tacit aim is to affirm the negative of what is on the literal level positively affirmed or vice versa. This consciousness of scepticism and ethical relativism involves a perspective 'that surreptitiously signals a denial of the assertion of similitude or difference ... [It is] a kind of attitude towards knowledge itself which is implicitly critical of all forms of metaphorical identification, reduction or integration of phenomena.'[7] It is of particular importance to my notion of reliability that an ironic mode of consciousness involves a 'real or feigned disbelief in the truth of [one's] own statements' (1973, 37). It will be recalled that disbelief is a quality of hallucination.

The important point for Hayden White is that 'in metaphor, metonym and synecdoche alike language provides us with models of the *direction* that thought itself might take in its effort to provide meaning to areas of experience not already regarded as being cognitively secured by either common sense, tradition or science' (White 1978, 73). The direction thought may take when guided by common sense, tradition, and Giambattista Vico's *New Science* appears to be elliptical. White parallels the tropological process in character and direction to Vico's four ages (of gods, heroes, men, and decadence) and implicitly gives it the ovular shape of the *corso-ricorso* (1978, 200–1). Whether the experience of a text is to occur within familiar or alien ground, the intersubjective treatment of narrative perspective must come to terms with the sense of direction in both the world of the text and the reader in the world: 'The dominant trope in which this constitutive act is carried out will determine both the kind of objects which are permitted to appear in that field as data and the possible relationships that are conceived to obtain among them' (1973, 430). The autonomy of the text ensures that there are multiple and '*necessary* combinations' that will vary in degree of impact and success within the text and within changing modes of effective-historical consciousness (1973, 29). New combinations of perspectives will create new meanings. These will be brought on by 'the dialectical tension ... [that] arises from an effort to wed a mode of emplotment with a mode of argument of ideological implication which is inconsonant with it' (29). Ricoeur has found in White's tropology a fundamental similarity with his own theory. This combination of perspectives and the resulting productive tension leads, as Ricoeur puts it, 'by way of a long detour to my theme of dissonant consonance' (Ricoeur 1984, 1:168). There are, of course, essential differences between historical and fictional narrative, not the least of which is the former's 'claim to speak about events which really happened' and its subsequent 'burden of proof' (1981a, 288). Nevertheless, each historian, reader, and writer participates, as White puts it, 'in the specific processes of sense-making which identify him as a member of one cultural endowment rather than another. In the process of studying a given complex of events, he begins to perceive the *possible* story form that such events *may* figure. In his narrative account of how this set of events took on the shape which he perceives to inhere within it, he emplots his account as a story of a particular kind' (1978, 86).

White's four types of discourse that provide entry into types of understanding help 'us understand how speech mediates between ...

supposed oppositions' (1978, 21). Yet these noetic types must in turn be approached from a noematic side that cannot be the facets of narrative voice and narrative world alone, precisely because they also *cross upon* ... the historical condition of man' (Ricoeur 1981a, 289). The medium, means, and sense of the process of perception can offer a tropological theory of discourse and the study of narrative perspective its noematic side.

The noematic side of these modes of consciousness may also be approached by means of the 'channel' or 'medium' through which a message passes in discourse. The question as to what may indicate a shift in mode of figuration and understanding can find an answer in the mode of transmitting a message in the course of dialogue. This is not to say that socio-political or economic changes do not indicate such a shift as well. What it does say is that the medium of literary communication will have an effect on understanding comparable to the role played by sense in the processes of perception and experience that linguistically constitute a world. Walter J. Ong has examined the changing modes of consciousness and culture by means of their passing through four channels of discourse: (a) primary orality, (b) chirographic script, (c) typographic script, and (d) electronic media that is accompanied by a second orality. He then establishes a dialectic between an oral noetic and a written noetic. The former maintains a strong link to the temporal 'Now' of a metaphorical perspective and an elliptical configuration that, in Ricoeur's words, 'can be indicated "around" the speakers, "around," if we may say so, the instance of discourse itself' (1981a, 148). The latter is intertwined with the spatial distances separating the voice and reader in the parabolic shape of an analytical or ironic perspective. Ong describes this dialectic of senses and noetic qualities as follows:

Sight isolates, sound incorporates. Whereas sight situates the observer outside what he views, at a distance, sound pours into the hearer. Vision dissects, as Merleau-Ponty has observed ... Vision comes to a human being from one direction at a time: to look at a room or a landscape, I must move my eyes around from one part to another. When I hear, however, I gather sound simultaneously from every direction at once: I am at the centre of my auditory world, which envelopes me, establishing me at a kind of core of sensation and existence. This centering effect of sound is what high-fidelity sound reproduction exploits with intense sophistication. You can immerse yourself in hearing, in sound. There is no way to immerse yourself similarly in sight.[8]

By relating understanding to these two senses, Ong's 'phenomenological history of culture and consciousness' explains the poetic of primary orality as fundamentally participatory and integrative (1977, 10).
It establishes a kind of continuum between the voice and the audience.
A community that cannot count on the written text 'to preserve [its]
knowledge and to recall it when needed' will rely heavily on mnemonic
devices that will be present in the configuration of the text (103). The
spoken word, tied to the flow of time, exists momentarily in the here
and now of the event. Knowledge and understanding lie rooted in
memory and oral consciousness is structured in mnemonic formulas
that stimulate recall of an integrating past. An oral noetic shuns any
disjunctive, analytical view of time as *distentio*. The refiguration carried
out by the audience tends to bring the schematization as close as possible to the pole of sedimentation in the dialectic of tradition. Innovation
is frowned upon because it threatens the identity and common perspective of the community. The mnemonic devices Ong brings to the
fore preserve the culture and its knowledge by 'constantly repeating
the fixed sayings and formulas – including epithets, standard paral-
lelisms and oppositions, kennings [and] set phrases' (284). These devices that emphasize the assimilative pole of appropriation and the
temporal pole of perception include

1) stereotyped or formulaic expressions
2) standardization of themes
3) epithetic identification for 'disambiguation' of classes or individuals
4) generation of 'heavy' or ceremonial characters
5) formulary, ceremonial appropriation of history
6) cultivation of praise and vituperation
7) copiousness (102)

The shift from an oral noetic to a chirographic noetic is a passage
from an aggregative and integrative consciousness of listening to a
'diaeretic or disjunctive or analytic' mode of consciousness (1977, 20).
Like vision, this shift 'corresponds to the drive to objectify knowledge,
to make it into something which is clearly thing-like, nonsubjective,
yielding meaning not in depth but off of surface, meaning which can
be spread out, ex-plained' (140). The audience is recast in a 'spectator's
rather than an interlocutor's role' and the spectator of the text 'is essentially a spectator, outside the action, however interested' (222). If
an oral noetic surrounds the narrative voice and the audience with an

elliptical time centred in a 'Now,' chirographic noetic disintegrates the circle by cutting it in half, alienating and distancing the foci of the event. The writer, as Ong puts it, 'creates his text in isolation,' but this alienation and 'cleavage, is not all bad' because literature is free to explain cause-effect relations and reflect a world in a more objective manner (222, 47). This 'realistic' explanation in space begins to reflect the form of time. It is *directed* 'to hold as 'twere, the mirror up to nature; to show virtue her own feature, scorn her own image, and the very age and body of time his form and pressure' (*Hamlet*, act 3, sc. 2).

The passage from a chirographic to a typographic noetic highlights the objective, spatial pole of perception even further. Typography 'makes words out of preexisting objects (types) ... it hooks up the words in machines and stamps out on hundreds or thousands of surfaces exactly the same spatial arrangement of words – constituting the first assembly line' (Ong 1977, 281). This greater alienation and distance allows for a relation between the foci in the manner I have characterized as parabolic.

The typographic noetic is not limited by the demands of mnemonic devices. Knowledge is stored in 'different places' rather than by 'people,' and the past can be retrieved in the future. The prefiguration of a text enjoys a greater freedom of abstraction and stresses the distanced reflection that is characteristic of academic, philosophical, and scientific subjects (Ong 1977, 287, 288, 25). It stresses space rather than time and explores things, conceptual networks, and places rather than people (140–1). The temporal field is disintegrated into ideas of past, present, and future and the refiguration of the text calls for a far greater interpretative activity. The innovative pole of tradition and the pole of distanciation come to the fore in the dialectic of appropriation.

The scattering or 'strewing' of typographic texts over a large area demands an increased hermeneutic activity in order to maintain the part-whole relationship between each text and the traditions in which it is received. A synecdochic mode of discourse would work to counteract disintegration. A relationship between primary orality and that typographic noetic that leads to second orality would then develop and give rise to what White has called a 'Metaphorical – Synecdochic mode of historical conceptualization' (1973, 80). Nevertheless, the more objective 'Mechanistic apprehension' characterized by White as 'Metonymical and Ironic' is also at work (80, 79). Ong states that the 'literate aesthetics of G.E. Moore' and the 'aesthetics of Bloomsbury' that developed in England illustrate an ironic noetic that began to explore the freedom of an 'artificial, contrived, fictionalized arrangement' through a 'multilayered irony' provided by an 'unreliable narrator' as their discourse moved into 'the electronic age.'[9] This ironic noetic presents a sequence of visual events in a fragmented manner, dismissing heavy figures of symbolic weight as 'dysfunctional' (Ong 1977, 292). The 'alternating current' of electronic media gives way to a 'play-within-the play' and 'voices within voices, or voices within voices within voices within voices ... [or an] echoing of voice within voice' (314, 275). These echoing voices would emerge from a configuration I have characterized in terms of the cave-like shape of a parabolic structure.

The 'cleavage' introduced by a metonymic-ironic noetic begins to separate 'the knower from the external universe and then from himself' (Ong 1977, 18). The metaphoric-synecdochic 'sense of continuity with life' and 'sense of participation' become problematic, thereby giving way to a 'search for means of integration to preserve it from total fragmentation' (21, 298).

It is essential to clarify that these modes of understanding concur in time and space, and are marked by a difference in degree and emphasis, with areas of transition in the process of transformation. This is not a system of discrete units of psychological conformation. In this way the 'oral residue persists in patterns of thought and expression not only for millennia after writing but for centuries even after the invention of letterpress alphabetic print' (Ong 1977, 282). Ong goes on to say that the oral 'thought process is still real and urgent today in developing countries and in the oral inner-city black culture and white hill-country culture of the United States' (290). If, for example, the transition from oral to electronic media has taken place in Africa 'not over six thousand years but in two or three generations,' it is perfectly understandable that a Caribbean writer such as Edward Kamau Brathwaite might attempt a 'phenomenology of orality' by recalling a common *History of Voice* in order to stem the historically conditioned disintegration of a people.[10]

If we are to speak of narrative perspective 'in literature,' not just in the literature of 'objectivist cultures,' then we must come to terms with what Ricoeur calls the 'qualitative aspect of graduated tension' that will be played out in the 'dialectic of intention and distention' between the metaphoric discourse of an oral noetic and the ironic discourse of a typographic-electronic noetic (Ong 1977, 290, and Ricoeur 1984, 1:85). To this mediative end, I propose that narrative perspective be considered as a mediation between the *reader* as language, perception, and experience, the *text* as a 'keyboard' of symbolic facets, and the *world* of figurative and technological channels of understanding. The four facets of narrative voice (person, dramatization, scope, reliability), as well as the temporal sequence and duration, mediate the symbolic phenomenon of the text and the subjective dimension of the reader. In this relationship the tension of interpretation comes to the fore. Mediating the text and the objective field of the first-order world are the facets of the narrative world (type, role, privilege, reliability), as well as the spatial field of foreground and background. Between this second-order and first-order world, the tension in the relational function of the copula becomes most apparent. The narrative world 'is not' the world around us and yet, while reading and listening, it 'is' our world. It is also this relationship that 'traverses' a semic field and brings to light the 'creative mechanism' mediating signs and referents in the world (Ricoeur 1977, 202). Mediating the work in the world and the reader in the hermeneutical experience of the text can be found the four tropological modes (metaphoric, metonymic, synecdochic, ironic) and four media (primary orality, chirographic script, typographic script, electronic media accompanied by a secondary orality) of discourse that characterize reader perspectives. This relationship brings out the tension in the statements about the world. These varying modes and media of sense-making cannot be divorced from the awareness that reaches out to the world called perception. The reader's perception of his or her first-order surroundings is not cancelled but only suspended while its energy is redirected towards the world of the text.

Each of narrative perspective's three dimensions comes into play when a text is realized. Thus, the mediation and tension between the hermeneutical experience of a reader, the symbolic dimension of the text, and the work as a product of a world each offer different but interrelated points of departure for the study of narrative perspective. One study will part from the relation between reader and text and seek to understand the voices of different and similar traditional worlds. Another will explain those structures in the world of the text that offer the reader different points of view. Yet another critical tradition will part from the relation between the reader and his or her world in order to comprehend the similarities in different texts' symbolic configurations. The point of departure and the direction followed will vary with the critic's tradition, one that is intertwined with a mode and medium of discourse. Central to all facets of narrative perspective, however, is appropriation's dynamic action of assimilation and movement of distanciation.

A text, then, is 'figured out' by perceptive readers and listeners with varying degrees of metaphoric, metonymic, synecdochic, and ironic perspectives. These enter into a dialogue of question and answer with the facets of the narrative voice and refigure the temporal dimension of sequence and duration. The reader's hermeneutic activity plays a vital role in realizing a narrative world. By narrating, the voice obviously refers to the narrative world. This second-order reference, however, does not stand alone. To the degree that the voice says something meaningful to someone about something, it also refers, however indirectly, to the first-order world. To use Robert Weimann's term, it also 'in-forms' the very world that has produced narrative works (1985, 276). The narrative world, in turn, offers both new and renewed, innovative and traditional perspectives to readers and listeners. While it certainly affects his or her perspective of other narrative texts, it also has an impact, however subtle, on his or her perspective of the world.

Hablar	– Parler		– To Speak
Fablar	– Parlier	–	*Sprek-
Fabulari	– Parabolare	–	*Spher(e)g-
Fable	– Parable	and	Ex-ploration

To this point, I have spoken of the noematic facets of narrative perspective and of the noetic figures of prefigurative and refigurative discourse as well as their corresponding noematic 'channels' of mediation in the world. I have yet to clarify the noetic configuration of sense in the symbolic dimension itself. Once again, to the degree that narrative is language and perspective is perception, the sense of narrative perspective is inextricably intertwined with the sense of discourse. I have chosen three verbs for the phenomenon of discourse to illustrate different modes of 'interfacing' through the 'I' in the symbolic dimension of the text.[11] I am proposing these action words only as heuristic devices illustrating the notion that different configurations of discourse are available. I am not proposing that all narrative perspective in their respective linguistic communities conform to the configuration represented by each verb. With this qualification in mind one can say that the Spanish *hablar* is a 'fabulous' configuration of the fable. The French verb *parler* is a parabolic configuration of the parable and the English *to speak* is a diaeretic, split configuration proceeding from the reconstructed base '*sprek-,' originally to shout, to cry (hence 'ex-ploration') and this, in turn, from the proposed base '*spher(e)g-': to strew, sprinkle, to sprout, burst.[12] A fabulous configuration of discourse would tend towards the metaphoric perspective of an oral noetic centred in the 'Here' and 'Now' of perception and its high-fidelity, primary level of faith. The elliptical configuration of time around the interlocutors binds them in a common interest of reporting or carrying once again the past to the present and the new to the old. The discovery of, say, a New World would bring the reporting function to the fore. The fabulous character of discourse might well have an impact on further discovery by lending itself to the search for a fountain that overcomes the flow of mortal time or to a search for some fabulous land. The fable would then appear as a configuration of resounding importance.[13] Germán Arciniegas has noted the degree to which both the discoverers and *conquistadores* of Latin America were attuned to fable:

The fabled wanderings of Ulysses were a prologue to the voyages of Columbus. Ulysses visited the land of the Lotus Eaters, the island of the Cyclops, the island of the winds, and the lands of the huge cannibalistic Laestrygonians, of the sorceress Circe, and of the Sirens. Inevitably the discoverers of the Antilles looked for those isles. Pliny the Elder mentions the pygmies who had been brought to the Indies from Africa; he describes the Astomi, men without mouths who fed themselves by drawing the perfume of the fruits and flowers into their nostrils, and, of course giants. Federmann saw pygmies on his search for El Dorado, Vespucci the giants of Curaçao. Pliny also describes the Monocoli, one-legged men who shaded themselves from the sun by lying down and raising their single enormous foot over their heads. Pigafetta reports that in the south Magellan found giants with abnormally large feet whom he named Patagonians. Peter Martyr confirms the report. Thus, as the fables of California and Florida marked the extreme northern point of Spanish exploration, that of the Monocoli – Patagonians – marked the extreme south. The America being born could trace many of its names back to a map of Greece. (79)

Arciniegas also notes that 'the elemental magic of the books of chivalry' played an important role in the conquest of America, for the 'few who knew how to read, read them aloud to the wandering, embattled, and illiterate crowd surrounding them. They delighted everyone; they made it seem there was something in the Conquest that might have occurred in the days of fable' (77).

I understand fable in terms that include the reader in an experience, achieved through dialogue, which must not dismiss 'the moral definition of man' (Gadamer 1975, 322). A fundamental question for the study of narrative perspective's role in the configuration of discourse becomes when and where the moral dimension is revealed and appropriated as the *self* of the *human* being. The fable contains a moral that is usually (but not always) explicitly stated at the ' "end point," which, in turn, furnishes the point of view from which the story can be perceived as forming a whole' (Ricoeur 1984, 1:66–7). This moral dimension that transforms 'the imminent end into an immanent end' through an 'apocalyptic model' is revealed at the point towards which the entire effort of narration has been directed (2:24, 23). This 'end point' is when and where the voice and the audience as the moral dimension of life are assimilated to the moral dimension of literature in the 'Here' and 'Now' of the moment of revelation. Again, the fabulous narrative perspective is revealed by a common point in time and space where the elliptical cycle and the two foci coincide in a critical 'Now' and 'Here' of apocalypses and revelation. Life and narrative coincide through and in discourse and time.

Hayden White has noted that the fabulous configuration is 'as old as Greek philosophy and was a mainstay even of Christian theology during the Patristic period' (1978, 143). According to White, this configuration characterized by a metaphorical dynamism between poles of truth and falsehood, good and bad, positive and negative, similarity and difference, was not admitted by the Enlightenment:

Where the Enlighteners failed was in their inability, once they had drawn the distinction between mythical thinking and scientific thinking, to see how these might be bound up with one another as *phases* in the history of a single culture, society, or individual consciousness. As long as they identified the 'fabulous' with the 'unreal', and failed to see that fabulation itself could serve as a means to the apprehension of the truth about reality and was not simply an alternative to or an adornment of such apprehension, they could never gain access to those cultures and states of mind in which the distinction between the true and the false had not been as clearly drawn as they hoped to draw it. (143)

The configuration of discourse in 'the mode of *contiguities*, i.e., spatial relations ... of *metonymy*' is far more appropriate for the enlightened science of which White speaks (253). This analytical and reflective mode of configuration finds its expression in the diaeretic exploration carried out by a voice that sprinkles or strews itself into the concave structure of parabolic discourse, which, in turn, reflects and echoes back upon the listener behind the exploring voice.

A parabolic configuration of discourse might come to the fore in an uncommon situation where past and future are bound together by a heritage of written texts. The explanation or laying out flat of existence through prophets' sacred scriptures and a corresponding 'drive to symbolize intellection and understanding by vision ... keyed to *reflected* light' would give rise to a configuration of discourse that 'parallels, detail for detail, the situation that calls forth the *parable* for illustration' (Ong 1977, 140, and Holman 357). It would not be unlikely that such parables might include tales of strewing mustard seed (Matt. 13:31–3) or a *Retour de l'enfant prodigue* (Gide). The sublimation of all discourse would bring the three acts of configuration into one appropriate perspective of absolutely brilliant resonance.

There are two moments in a parabolic configuration. The first is the exploration or 'crying out' from focal point F and the strewing, sprinkling, or sowing of words in a field (P) of narrative events. Thus: 'A sower went out to sow' (Matt. 13:3).[14] The field of events (P) is a point-by-point, detail-for-detail reflection of the telling situation and the process of language, perception, and perspective of its own making. The second moment is when all points (P) reflect back, behind the sowing voice at F to the reader-audience who sees the display of language in the text and listens to the echo of the reflected voice. Thus: 'He who has ears, let him hear' (Matt. 13:9) and the words of Isaiah: 'For this people's heart has grown dull, and their ears are heavy of hearing and their eyes they have closed, lest they should perceive with their eyes and hear with their ears, and understand with their heart, and turn for me to heal them' (Matt. 13:15). I have insisted that the moral definition of man and the moral of the text not be dismissed. I have also suggested that a fundamental question for narrative perspective is the role it plays in the revelation of this moral dimension. If the fable ends with a moral and a point of view whereby the whole is made available through the 'Now' of revelation, when and where is the moral of the parable? The end of the parable offers no encapsulated proverb fusing man and narrative. On the contrary, the reader-audience is usually left bewildered as to just what it all means. Thus: 'And his disciples came to him, saying, "Explain to us the parable of the weeds of the field" ' (Matt. 13:36). Now, every echoing voice, every line drawn, every letter on every page seen, all converge at one point that is apparently not in the world of the text: each and every *individual* reader who listens. Thus, verse nine is repeated: 'He who has ears, let him hear' (Matt. 13:43). The text does not end with the last word written, for the last word is not the moral of the story. The reader *is* the moral. The parable does not explicitly state a moral 'end point' because it is the reader's perspective and very perception that must open and 'realize' by acting to appropriate that core of mankind that is our definition. It is only through this 'action,' this opening of eye and ear that self-appropriation comes 'to Be' and it is in this way that the reader-audience transforms and does 'turn for me to heal them' (Matt. 13:15). A parable does not and cannot end on the printed page. It passes into the listening reader. When the reader-audience acts to appropriate his and her true self, 'Then' and 'There' do dogma and scepticism fall away to reveal that moral dimension of narrative that *is humanity*. Then and there is the parable complete, the 'point of the view' achieved.

I have explained my understanding of narrative perspective as a fabulous 'here and now' and as a parabolic 'then and there' within a text's symbolic dimension. I have also explained a fourfold typology of discourse that will come to bear upon the manner in which an author prefigures a text and upon the way in which a reader refigures it. Between the oral noetic of a metaphorical perspective, the chirographic noetic of a metonymic perspective, the typographic noetic of a synecdochic perspective, and the electronic noetic of a highly ironic perspective there is room for multiple combinations and an infinite degree of variation.

I have yet to account for their underlying generative principle. This question of a generative principle brings the consideration of narrative perspective in full circle back to the energy produced within the tension of the metaphoric copula. The dialectic of appropriation, that is, assimilation or making similar, and the 'is not' of distanciation lies at the heart of the process's action-movement. Narrative perspective is a dialectic of distanciation and assimilation because it involves 'the way in which the text is addressed to someone' (Ricoeur 1981a, 183). It is not the projection of a reader's perspective onto the text but rather by figuring out the narrative perspective the reader receives an enlarged perspective 'from the apprehension of proposed worlds which are the genuine object of interpretation' (1981a, 182–3). This enlarged outlook, sense, attitude can never cover the full dimension of the text, just as no one perspective can cover all sides of a cube at one time. In every acquired perspective there is an inherent fleeing of the world. It always remains a figurative construct. In turn, it is only by means of the text's facets that the reader becomes aware of his own historical perspective of the world. This new self-understanding is not a re-affirmation of the ego but rather an inevitable release from opinion in which a reader's perspective might otherwise become trapped and stagnate (192–3). Narrative perspective, in that it contributes to the construction of the text, is a liberating process, an opening of the self to the world, as is the question of Gadamer and the perception of Merleau-Ponty. Narrative perspective cannot be reduced to any one of its facets. It is not just first, second, or third person nor is it an isolated effect in the reader. It is a process of gaining a perspective of one's 'self' and an enlarged perspective of the world.

This process of appropriation as assimilation and distanciation is one of playing. To play in this sense 'is an experience which transforms those who participate in it' (Ricoeur 1981a, 186). Rather than drawing an analogy between appropriation and playing a game with rules, I believe a more appropriate analogy can be drawn with playing music on an instrument.[15] One can play on one's own or in a symphony orchestra that involves an intersubjective tradition of interpretation. The former allows maximum freedom and the latter is directed by the rules of harmonious dialogue by which one must abide if one wishes to be heard. A reader is not free to impose his or her individual perspective as an absolute closure on the text, for the text's multiple facets always resist closure. Narrative perspective, as it acts to play upon different notes of person, role, scope, reliability, and all of its other aspects, moves through the major, minor, and chromatic scales of its three dimensions. A narrative perspective may range in complexity from a simple satisfying tune played absent-mindedly on a summer's evening, to the complexity of a baroque fugue, to an electronic piece that leaves the reader bewildered and amazed. It is an act of recreating a text through question and answer. It is also a movement for it moves the reader's perspective to the text where he or she is made available to him or herself and where a new world is opened. Each change in narrative perspective is by its very nature a movement in standpoint. The facets of voice and world will be played differently by a metaphoric reader perspective than by an ironic reader perspective. The reader's perspective in an audio-oral society is more decidedly metaphoric than ironic. The perspective of a reader in the highly typographic society of, say, early twentieth-century England would begin to be quite ironic. Both readings are valid but both must be aware of the nature of their own standpoint and that narrative perspective is what mediates them through the text.

The present development of narrative perspective does not claim to be exempt from its own considerations. The main thrust of my inquiry has been to integrate narrative perspective's parts – through language, perception, experience, and concept – into a balanced and consistent whole. As such, I believe my standpoint to be within what Hayden White calls an 'organist' mode of argument, a 'conservative' mode of ideological implication, and a 'synecdochic' mode of discourse (1973, 29–31). In so stating I dismiss any claim to closure on the issue and, I hope, open narrative perspective to new potential and new paths for productive debate.

Part Two

PLAYING NARRATIVE PERSPECTIVE

6

Narrative Perspective in the Reading Experience

To this point my inquiry has centred on explaining an understanding of narrative perspective through the fourfold process of language, perception, experience, and concept. This understanding stems from the principles of similarity and difference as well as the sense of direction mediating the two. Hans-Georg Gadamer's concept of consciousness provided a point of departure. Language, as *energeia*, was characterized as a dialogue and structured as a dialectic of question and answer. Gadamer's sense of hermeneutics emphasizes the importance of listening to the voice of tradition, for it is this voice that directs the attitudes of speakers in a dialogue and guides their questions in finding answers. Each sensible answer, in turn, reflects the question from which it proceeds. There is, then, a primary centrifugal direction of the question and a reflective, centripetal direction from the answer. Together they make sense through the experience of a hermeneutical situation.

Maurice Merleau-Ponty's phenomenology of perception mediates Gadamer's hermeneutics of language and Paul Ricoeur's temporal experience of narrative. Merleau-Ponty explains perception as a reaching out from a primary level of faith and non-sense towards the world in awareness. It proceeds through the senses towards the world in order to grasp things by bringing their parts into consistent units. The centrifugal reaching out to the world is directed from the temporal character of subjectivity towards the objective structures of space. These objective structures in space provide a point of departure for the phenomenon of reversibility. Here an abstract perspective looks back through the natural or common perspective and reflects upon the process of perception from which it proceeds. The sense of an integrated whole becomes the non-sense of a disintegrated paradox. While both the echo of speaking and the ambiguity of focusing reflect this phenomenon, Merleau-Ponty explores reversibility primarily through an 'artificial perspective' of the visual arts. The audio-oral system cannot achieve the objective illusion demanded by reversibility as readily as can sight. Perception, then, also involves two directions: the first from subjective time to objective space and the second from the illusion of an objective standpoint in space through the level of intersensory communication and into the abyss of non-sense. Finally, Merleau-Ponty gives both directions the value of reality. It is only perception, however, that is directed towards a world held in common. Hallucination is directed towards a private world of alienation.

Paul Ricoeur's approach to narrative experience brings the noetic character of time, discourse, and the voice of tradition together with the noematic structure of prefiguration, configuration, and refiguration. With Ricoeur question and answer, time and space, non-sense and sense enter into a dynamic relationship of muthos and mimesis. Muthos is a dialectic of the soul's action and passion. On the one hand, *intentio* provides an action that brings events together in the unity of a story. On the other hand, the wandering of *distentio* reflects back upon the aporias or paradoxes of the experience of time by way of reversals or *peripeteia*. What is achieved is a direction from *intentio* to *distentio* and vice versa, as well as a dynamic tension mediating the two. This dynamic relationship generates innumerable temporal experiences that can range from concordance to discordant concordance. If muthos is the temporal unity of narrative, mimesis is the objective explanation reflecting this unity. Mimesis one, or prefiguration, is a competent act that creates a text. The resulting configuration, or mimesis two, reflects the conditions of its creation but is not bound to the subjective intentions of its author. The third moment of mimesis, or refiguration, calls the active participation of the reader into play. He or she must realize the text through the process of appropriation. If muthos and mimesis involve a direction from a subjective act to the world of a text, and then a reflection back upon the action itself, appropriation brings both directions into play. Appropriation reveals both the text as a mode of being in the world and the reader's self.

The concept of narrative perspective can be understood as different moments in the history of a theoretical process that highlights either the subjective notion of person or the objective idea of a central reflector or point of view. While the former has developed perspective in terms of the relations between persons in a dialogue, the latter has done away with person in favour of a standpoint within the structured space of the narrative world. Once the author's subjective intentions could no longer serve as a criterion for establishing the narrative perspective of a text, the structures of the text's world were shown to reflect a narrative focalization. The predominance of an objective spatial criterion has slowly moved towards including once again the subjective notion of person, only now in the form of a reader. This reintroduction of the personal dimension has put the objective concept of narrative focalization into question. An effort to include the subjective notion of a reader as part of the objective structures of the text results in 'he' or 'she' being objectified as an 'it.' In answer to this paradox three positions present the question of a historical reader. The reader's historical perspective is introduced: first, at the level of prefiguration when he or she encounters the conditions of the text's production and the author's ideology; second, at the level of configuration where the reader reacts to textual strategies; and third, at the level of refiguration when an aesthetic perspective of one moment in history meets the aesthetic perspective of a previous age. The first gives priority to socio-economic concerns in the world, the second gives priority to fiction as a structured reaction against the social norms of the world, and the third divorces an aesthetic or interpretive perception from the proceess of everyday perception. Although all three share a common question, each tends to stress their differences rather than their similarities when providing answers.

The search for a tertium quid capable of mediating all three positions leads the process of explanation back to its point of departure in language. All three moments of figuration are inextricably intertwined with consciousness as discourse. Consciousness does not unfold within one tradition of discourse alone. It figures out time and space in a variety of interconnected ways. Narrative perspective, when understood in terms of a tropology of discourse, comes to bear upon all three moments of 'figuration.' This is true to the degree that prefiguration, configuration, and refiguration work in discourse to figure an experience of time. This epistemological dimension of narrative may serve to characterize the tropological sense that underlies a perspective, but narrative perspective must be approached from its noematic side. Once again my explanation moves from language to perception. While narrative perspective brings all of the senses into the experience of a text, the senses of hearing and sight have played major roles in constituting the technical medium through which the narrative experience is achieved. A change in medium has repercussions at all levels of narrative perspective. When the appropriation of narrative calls upon the audio-oral system of perception then a 'common perspective' will likely figure a metaphoric fable of time and echo a sense of tradition. Where narrative looks to the written text as its primary medium of appropriation, the sense of sight will permit a greater freedom to wander through perception's spatial dimension. Here an artificial perspective will likely explore the *facettes* of non-sense in a parable that reflects an impersonal world of alienation and the monumental experience of time.

Needless to say, the explanation of my understanding cannot pass from language to perception without subsequently 'comprehending' an experience of texts. This experience of texts cannot prove my theoretical understanding and explanation of narrative perspective. Nor can it prove that the texts chosen call only for a metaphoric perspective or reflect an ironic perspective alone. The experiential playing of perspectives can only present a logic of probability and reveal the texts in one of a range of possible narrative perspectives. My comprehension of *Cien años de soledad* by Gabriel Gracía Márquez and *Jacob's Room* by Virginia Woolf will offer this experiential dimension.

7

The Fabulous Metaphor of
Cien años de soledad

If there is any particular facet of a text that is first perceived by a reader, it must be the cover page. The text's experience begins with its title, the author's name, and more often than not some point of departure for the action. *Cien años de soledad*, Gabriel García Márquez, and Riohacha on the remote Guajira peninsula all speak of a part of today's world where everyday events are worked into stories and pass by 'word of mouth' from village to village and generation to generation. The title brings together the notion of a temporal unity on the one hand and the alienation of solitude on the other. It is undoubtedly a tale about time; a unity of time that brings with it an experience of solitude. Gabriel García Márquez is a name that speaks of literary competence achieved during the first half of this century in Aracataca, 'ese pueblecillo de la costa atlántica de Colombia' (Herrera 346). His preliminary competence will have developed within a mode of being in the world than can be described as 'aislada, iletrada y homogénea, ... La conducta es tradicional, espontánea, no crítica, personal ... el grupo familiar es la unidad de la acción. Lo sagrado prevalece sobre lo secular. La economía es de autoconsumo más bien que de mercado ... la cohesión del grupo se opera no en función de razones mecánicas sino de motivaciones orgánicas' (R. Redfield, quoted in Guzmán Campos 277). His linguistic competence will have been achieved within a mode of discourse that has not as yet felt the full impact of writing. More than a decade after the text's first appearance, illiteracy was calculated at between 29 and 49 per cent of the Latin American population over the age of fifteen.[1] This figure was exceeded only by 50 to 74 per cent illiteracy in East Africa and 75 to 100 per cent in West Africa (UNESCO 6). Much like Africa, Latin America relies heavily on mnemonic techniques and devices for the audio-oral transmission and survival of its heritage. Colombia in particular was calculated as having 90 per cent of the population illiterate at the turn of the century and 40 per cent sixty-three years later.[2] Most of the illiterate population is to be found in rural areas. Working with acts of symbolic weight within this conceptual network would most probably concentrate on the here and now of temporal duration characteristic of a predominantly oral mode of discourse. Again, there is a high probability that the linguistic competence underlying this text's prefiguration was achieved with the rules of composition and the relations of intersignification that employ techniques and strategies available to an audio-oral medium of narrative and an oral noetic. Oral narrative was also an integral part of García Márquez's upbringing. He spent much of his youth listening to his grandmother's 'anécdotas de las cruentas guerras civiles de Colombia,' and it was in search of 'las gentes en quienes ve reencarnados los fantasmas creados por sus abuelos' that he left his university career unfinished (Herrera and Fernando Alegría, quoted in Herrera 347).

When the audio-oral system of perception carries the responsibility of a tradition's survival, then a metaphoric perspective will likely prevail. Metaphor opens the core of perception that 'stands under' the discrete dichotomies of life vs. death and reality vs. fiction. A metaphoric perspective is closely tied to the dialogical situation of speaking and listening as well as to the temporal unity of the present. This experience of the present would not be shared by those traditions that have been transformed by both chirographic and typographic script. A metaphoric perspective in the twentieth-century, European community of letters would be a solitary perspective indeed and this is brought to the fore in a 'speech' to the world:

Me atrevo a pensar que es esta realidad descomunal, y no sólo su expresión literaria, la que este año ha merecido la atención de la Academia Sueca de las Letras. Una realidad que no es la del papel, sino que vive con nosotros y determina cada instante de nuestras incontables muertes cotidianas, y que sustenta un manantial de creación insaciable, pleno de desdicha y de belleza del cual este colombiano errante y nostálgico no es más que una cifra más señalada por la suerte ... todas las criaturas de aquella realidad desaforada hemos tenido que pedirle muy poco a la imaginación, porque el desafío mayor para nosotros ha sido la insuficiencia de los recursos convencionales para hacer creíble nuestra vida. Este es, amigos, el nudo de nuestra soledad. (García Márquez 1982b, 212–13)

This solitude is the experience of a metaphoric perspective that is just beginning to be recognized in an ironic world. It is understandable that 'los talentos racionales' of Europe, 'insistan en medirnos con la misma vara con que se miden a sí mismos' precisely because they have been left 'sin un método válido para interpretarnos' (213). It is, nevertheless, essential to remind these rational perspectives that the 'interpretación de nuestra realidad con esquemas ajenos sólo contribuye a hacernos cada vez más desconocidos, cada vez menos libres, cada vez más solitarios' (213).

   Cien años de soledad, García Márquez, and the Guajira peninsula of Colombia are not alone, however, in the solitude of a metaphorical perspective. As Walter J. Ong has noted above and as the levels of illiteracy have suggested here, similar techniques and a similar notion of time can be found in the narrative strategies of Africa. The oral narrative tradition of the French Sudan describes space in terms of the elliptical shape of time, that is, 'La terre a la forme d'un oeuf' (Zahan et Ganay 13). This notion of time is not derived from 'un enseignement purement théorique,' but is 'une partie intégrante de la vie même du groupement humain.' The action that unfolds through techniques of oral narration takes the form of a spiraling helix. Narrators represent their act of artistic creation as a 'distending' from one concentrated centre: 'C'est ainsi que pour faire le ciel et la terre, partant d'un point central, il s'étire en hélice conique ... Les rebroussements de cette spirale sont figurés graphiquement par les côtés de deux angles, qui représentent aussi l'espace d'en haut et l'espace d'en bas' (20). A resumé following the study of this cosmology notes that 'the mentality [of these people] as revealed in their myths, is at once so complex and so strange to European minds that long and detailed researches, as well as caution in offering interpretation, are most necessary' (23). For all of their innumerable differences, and as strange as it may appear, the remote Guajira peninsula and regions of illiterate Africa may share a metaphoric perspective and a history of voice.

   Cien años de soledad consists of twenty chapters, none of which are numbered. The reader's memory arranges the text through the experience of a concentrated reading and in accordance with its temporal order. The point of departure for the action is real but the world of the action is mythical. Riohacha is separated from Macondo by a swamp, thereby setting up a dialectic of 'real' and 'mythical' that dominates the entire narration. The founding family of Macondo is the Buendía, whose twenty-three members (excluding the seventeen illegitimate children of Col. Aureliano) constitute the text's principal characters, and whose history is narrated through one hundred years from a genesis to an apocalypse.

The narrative voice takes full command of the text from beginning to end. As Ricardo Gullón has pointed out:

En la novela sólo se oye la voz del narrador ... La voz narrativa es, como el tono sugiere, amistosa, familiar; una voz que infunde confianza en quien la oye, que consigue hacerse escuchar y que se admite cuanto dice sin objeciones. La relación entre ella –entre el narrador– y el lector, es también relación de familiaridad, por lo tanto próxima. Acontecimientos y personajes van ocurriendo y presentándose al lector como cosa corriente, cercana y situándose a la misma distancia material y psicológica de él. (23–4)

This familiar relationship between the voice and the reader, in which the former tells 'cosas corrientes' to which the latter has no 'objeciones,' is true only for a reader sharing the metaphoric perspective. For a European reader such as Mieke Bal the relationship is neither a familiar one nor are the events narrated common to her everyday experience. Such a reader might certainly object to seeing *Cien años de soledad* as a credible view of the world and might vacillate between the 'real' world of Riohacha and the 'fantastic' world of Macondo. Thus, Bal finds herself 'powerless in face of *One Hundred Years of Solitude*' (42). She tells her readers:

But even without such indications in the text there are data in the contents which we, with our sense of everyday logic, can combine in such a way that we can say, ... [an event] 'is likely to be the result of the occurrence of the desire.' It is not always possible to reconstruct the chronological sequence. In many experimental modern novels, we find, for instance, that matters are intentionally confused, the chronological relations expressly concealed. In such a case, obviously, we are powerless. But what is striking in these cases is that the chronological chaos we note is often still quite meaningful. This chaos can even be concealed behind apparent chronology, as in Márquez's [that is, García Márquez's] *One Hundred Years of Solitude* ... The effect of Márquez's novel is to let people, generations, social contexts succeed each other in rapid turmoil in the course of a hundred years which seem to contain a history of mankind, to terminate in the absurd failure of (communal) life. (51–2)

At this point I shall not dwell on whether the text's moral is a familiar success or an absurd failure. What I shall insist upon is that between Gullón and Bal there are two different reader perspectives at work and therefore two different narrative perspectives and different herme- neutical experiences.

While a reader with an ironic or metonymic perspective may find some 'objeciones', the 'familiarity' soon becomes apparent because the text is narrated in the third person. The choice of third person brings with it an implicit union of the first person, who is narrating, and the second person who is listening in a tacit first-person plural within the subjectivity of discourse. The third person of the text stands before the narrrator and the reader to be viewed as the object or 'non-person.' This dialectic of person–non-person, that is, narrator and reader-nar- rative world, creates the familiar tone and the intimacy of a dialogical situation. It helps create a common standpoint in time and space from which the events of the narrative can be perceived. The third person brings the voice and the reader together in this shared standpoint through the function of the pronoun within the structure of discourse. There can be no narration in the third 'non-person' that does not pre- suppose the first and second persons of the dialogical situation. The inherent subjectivity of the personal pronouns organizes relations of time and space around the standpoint of the subject. Person in dis- course is characterized by its emptiness of form. The narration of the text in the third 'non-person' implicitly situates both narrator and reader in the very emptiness of the subjective pronominal form. The reader, in taking up the narrative, fills the emptiness with his *self* and listens to the voice of the narrator in the telling situation.

The choice of third 'non-person,' and the resulting dialectic, places the reader with the narrator in the temporal domain of the present. The 'I' and the 'you' observing the 'he, she, it' of the narrated world are implicitly situated in the ever-present 'now' of the speech situation. The subjective axis of the narrator and reader form the referential present that divides the objective past and future of the narrative events:

Il n'y a pas d'autre critère ni d'autre expression pour indiquer 'le temps où l'on *est*' que de le prendre comme 'le temps où l'on *parle*.' C'est là le moment éternellement 'présent,' quoique ne se rapportant jamais aux mêmes événe- ments d'une chronologie 'objective,' parce qu'il est déterminé pour chaque locuteur par chacune des instances de discours qui s'y rapporte. Le temps linguistique est *sui-référentiel*. En dernière analyse la temporalité humaine avec tout son appareil linguistique dévoile la subjectivité inhérente à l'exercice même du langage. (Benveniste 1:262–3)

The choice of a third-person technique of narration for *Cien años de soledad* places the reader in the *present* that is the temporal domain of experience, perception, and the dialogical realization of discourse. The narrative voice, as an implicit, subjective person, stands in the present forming a link between the implicit non-subjective person of his present audience and the 'non-person,' objective world of past and future in the text. While the consistent use of a third person is important because it invokes a common perspective mediating voice and reader, this alone is not sufficient to maintain a common standpoint. If the symbolic speech situation is to be obtained as an experience, it must be sustained by all other devices at the disposal of the narrating voice.

The question of the narrator's dramatization also involves a dialectic. Gullón has noted that the text appears to have been written twice; once in Sanskrit and once in Spanish. He goes on to ask: '¿Es el narrador reflejo de Melquíades, o, dicho en los términos de esta obra, reencarnación de Melquíades?' (1970, 22). He settles for: 'En cualquier caso sabemos que entre su crónica y la del anciano inmortal, no hay discrepancia; la una es reproducción literal de la otra, por un milagro semejante al acontecido cuando Pierre Menard reescribe, sin saberlo, un *Quijote* idéntico al de Cervantes' (22). His question is brought on by the revelation in the last chapter. This revelation not only places Melquíades, as narrator and scribe, between the voice and the events but also places Aureliano Babilonia as reading character and translating reader between the reader's position and the world of the text. Gullón's question is presented in terms of a 'reflective,' either/or dichotomy, that does not necessarily function adequately in the case of Melquíades. The fact remains that, relative to the experience of the text, Melquíades both *is* the narrator and again *is not*. The 'reproducción literal' gives the reader his 'pergaminos.' The reader accompanies his perspective of the Buendía saga throughout 'Cien años' standing next to him in a shared standpoint. The final revelation converts the *is not* dramatized to a resounding *is* dramatized. When the 'character' Melquíades is elevated or taken from his role as a character and then dramatized as the 'narrador,' the inverse occurs with the reader and the narrative voice. Both become characters. The reader, who has stood next to the narrating voice for one hundred years, now finds himself fusing with Aureliano Babilonia who is reading 'en voz alta ... las encíclicas cantadas que el propio Melquíades le hizo escuchar a Arcadio' and it is also 'en voz alta' that the reader is left to 'descifrar' the written signs of the magician philosopher.[3] When the character is dramatized as the 'speaker of the voice,' the reader is also dramatized as a character. The narrator *is not* a character and then suddenly he *is*. The narrative world *is not* that of the reader and then suddenly it *is* his or her world. A mimesis of action becomes a character's action and then a character's discourse about action (Ricoeur 1984, 2:88).

It is, of course, the affirmative of the copula that carries the weight of the revelation. The reader can then read the text once again and note how the standpoint he or she shares with the narrator is brought into close proximity with characters and events and then suddenly withdrawn to a distance. The nature of discourse in the third person is an open invitation to accompany the narrative voice in its creative act, just as the text's apocalypse is an open invitation for the reader to appropriate the narrative world and reveal his or her self in the role of a reader.

The function of the narrator as 'speaker of the narrative voice' makes Melquíades and the voice inseparable (Ricoeur 1984, 2:96). This function of the narrator is dramatized by the role Melquíades plays in the text's world. In the very first paragraph he presents 'la octava maravilla' of the world. He introduces two inventions to the world of Macondo: the magnet and the magnifying glass. While the latter is a glass ground into the form of an ellipse, the magnet is a dialectic of positive and negative poles that, when placed at odds with another magnet, produce the dynamo. The dynamic energy that flows forth from the tension between the positive *is* and the negative *is not* of the magnets' copula is the dynamo's creative power. It is with this dynamic structure in mind that the narrator can proclaim at the top of his voice: 'Las cosas tienen vida propia ... todo es cuestión de despertarles el ánima' (59).

If the Jewish philosopher Spinoza ground and polished lenses in Amsterdam, it is Melquíades who brings the philosopher's elliptically shaped glass to Macondo. The function of this 'último descubrimiento de los judíos de Amsterdam' is to reduce distance and give the viewer a universal perspective: 'Dentro de poco, el hombre podrá ver lo que ocurre en cualquier lugar de la tierra, sin moverse de su casa' (60). Dynamism and universal perspective are what the narrator introduces to Macondo. This universality allows Melquíades to know 'el otro lado de las cosas' (63). The navigational instruments he gives José Arcadio Buendía serve to discover the circular nature of the world, and his laboratory of alchemy serves as an impetus to search for the '*huevo filosófico* ... la piedra filosofal' that lie as 'huevos prehistóricos' on the bank of the river (64).

By the end of the first chapter the dramatized narrator function has faded away to old age and death, only to reappear again in the third chapter. Here it deals with a singularly important function: that of saving the world from forgetting its history. The written words begin in a sign-referent relation and rapidly grow to form the first semantic units: '*Esta es la vaca, hay que ordeñarla todas las mañanas para que produzca leche y a la leche hay que hervirla para mezclarla con el café y hacer café con leche*' and '*Dios existe*' (102–3). The written word is, nevertheless, no match for the disease of forgetting one's history. The written word as a sign, 'exigía tanta vigilancia y tanta fortaleza moral, que muchos sucumbieron al hechizo de una realidad imaginaria, inventada por ellos mismos, que les resultaba menos práctica pero más reconfortante' (103). It is from this 'Fetichismo de la letra' that the narrator must save the people of his narrative world which, of course, includes the reader.[4] The narrator animates the memory of a tradition through the celebration of his narrative art: 'Mientras Macondo celebraba la reconquista de los recuerdos, José Arcadio Buendía y Melquíades le sacudieron el polvo a su vieja amistad' (104).

The narrator does not reject writing as such; only writing that does not animate memory. His function is also that of the writer: 'Sólo iba al taller de Aureliano, donde pasaba horas y horas garabateando su literatura enigmática en los pergaminos' (125). The onomatopoeic quality of his written words appeals directly to the sense of hearing and all his efforts are directed towards communication:

Aureliano terminó por olvidarse de él, absorto en la redacción de sus versos, pero en cierta ocasión creyó entender algo de lo que decía en sus bordoneantes monólogos, y le prestó atención. En realidad, lo único que pudo aislar en las parrafadas pedregosas, fue el insistente martilleo de la palabra equinoccio equinoccio, equinoccio, y el nombre de Alexander Von Humboldt. Arcadio se aproximó un poco más a él cuando empezó a ayudar a Aureliano en la platería. Melquíades correspondió a aquel esfuerzo de comunicación soltando a veces frases en castellano que tenían muy poco que ver con la realidad. (125–6)

Here, the experience of discourse in literary communication is an equinox between the past and the future. The narrative voice animates past traditions through writing in order to communicate them to future generations through the present. The narrator's function has little to do with an empirical configuration of reality. His invocation of the von Humboldt name is an invocation of history, discovery, and a new world. The narrating voice, in recalling the historian's name, dramatizes a different mode of historicity and discovery: that of language and that of metaphor. In the words of Paul Ricoeur, 'This semantic dynamism, proper to ordinary language, gives a "historicity" to the power of signifying. New possibilities of signifying are opened up, supported by meanings that have already been established. The "historicity" is carried by the attempt at expression made by a speaker who, wanting to formulate a new experience in words, seeks something capable of carrying his intention in the network of meanings he finds already established.' (1977, 298). The work of Alexander von Humboldt, in representing the New World to the Old World through language, and the work of the narrator, in presenting a new world in *Castellano*, call upon the work of metaphor. The 'equivocalness' of metaphor, its 'logic of discovery,' the dramatized function of the narrator pounding away at 'equinoccio,' and the historian Alexander von Humboldt become intertwined (Ricoeur 1977, 262, 240). Consider Ricoeur's description of the function of metaphor in conjunction with von Humboldt's historical task and the narrator's task: 'Metaphor's power of reorganizing our perception of things develops from transposition of an entire "realm." Consider, for example, sound in the visual order. To speak of the sonority of a painting is no longer to move about an isolated predicate, but to bring about the incursion of an entire realm into alien territory. The well-worn notion of "transporting" becomes a conceptual migration, if not an armed and luggage-laden overseas expedition' (1977, 236).

The setting for the dramatized narrator is also significant. He is located in a scientific laboratory and the Gypsies are 'los últimos herederos de la ciencia de Melquíades' (380). If this is the science of 'los sabios alquimistas de Macedonia,' then this ancient sense of things is not restricted to a science of positivistic thought (59). As Gadamer has pointed out, the 'difference between Greek theoria and modern science is based, in my opinion, on different attitudes to the linguistic experience of the world. Greek knowledge ... was so much within language, so exposed to its seductions, that its fight against the dunamis ton onomaton never led to the evolution of the ideal of a pure sign language, whose purpose would be to overcome entirely the power of language, as is the case with modern science and its orientation towards the domination of the existent' (1975, 413).

The room of Melquíades is 'protegido por la luz sobrenatural, por el *ruido* de la lluvia, por la sensación de ser *invisible*' (349; emphasis added). The narrator's function is a 'presencia invisible' whose death gives the characters a place in the world: 'Uno no es de ninguna parte mientras no tenga un muerto bajo la tierra' (128, 71). The spiritual nature of the narrator is underscored by the reservation of tombs neighbouring his for such saints as Pietro Crespi (161). In keeping with oral tradition, his room is one of exaggeration, an exaggeration that sparks the interest of an investigating official: 'el oficial siguió examinando la habitación con la linterna, y no dió ninguna señal de interés mientras no descubrió las setenta y dos bacinillas apelotonadas en los armarios. Entonces encendió la luz' (348). The narrator's function is not to translate the manuscripts. That he leaves to the reader: 'Melquíades le hablaba del mundo, trataba de infundirle su vieja sabiduría, pero se negó a traducir los manuscritos. "Nadie debe conocer su sentido mientras no hayan cumplido cien años," explicó' (231). The narrator's immanent self-reference is imminent until the moment of revelation at the end of the text. The end of the text is precisely that point which offers a perspective of the whole narrative world.

The narrative scope is in keeping with the metaphorical function of the voice. It is dialectic in nature, stereoscopic in time, and binocular in space. In that the standpoint of the voice lies at the prehistoric centre of the myth, it proceeds from the centre of language and perception. This centre of perception does not concern itself with the difference between life and death. In the realm of experience, life and death are but inventions of an analytical mind. At the more fundamental levels of language and perception they can pose no real barriers, and for the singular perspective of Melquíades these barriers offer no problem. He can pass from one to the other because, as narrator, they do not belong to his realm, that is, that of language. There is nothing 'magical' about a scope that mediates two dialectical poles through experience. He can enter the mind of Prudencio Aguilar who, since his death in a duel of honour, has been suffering 'inmensa desolación ... honda nostalgia ... [y] ansiedad' (79). In the third chapter Melquíades returns from death, which is described not as an absence of sensation but rather as an alienation and distanciation: 'Había estado en la muerte, en efecto, pero había regresado porque no pudo soportar la soledad' (104). Upon entering death, it is Melquíades who tells Prudencio Aguilar the where-abouts of José Arcadio Buendía (131). When Prudencio touches the patriarch's shoulder, he is caught in an intermediary room between life and death and it is here that Ursula has visions of Melquíades: 'Dios mío –pensó Ursula– Hubiera jurado que era Melquíades' (189).

For the narrative voice the dialectic of life and death can function the other way around. The living can be as dead, as the dead living: 'Rebeca cerró las puertas de su casa y se enterró en vida' (183). When Amaranta Ursula does not hear her great, great grandmother, Ursula exclaims, 'Dios mío ... De modo que esto es la muerte,' and the next day 'amaneció muerta,' she 'woke up' dead (377–8).

The omniscience, or total science, of the voice does not function only at the deep levels of perception. His scope also has height. Throughout the narration, the voice centres on an event and then, as if with bi-noculars, brings it very close and then distances it again. In chapter 1, the voice narrates as from above while 'José Arcadio Buendía echó treinta doblones en una cazuela, y los fundió con raspadura de cobre, oropimente, azufre y plomo' (65). In the second chapter he leaves Ursula's smoldering inheritance and focuses on the intimate world of José Arcadio (primogénito). The reader is brought so close that he can hear Pilar Ternera's 'risa explosiva' and can listen to José 'respirar hacia dentro' to 'controlar los golpes del corazón'. Then, from this intimate proximity, the voice suddenly draws back and again commands a wide scope from above. Here both events are brought together in a single sentence: 'Estaba tan ensimismado que ni siquiera comprendió la al-egría de todos cuando su padre y su hermano alborotaron la casa con la noticia de que habían logrado vulnerar el cascote metálico y separar el oro de Ursula' (85). The voice brings his equivocal scope back un-expectedly from its detailed proximity to the more general account and then continues, 'En efecto, tras complicadas y perseverantes jornadas, lo habían conseguido' (85). The reader is left to wonder where José Arcadio has gone only to find him again, at the end of the paragraph, at an intermediary distance, in a clipped dialogue with his father.

This same technique of amplifying and narrowing the scope gives way to a magnification of everyday events and characters. Aureliano Segundo's wealth is as exaggerated as are the feats of the colonel. Six men are needed to carry José Arcadio Buendía to his bed and Remedios la bella is a beauty not of this world. It is because of the lengthy queue of Meme's schoolmates that Fernanda buys the seventy-two 'bacinillas' that are kept in the narrator's room: 'Devolvió las camas y taburetes prestados y guardó las setenta y dos bacinillas en el cuarto de Melquíades. La clausurada habitación, en torno a la cual giró en otro tiempo la vida espiritual de la casa, fué conocida desde entoces como *el cuarto de las bacinillas'* (302). This exaggeration does not contradict the universal scope of the narrator's metaphoric perspective. In the text's second paragraph, Melquíades introduces the 'lupa del tamaño de un tambor ... la lupa gigantesca' through which he has detailed access to any aspect of the narrative world (60).

The scope also presents apparent contradictions that are later resolved. The contradictions can be resolved only if the reader remembers his standpoint next to the stereoscopic perspective of the voice. The reader must keep past events in mind and be open to future possibilities. He or she is asked to read back through previous pages and then forward to where the apparent contradiction presents itself. The breadth of the reader's scope and his memory are both put to the test if he is to resolve the contradictions and recognize the narrative voice's claim to authority and truth over his world. At the end of the sixth chapter Arcadio expresses one last wish before his execution: 'Díganle a mi mujer –contestó con voz bien timbrada– que le ponga a la niña el nombre de Ursula –hizo una pausa y confirmo–: Ursula, como la abuela' (170). The moment before his death the voice centres on his last thought: '¡Ah, carajo! –alcanzó a pensar–; se me olvidó decir que si nacía mujer le pusieran Remedios' (170-1). Halfway through the next chapter the reader finds: 'Contra la última voluntad del fusilado, bautizó a la niña con el nombre de Remedios. "Estoy segura que eso fue lo que Arcadio quiso decir –alegó–. No la pondremos Ursula, porque se sufre mucho con ese nombre" ' (181). At this point the reader can only search page by page, back through his past reading until he finds that the last wish of Arcadio both *is* overruled and again it *is not*. His expressed wish is ignored by the character, who is not privileged, yet his unexpressed wish is fulfilled. Again, the reader is not faced with contradiction but rather with a tension in the relational function of the copula. The contradiction can be resolved only with an 'It *is* his last wish and again it *is not*.'

The reliability of the narrative voice lies beyond doubt. Every apparent contradiction is resolved because the perspective issues forth 'from the postulate of perceptibility that comes from our human forms of perception,' which is the here and now of experience (Gadamer 1975, 409). It is from this postulate that 'modern physics has departed radically,' and it is for this reason that the perspective of the text presents a chaos to the empirical mind (409). The narrative voice assumes the reliable attitude of a chronicler. He is reporting things exactly as they are and from the beginning offers no opinion. The impersonal, unintrusive attitude he adopts is strengthened by phrases like 'Melquíades, que era un hombre honrado ... y el gitano dió entonces una prueba convincente de honradéz' (60–1). In chapter 4 the narrator tells us that 'Arcadio había de acordarse del temblor con que Melquíades le hizo escuchar varias páginas de su escritura impenetrable,' and two chapters later Arcadio stands before the firing squad and hears 'letra por letra las encíclicas cantadas de Melquíades' (126, 170). Each prediction is fulfiled. The miraculous shot that passes through the colonel's chest 'sin lastimar ningún centro vital' (155) does so because his doctor paints a circle of iodine on 'el único punto por donde podía pasar una bala sin lastimar ningún centro vital' (222, 225). The chronicle also states that the mystery of José Arcadio's death at the hands of his beloved Rebeca will not be solved, and it is not (182). This universal control that ties up each loose string and resolves each paradox is possible only in the realm of language, which obeys its own laws.

There is one contradiction that is clearly left for the reader to resolve. At the beginning of the *sixth* chapter the narrator tells us that colonel Aureliano Buendía had 'diecisiete hijos varones de diecisiete mujeres distintas, que fueron exterminados uno tras otro en una sola noche' (155). This is not the case, for at the end of the *eighteenth* chapter 'Aureliano Amador, el único sobreviviente de los diecisiete hijos del coronel Aureliano Buendía,' appears at the Buendía door and is only then shot by the police (408). This paradox can be resolved if the reader accepts the *Cien años* as existing simultaneously in the one night of the narrator's telling. Again, the abstraction of past and future is concentrated in the real experience of the chronicler's present telling.

The attitude of chronicler, and the reliability of the telling, mediate the distinction normally established between a narrative fiction and a chronicle. The narrative voice presents the world as he perceives it, that is, from language leading to experience, and yet with the objectivity of a chronicler. Unlike a chronicle, however, the text has a beginning, middle, and an end. It proceeds from a genesis to an apocalypse. It is a chronicle, yet it links beginning to end and its circular structure is more like a spiral than the 'círculo vicioso que se prolongaba por noches enteras' of the 'gallo capón' (101). The questions that might be presented by a historian are answered metaphorically: 'Does the world really present itself to perception in the form of well-made stories, with central subjects, proper beginnings, middles, and ends, and a coherence that permits us to see "the end" in every beginning? Or does it present itself more in the forms that the annals and chronicle suggest, either as a mere sequence without beginning or end or as sequences of beginnings that only terminate and never conclude?' (White 1981, 23). The first sentence does begin *in medias res* as does the chronicle, for the firing-squad event is presented half-way through the seventh chapter. It also begins at a genesis for it begins with the beginning of memory, the experience of a solid liquid: ice. The tension between these two questions is put into productive play by the reliability of the narrating voice. Truth and fable, narrative fiction and history are mediated from within language. Thus, Carlos Fuentes can exclaim: 'Toda la historia "ficticia" coexiste con la historia "real" ' and the 1982 edition of *Encyclopaedia Britannica* gives *Cien años de soledad* as a suggested background reading for the history of Colombia (Fuentes, quoted in Vargas Llosa 78). The text *is* a chronicle and again it *is not*. The narrative voice speaks from the reliable standpoint of perception, but knows well that perception is subject to the priority of language.

The stereoscopic understanding of time is closely tied to the sequential structure of *Cien años*. The forward and backward action of the reader is a 'real' enactment of the experience of time that is expressed in the first sentence of the text: 'Muchos años después, frente al pelotón de fusilamiento, el coronel Aureliano Buendía había de recordar aquella tarde remota en que su padre lo llevó a conocer el hielo.' What first strikes the reader is the rearrangement of a traditional 'Había una vez' opening to narrative fiction. Although the sentence is read in a chronological and syntagmatic progression, it is assimilated by means of a semantic structure that not only points to a specific event in the distant future as well as to a specific event in the distant past, but also establishes a direction of temporal movement. The standpoint of the narrator is elevated and provides a singular point from which to observe the elliptical swing to the future and then to the past. Whereas the 'Había una vez' formula is a reference to the past, the 'Muchos años después ... habiá de recordar' *is* a reference to the past and then again *is not*. The dialectical progression is elliptical in shape as is the prehistoric egg, the '*huevo filosófico*,' and the 'piedra filosofal' of Melquíades (59, 64). It is also striking that the first adverbial group, the point of genesis, has no syntagmatic antecedent. Rather than preceding the phrase, a semantic antecedent is found at the end of the sentence and *it is towards this semantic antecedent that the sentence as a whole tends.* The *whole* sentence must be read for the adverbial group 'Muchos años después' to have any meaning. The same structure, which forms an iterated point of departure throughout the text, gradually acquires an antecedent by means of its own creation. Half-way through the text the reader finds the same structure, only now with a clearly defined antecedent, in the usual position: 'Escupió el espectacular montón de monedas, lo metió en tres sacos de lona, y lo enterró en un lugar secreto, en espera de que tarde o temprano los tres desconocidos fueran a reclamarla. Mucho después, en los años difíciles de su decrepitud, Ursula solía intervenir en las conversaciones de los numerosos viajeros' (239).

The future event of the first sentence is understood in terms of a temporal clause, that is, *'cuando se encontraba* frente al pelotón de fusilamiento, only there is a marked *ellipsis* of the conjunction, subject, and reflexive verb. The ellipsis is made even more evident when, just before the end of the first chapter, the same structure is presented again, only now with the ellipsis filled:

Aquellas alucinantes sesiones quedaron de tal modo impresas en la memoria de los niños, que muchos años más tarde, un segundo antes de que el oficial de los ejércitos regulares diera la orden de fuego al pelotón de fusilamiento, el coronel Aureliano Buendía volvió a vivir la tibia tarde de marzo en que su padre interrumpió la lección de física, y se quedó fascinado con la mano en el aire, y los ojos inmóviles oyendo a la distancia los pífanos y tambores y sonajas de los gitanos que una vez más llegaban a la aldea pregonando el último y asombroso descubrimiento de los sabios de Memphis. (73)

The ellipsis has been filled to a point of almost exploding. The ellipsis in the generative sentence gives the appearance of a phrase stating 'where' or giving a precise locale of action, that is, 'frente al pelotón.' Yet it is actually stating a specific time. The missing conjunction is found later in sentences such as 'Muchos años después, el coronel Aureliano Buendía volvió a travesar la región, *cuando* era ya una ruta regular del correo, y lo único que encontró de la nave fue el costillar carbonizado en medio de un campo de amapolas' (69; emphasis added). The ellipsis of the temporal *cuando* and the presence of the spatial *frente* create an intermediary point of perception where time and space intermingle. This point of mediation between time and space is the stand-point of both the narrative voice and the reader. It gives a scope of temporal understanding that has access to both past and future. The only standpoint that coincides with these characteristics in the 'real' world is the very 'real' standpoint of the reader in the precise *'here and now'* of perception, experience, and his or her interpretive activity (Ricoeur 1981a, 161).

The direction discourse takes between the two points in time, that is, that of the firing squad and that of the discovery of ice is a dialectic of dynamic circularity. Again, if 'Muchos años después' is a quantitative assessment carried out from an invisible standpoint co-ordinating a past and a future, it could only reasonably consist of an ever-present 'Now,' an anchor point in the present moment of the real world of action. The adverb 'después' points from 'that remote afternoon' forward to the firing squad. This moment charged with impending death is a moment in space and time that, because of the intensity of the lived experience, refers back through memory to the equally intense experience of discovering water in its congealed state.

This jumping to the future, which refers through memory to the past, which in turn refers, through the narrating technique, to a point in the future where a meaning will be revealed, appears to underlie the forward-backward dialectical ellipse not only of the text as a whole but also of the very act of reading anchored in the 'Now' of the reading experience. Through the temporal sequence, the reader finds his activity clearly dramatized but is not aware of it until it is revealed through an apocalypse or transformational revelation.

A subtle change in temporal direction mediates the two directions of the temporal ellipse. The voice's standpoint begins above the river bank away from the 'huevo prehistórico' and watches Macondo, the Gypsies, and the river from afar. From this standpoint he observes the temporal flow. It is like the river flowing by the prehistoric stones and washing them smooth: 'We say that time passes or flows by. We speak of the course of time. The water that I see rolling by was made ready a few days ago in the mountains, with the melting of the glacier; it is now in front of me and makes its way towards the sea into which it will finally discharge itself. If time is similar to a river, it flows from the past towards the present and the future' (M.M-P. 1962, 411). This is the direction of time in the first half of the sentence. It is directed towards the future 'pelotón de fusilamiento.' The second half of the sentence runs time round to the other direction: from the firing squad in the future back round the present to the past of 'aquella remota tarde en que su padre lo llevó a conocer el hielo.' In this same way, two directions are brought together in the chronological and syntactic presentation. The former becomes an inverted figure of the latter. The sequence of events is from 'aquella remota tarde' to the 'pelotón de fusilamiento.' The syntactic order of emplotment, however, puts the 'pelotón de fusilamiento' at the beginning of the sentence and 'aquella remota tarde' at the end. Two directions are mediated by the metaphoric experience of time. The narrative voice brings together two views of time that are relative to and mediated by the standpoint of the perceiving subject:

Now, no sooner have I introduced an observer, whether he follows the river or whether he stands on the bank and observes its flow, than temporal relationships are reversed. In the latter case, the volume of water already carried by, is not moving towards the future but sinking towards the past; what is to come is on the side of the source, for time does not come from the past. It is not the past that pushes the present, nor the present that pushes the future, into being; the future is not prepared behind the observer, it is a brooding presence moving to meet him, like a storm on the horizon. If the observer sits in a boat and is carried by the current, we may say that he is moving downstream towards his future, but the future lies in the new landscapes which await him at the estuary, and the course of time is no longer the stream itself: it is the landscape as it rolls by for the moving observer. (M.M-P. 1962, 411–12)

This first sentence or 'cornerstone sentence' establishes the sequence that is followed by the larger semantic units, or unnumbered chapters of the text (Ricoeur 1981a, 212) The opening phrase 'muchos años después' becomes 'muchos años antes' in the seventh chapter, back to 'años después' in the eleventh, and by the nineteenth chapter it is turned again: 'Años antes cuando cumplió los cuarenta y cinco, había renunciado' (59, 186, 228, 427). The text's genesis is centred in the 'Now' of narrating and reading as an experience. This empty zero point is again brought to the fore at the end of the text's first quarter. The sixth chapter tells of the miraculous pistol shot that hits colonel Aureliano Buendía in the chest, yet 'el proyectil le salió por la espalda sin lastimar ningún *centro vital*' (155; emphasis added). The importance of this shot is not revealed until the text begins to enter into its second half, that is, between the ninth, tenth, and eleventh chapters. The elliptical design of the sequence intertwines and centres the narrative voice, the character, and the reader all along the same axis of language. The voice centres on Aureliano Buendía now placed in 'el centro del círculo de tiza que sus edecanes trazaban dondequiera que él llegara' (212). This circle around the character disappears only to be replaced by the circle on his chest. At a quarter after three, when both hands of the clock point to the dead centre of the text, 'se disparó un tiro de pistola en el círculo de yodo que su médico personal le había pintado en el pecho' (224–25). The verb and action are reflexive. This vital centre, however, is not a centre of life vs. death. Although he shoots himself, the colonel does not die. This is a centre that has been drawn with great care. The shot passes through the centre of the character, the text, and the reading activity. The carefully drawn circle is much like the 'masterpiece' of language found at the core of the reader, the voice, and the text: 'El proyectil siguió una trayectoria tan limpia que el médico le metió por el pecho y le sacó por la espalda un cordón empapado de yodo. "Esta es mi obra maestra –le dijo satisfecho–. Era el único punto por donde podía pasar una bala sin lastimar ningún centro vital" ' (225). The shot is followed by a string that the doctor passes carefully through the centre of the main character, and through the centre of the text. It is much like a thread passed 'through the eye of a needle.' It is the unifying *energeia* of language and perception reaching out in awareness to the world. Reader, voice, and character in the narrative world are brought together like beads on a string. Recalling the heuristic structure of an ellipse, the projectile follows a straight course that passes the string of language L' through the primary level of perception o, carefully through the reader at F', carefully through the voice at F, and carefully through the character at P in the middle of the narration between the ninth and eleventh chapters of the text.

This unifying thread, however, also directs the reader, the voice, and the character into the most distant curve of the ellipse. Here the perspective would appear quite parabolic, for F' and F look into the centre of the narrative between chapters 9 and 11. In this light a radical change comes about in the text and a mirroring effect begins. Here 'coronel Gerineldo Márquez fue el primero que percibió el vacío de la guerra' (209). Aureliano is alienated from the rest of the world within his circle of chalk. When he moves out of this abstract circle it is to

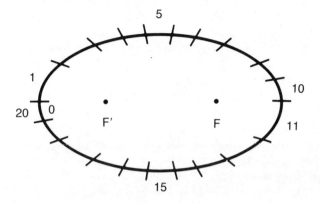

Figure 2

Let 0–F'–F–10 be the course of the projectile and the string of language passing through perception, the reader, the voice, and the character.

sign the surrender, even though his advisors tell him it is a 'contra-sentido' (215). He tells his doctor not to lose time and then (much like Charles Steele's suspended paintbrush in the first pages of *Jacob's Room*) the colonel 'detuvo en el aire la pluma entintada, y descargó sobre él todo el peso de su autoridad' (216). He also removes all but 'objetos impersonales' from his room and, much to the dismay of the character most heavily identified by epithets, he also removes anything that will stimulate memory of him: 'Santa Sofía de la Piedad, la silenciosa, la condescendiente, la que nunca contrarió ni a sus propios hijos, tuvo la impresión de que aquel era un acto prohibido' (221).

The last supper before Aureliano is shot also brings about a mirroring effect. Aureliano Segundo is seated at the same table as José Arcadio Segundo, and 'era tan precisa la coordinación de sus movimientos que no parecían dos hermanos sentados el uno frente al otro, sino un *artificio de espejos*' (220; emphasis added). At this meal Ursula is the only character who dares 'perturbar [la] abstracción' of colonel Aureliano Buendia (220). This she does by stating, 'Si has de irte otra vez– le dijo a mitad de cena–, por lo menos trata de recordar como éramos esta noche' (220). This sentence reverses the direction of time half-way through the text in the same manner as it is reversed half-way through the first sentence. Here, a hypothetical future event of leaving becomes a point of departure from which the character is asked to remember back to the present supper, which by then will have become a past. Thus, a future points to the lived present, which is its past. Time has been reversed.

This impersonal, half-way point is also filled with the main character's moment of sudden self-realization: 'En un instante descubrió los arañazos, los verdugones, las mataduras, las úlceras y cicatrices que había dejado en ella más de *medio siglo* de vida cotidiana, y comprobó que esos estragos no suscitaban en él ni siquira un sentimiento de piedad' (220; emphasis added). This extreme of the ellipse is not betrayed by any trace. Here the colonel sets out to 'destruir todo rastro de su paso por el mundo' (221). Once the shot is fired, however, a new beginning occurs. All the windows of the hosue are opened, Amaranta's heart is 'purificado por el tiempo,' and on this New Year's day Ursula invites the guards to supper, gives them shoes, and clothing and 'les enseñaba a leer y escribir' (227).

Chapter 10 begins with the same sentence structure as the first sentence, only now with Aureliano Segundo taking the place of the colonel. The presence of the narrator once again reverberates with metaphoric presence. We find: 'Contra la reverberación de la ventana, sentado con las manos en las rodillas, estaba Melquíades. No tenía más de cuarenta años. Llevaba el mismo chaleco anacrónico y el sombrero de alas de cuervo, y por sus sienes pálidas chorreaba la grasa del cabello derretida por el calor, como lo vieron Aureliano y José Arcadio cuando eran niños. Aureliano Segundo lo reconoció de inmediato, porque aquel recuerdo hereditario se había transmitido de generación en generación, y habia llegado a él desde la memoria de su abuelo' (231). While the text's beginning, middle, and end all lie upon the same axis, the middle is not the end. The sense is not yet revealed. No one must know the text's 'sentido mientras no hayan cumplido cien años,'' explains Melquíades (231).

The third quarter of the elliptical structure is also linked to the first half and to the end, through time and corresponding events. In chapter 15 Ursula also has a moment of discovery, exclaiming, 'Es como si el mundo estuviera dando vueltas' (335). This discovery does not reach its full potential until the seventeenth chapter when 'se estremeció con la comprobación de que el tiempo no pasaba, como ella lo acababa de admitir, sino que daba vueltas en redondo' (371). It is in chapter 15 that José Arcadio Segundo 'sweats ice' while holding a boy upon his shoulder and once again, 'Muchos años después, ese niño había de seguir contando, sin que nadie se lo creyera, que había visto al teniente leyendo con una bocina de gramófono el Decreto Número 4 del Jefe Civil y Militar de la provincia' (341–2). It is here also that José Arcadio Segundo finds refuge in Melquíades's room. There he is 'protegido por la luz sobrenatural, por el ruido de la lluvia, por la sensación de ser invisible' (349). It will be recalled that here José Arcadio Segundo 'leía en el cuarto de Melquíades las prodigiosas *fábulas* de los tapices volantes y las ballenas que se alimentaban de barcos con tripulaciones' (353; emphasis added). At the end of chapter 6 Arcadio hears the 'encíclicas cantadas por Melquíades,' and then cries out to the firing squad, '–¡Cabrones! –gritó– ¡Viva el partido liberal!' (171). In chapter 15 we find José Arcadio standing before an army, and '–¡Cabrones! – gritó–. Les regalamos el minuto que falta' (342). By this time the text's unifying string of characters is seen 'en la primorosa caligrafía de Melquíades [que] parecían piezas de ropa puesta a secar en un alambre' (384). As the first quarter is linked to the middle so the third is linked to the last chapter. Chapter 17 finds that Pilar Ternera has now reached the age of one hundred and the seller of lottery tickets calls out: 'Aquí está la Divina Providencia ... No la dejen ir, que sólo llega una vez cada cien años' (385). In chapter 15 we find 'la muchedumbre centrifugada por el pánico' and a 'descomunal potencia expansiva' erupts like a volcano in its centre (343). The same occurs in the final chapter.

The end of the text finds the same circle around a character as does the middle. In chapter 19 'pasaron varias semanas antes de que Aureliano descubriera que ella tenía alrededor de la cintura un cintillo que parecía hecho con una cuerda de violoncelo, pero que era duro como el acero y carecía de remate, porque había nacido y crecido con ella' (419). By the end of this same chapter Amaranta Ursula is rooted in a dialectical centre that finds her and Aureliano 'al mismo tiempo adversarios y cómplices' (429). It is here that 'una conmoción descomunal la inmovilizó en su centro de gravedad, la sembró en su sitio, y su voluntad defensiva fué demolida por la ansiedad irresistible de descubrir qué eran los silbos anaranjados y los globos invisibles que la esperaban al otro lado de la muerte' (430). Once again the text passes through the eye of a needle and there is nothing absurd about its synaesthetic passage.

The twelfth chapter of the text reveals a very subtle change in the voice's unintrusive posture. As he prepares to dramatize the narrator's function and bring the reader into the text as a character, he introduces a rejection of the mechanistic world. This rejection is difficult to conjugate within the paradigm of archetypes that has been sustained to this point. Thus, the reader finds that

se supo de señoras respetables que se disfrazaron de villanos para observar de cerca la novedad del gramófono, pero tanto y de tan cerca lo observaron, que muy pronto llegaron a la conclusión de que no era un molino de sortilegio ... sino un truco mecánico que no podía compararse con algo tan conmovedor, tan humano y tan lleno de verdad cotidiana como una banda de músicos. Fue una desilusión tan grave ... Era como si Dios hubiera resuelto poner a prueba toda capacidad de asombro, y mantuviera a los habitantes de Macondo en un permanente vaivén entre el alborozo y el desencanto, la duda y la revelación, hasta el extremo de que ya nadie podía saber a ciencia cierta dónde estaban los límites de la realidad. (268)

The reader has the feeling that it is the voice commenting on his own activity and expressing his own rejection of mechanization. If in chapter 12 he still attributes the opinions to 'señoras respetables' (and who would dare question them?), by the seventeenth chapter the narrator's intervention is more direct: 'En realidad, a pesar de que todo el mundo lo tenía por loco, José Arcadio Segundo era en aquel tiempo el habitante más lúcido de la casa' (383). If the whole world takes José Arcadio for a madman, who takes him for a lucid occupant of the house? It can only be the voice.

This very subtle change from non-intervention to a touch of intrusion is coordinated with a change in the temporal duration of the text. The stereoscopic temporal flow that gyrates forward in the dialectic of 'muchos años después' and 'había de recordar' slowly narrows as it sinks into the narrative world. The wide sequence of future-past-future gradually narrows, causing the pendulum to gyrate very rapidly when it nears its centre and point of rest at the instant of revelation. The gradual reduction in duration of the narrated events is accompanied by a reduction in the sequential distance separating them. The text begins with 'muchos años después' and proceeds to 'pocos años después' (chap. 5), 'pocos meses después' (chap. 6), and 'meses después' (chap. 11), and by the end of the thirteenth chapter it has become 'un momento después.' The one hundred years of the text is slowly concentrated as the narrative voice moves away from the beginning towards the future end.

The end of the text does not point into the future, however. Just as there is no 'habia una vez' at the genesis, there is no y vivieron muy felices para siempre' at the end. The dialectic demands an apocalypse and this lies in the elliptical progression of the gyrating pendular swing from future to past and past to future that vibrates as it centres in the present: 'Melquíades no había ordenado los hechos en el tiempo convencional de los hombres, sino que concentró un siglo de episodios cotidianos, de modo que todos coexistieran en un instante' (446). From here on, the duration of events is minimal: 'Aureliano dió un salto' (447). As the reader becomes a character he begins to read the end of his own reading of *Cien años*: 'y empezó a descifrar el instante que estaba viviendo, descifrándolo a medida que lo vivía, profetizándose a sí mismo en el acto de descifrar la última página de los pergaminos, como si se estuviera viendo en un espejo hablado. Entonces dió otro salto' (447). The reader skips with Aureliano like a stone across the river only to come to rest with the 'huevo prehistórico,' the philosopher's stone, neither high above the bank nor in the river but mediating both. The reader, like Aureliano, does not have a 'segunda oportunidad sobre la tierra [empírica],' for he is planted firmly in the ever-present instant of experience in language (448).

The text's duration, then, is also a dialectic of dynamic tension. The first sentence is the smallest semantic unit, yet it lasts, both in character and structure, throughout the entire *Cien años de soledad*. The last chapter counts among the largest units of the text, that is, the unnumbered segments. Its duration, however, is more or less three months and it is experienced primarily as a single instant of discovery (433). The shortest sentence can have the longest duration and the longest chapter can have the shortest duration. The first sentence is short and then again it is not. The final chapter is long and then again it is not. The instantaneous standpoint of the reader leaves the first order in chaos in order to reveal a metaphoric world and its truth. The reader grasps the whole of this world of discourse, which is the text, to the degree that he interprets the 'pergaminos.' To the same degree that both reader and text encounter time and language itself at their centre both are as 'real' as is 'language' and 'time.' The dramatized narrator, the narrative voice, the character, and the reader meet in the discourse of the text. Along the central axis there is a fusion of horizons. The fusion of horizons occurs at a moment when the dynamic tension between the relational function of the copula, the interpretation by the reader, and the statements of the voice is most concentrated. The narrator is dramatized and again he is not. The reader is interpreter of the text and again he is not, for his role is dramatized as a character in the text. The reader thus belongs to the first-order world but also to the world of the text. Finally *Cien años de soledad* is but a world of fiction and again it is not, for its 'muthos' is a temporal world of fabulous language that reverberates at the *personal* centre of humanity. If *dramatization* is the degree to which the narrator enters into the cause-effect relations of the text, then the dramatization of Melquíades as the 'narrador' is cause enough for a reverberation in a bewildered reader. The *scope* of the text's action *is* metaphor itself, and upon this metaphor the reader either can or cannot rely. It depends upon his or her perspective.

The temporal dimension of the text is, then, a mediative enterprise. It mediates St Augustine's *intentio* and *distentio animi*, on the one hand, and the Aristotelian *muthus* and *peripeteia*, on the other. It answers St Augustine's question 'Can a hundred years be present at once?' with a resounding ¡Sí! and yet it affirms Aristotle's 'beginning, a middle and an end' of emplotment (Ricoeur 1984, 1:8, 30). It is a mediation made possible through the productive tension in the relational function of the copula that, in turn, is made possible by the voice's standpoint at the heart of language. The two modes of perceiving time, either in the experience of its flow or through its emplotment from the bank, are presented not as an irresolvable opposition, nor as an absurd chaos, but as an active dialectic to be played through a dynamic and productive figure. The temporal dimension of the narrating voice presents both sides of this figure from the very first sentence. As a figure who spins a rope from one side to another, while jumping through the centre, so the narrating voice spins the temporal perspective. If the initial elevated standpoint mediates the future and the past, the past and the future, it must be located directly above the elliptical philosopher's stone upon which the gyrating pendulum of time finally comes to rest. This point of rest is the ever-present 'Now' of the experience of one's own 'self' as it realizes the reading process. The temporality of the narrating voice 'temporalizes itself as future-which-lapses-into-the-past by coming-into-the-present' of the act of reading (M.M-P. 1962, 420).

The narrative world emerges from this perspective of the narrating voice. The twenty-three characters that make up the Buendía family are concentrated in a progressively diminishing number. The reader is presented first to José Arcadio Buendía, Ursula Iguarán, and their three children: José Arcadio (primogénito), Coronel Aureliano, and Amaranta. Rebeca Montiel and Remedios Mascote are introduced to form a family of seven. The seventeen children of colonel Aureliano are eliminated, leaving only two grandchildren by way of José Arcadio (primogénito) and Pilar Ternera. Of these two, again, Aureliano José does not have children and Arcadio, by way of Santa Sofía de la Piedad, renews the cycle of children with three: Remedios la bella, Aureliano II, and José Arcadio II. With Arcadio's death the family is reduced to five, for Petra Cotes always maintains her distance. Aureliano II has three children with Fernanda del Carpio, and José Arcadio II does not, thereby reversing the Aureliano trend. The changes in names and confusion between the twins is also a sign of this change in the narrative world. Of the three children, José Arcadio, Meme, and Amaranta Ursula, only Meme has a child, Aureliano, by Mauricio Babilonia. The family is reduced to one and the marital situation is reversed. Colonel Aureliano did not have children by his wife, Remedios Mascote, but had seventeen outside of marriage. Amaranta Ursula does not have children with her husband Gastón but has one child with her nephew Aureliano. The process comes to rest in 'el último Aureliano' who, much like the philosophical egg, 'era un pellejo hinchado y reseco, que todas las hormigas del mundo iban arrastrando trabajosamente hacia sus madrigueras por el sendero de piedras del jardín' (446). The Buendía dynasty is slowly reduced to one and this 'one' initiates the revelation: 'Aureliano no pudo moverse. No porque lo hubiera paralizado el estupor, sino porque en aquel instante prodigioso se le revelaron las claves definitivas de Melquíades, y vió el epígrafe de los pergaminos perfectamente ordenado en el tiempo y el espacio de los hombres' (446). When Aureliano begins to read 'en voz alta' he, the narrator, and the newly dramatized reader function are fused into one: 'el narrador y lo narrado no son realidades diferentes ... el narrador salta de ese centro desde el cual dominaba todo el círculo al círculo mismo' (447 and Vargas Llosa 547). In one instant narrator, narration, and reader fuse horizons through the revelation. All have reached the same standpoint in language from which to view the narrative world of Macondo: 'Melquíades no había ordenado los hechos en el tiempo *convencional* de los hombres' and 'vió el epígrafe de los pergaminos perfectamente ordenado en el tiempo y el espacio de los hombres' (446; emphasis added). Conventional, first-order understanding is left behind to achieve a unified perspective in the language experienced through the text.

The names of the characters follow the same centripetal movement. The reader spends much of his time at the beginning of the text reading, or rather jumping backward and forward, trying to identify which Aureliano, José Arcadio, or Amaranta is being presented. Epithetic identification and nicknames such as Remedios la bella, El cachorro, Santa Sofía de la Piedad, la silenciosa, Aureliano Segundo, and José Arcadio Segundo all allow for the characters to be seen as part of a tradition and lineage on the one hand and as individuals on the other.

The characters of Macondo are of an oral tradition. This is seen not only in what Walter J. Ong has called the 'epithetic identification for "disambiguation" of classes or of individuals' (1977, 108), but also in such types as 'Francisco el Hombre ... así llamado porque derrotó al diablo en un duelo de improvisación de cantos' (106). The *juglar* is placed 'como un camaleón monolítico, sentado en medio de un círculo de curiosos. Cantaba las noticias con su vieja voz descordada' (106). When José Arcadio Buendía is told of the possible misfortune his offspring may suffer if he marries his cousin Ursula, he replies, 'No me importa tener cochinitos, siempre que puedan hablar' (77). When Don Apolinar Mascote paints 'en la puerta el letrero: "*Corregidor*," ' José Arcadio tells him, 'En este pueblo no mandamos con papeles' (111). The Gypsies that visit Macondo after the band of Melquíades are different because they speak another tongue. The Indians of Macondo also speak another tongue and are therefore on the fringe of its world. When Don Apolinar Moscote wants a guarantee from José Arcadio it is not in any written form but as a 'palabra de honor' (113). Folk sayings such as 'un clavo saca otro clavo' pass wisdom on in the oral tradition of Macondo (150). For the characters of Macondo 'the end' is signaled not by a revelation through the written words on parchment but by the death of Pilar Ternera, that is, the last character old enough to remember their history: 'Pilar Ternera murió ... Era el final. En la tumba de Pilar Ternera ... se pudrían los escombros del pasado' (431). Melquíades did not discover Macondo by looking at a map but by listening: 'los gitanos confesaron que se habían orientado por el canto de los pájaros' (67).

That the characters form archetypes with specific roles to play is made clear by the narrator's dividing them according to names: 'En la larga historia de la familia, la tenáz repetición de los nombres le había permitido sacar conclusiones que le parecían terminantes. Mientras los Aurelianos eran retraídos, pero de mentalidad lúcida, los José Arcadio eran impulsivos y emprendedores, pero estaban marcados por un signo trágico' (228). José Arcadio is referred to as 'aquel protomacho' (144). The six roles – 'mother, temptress and symbol' for the women and 'warrior, lover and philosopher' for the men – are eventually reduced to the specific role of reader in the character of Aureliano (Valdés 1982, 70). The role of the reader Aureliano and the 'real' reader become one when the elliptical shape of time and the world of the philosophical egg are appropriated. This allows for an interpretation 'antes de llegar al verso final,' and the reader's self is revealed in the realization of his reader role (448).

None of the characters that make up the world of Macondo is privileged beyond the capacities implied by his or her role. Melquíades is the only privileged character for he is the narrator. Aureliano can know when an assassin approaches in the seventh chapter only because his role is to survive. Ursula cries out, '¡Han matado a Aureliano!' while watching the milk boil, not because she is privileged, but because intuition is a maternal trait and her role is that of the mother (225). Her intuition and insight grow to the degree that by the thirteenth chapter she watches the family 'con sus cuatro sentidos' not needing her eyesight (289). As has been pointed out above, Santa Sofía de la Piedad christens the girl Remedios, not because she is privileged and knows her husband's last thought, but because her role, like that of Ursula, is a maternal role. Intuition tells her 'que eso fué lo que Arcadio quiso decir' (181).

The characters are also reliable. Each develops not as an individual but as a role player in a society. The roles must be played and are independent of any individual wish. The patriarch sits at the foot of the family tree because he is the root of the dynasty. He is moved away from his seat only by the arrival of the gramophone and other modern inventions that break the traditional world: 'Era un intrincado frangollo de verdades y espejismos, que convulsionó de impaciencia al espectro de José Arcadio Buendía bajo el castaño y lo obligó a caminar por toda la casa aun a pleno día' (268). Aureliano is the character to interpret the manuscripts because his role is that of the reader. It is he who begins with a study of language itself, that is, Sanskrit, and it is he who frequents the bookstore. He is the one to read books 'que sólo había leído Beda el Venerable' and it is he who enters into intersubjective debate with 'Alvaro, Germán, Alfonso y Gabriel.' Aureliano is 'encastillado en la realidad escrita' (421).

The play between foreground and background follows the temporal structure of the narrating voice. Time and space are two sides of the same dialectic. Once again, Ursula sees both the changes and the constants of time as part of the movement of space: 'Es como si el mundo estuviera dando vueltas' (335). At the outset of the reading experience, the foreground is the historical world. Riohacha and the Guajira peninsula are as real as 'Sir Francis Drake' and 'la reina Isabel' (67). It is from this real world that the 'exodus,' provoked by a duel of honour, takes place. The foreground becomes more restricted as Riohacha falls into the background and Macondo, on the banks of a river, takes its place. The distance between the background and the foreground is not given in spatial terms, but in terms of the time it takes news to reach the characters' ears: '¡Estalló la guerra! En efecto, había estallado hacía tres meses. La ley marcial imperaba en todo el país' (152). The foreground is isolated from the background in both time and space. As the gyrating temporal pendulum draws ever smaller elliptical circles, so the narrating voice focuses the giant microscope closer. The foreground of 'la posición de las casas, que desde todas podía llegarse al río y ... las calles con tan buen sentido' becomes the background when Ursula 'decidió que Melquíades se quedara viviendo en la casa' (66, 105). The house is the new foreground and Macondo becomes the background: 'Entonces sacó el dinero acumulado en largos años de dura labor, adquirió compromisos con sus clientes, y emprendió la ampliación de la casa' (109). By chapter 17 the house begins to fall into the background and different rooms become the foreground. José Arcadio leaves behind the social conflicts of Macondo and dedicates all of his energy to study in *Melquíades's room* 'era el único que había dispuesto de bastante lucidez para vislumbrar la verdad de que también el tiempo sufría tropiezos y accidentes, y podía por tanto astillarse y dejar en un cuarto una fracción eternizada,' and again, 'el propio Aureliano parecía preferir el encierro y la soledad, y no revelaba la menor malicia por conocer el mundo que empezaba en la puerta' (384, 383). The rooms and halls of the Buendía house in turn become the background as the narrative world is concentrated almost entirely on Aureliano and José Arcadio in the study.

The last two chapters mark a change in the world of the text. The arrival of Amaranta Ursula from abroad forces Aureliano out of the room: 'Lo obligó a cambiarse los escuálidos pantalones que heredó del coronel Aureliano Buendía, le regaló camisas juveniles y zapatos de dos colores, y lo empujaba a la calle cuando pasaba mucho tiempo en el cuarto de Melquíades' (411). From the background of his *private* reading room a new foreground develops: 'Después de la muerte de José Arcadio, se había vuelto un cliente asiduo de la librería del sabio catalán' (417). The room, the house, and Macondo in ruins form a background for his function as a reader. 'Trató de reconstruir con la imaginación el arrasado esplendor de la antigua ciudad' and 'siguió reuniéndose todas las tardes con los cuatro discutidores, que se llamaban Alvaro, Germán, Alfonso y Gabriel' (417, 421). It is in the foregrounded bookstore that, through intersubjective debate, the first part of the revelation occurs: 'Para un hombre como él, encastillado en la realidad escrita, aquellas sesiones tormentosas ... fueron una revelación' (421). The bookstore in turn falls into a background that is once again the historical world of Europe and America. The house takes its place one again as the foreground: 'Volvieron a cerrar puertas y ventanas para no demorarse en trámites de desnudamientos' (437). The attention switches again to Macondo as Aureliano searches through the archives for his identity, then again to a room in the house when Amaranta Ursula dies. Again, the town becomes foreground as Arcadio wanders aimlessly in search of 'un desfiladero de regreso al pasado,' and then switches to his room, then to the child's room, and finally comes to rest 'entre las plantas prehistóricas,' foregrounding the text itself. Instead of the text being the frame of Macondo, Macondo and the Buendía house become the frame for the text. The text is constructed dialectically in 'versos pares' and 'impares' and in the concentrated time of experience (444, 446). The dialectic play between foreground and background, frame and focus follows the same structure as that of time. The variation is wide and slow at the beginning but narrow and fast as it gyrates to a stop on the text itself in the end.

The narrative world of *Cien años de soledad* is the world of Macondo. The name Macondo is African in origin. It is the Bantu word for the banana tree (Herrera 346). This narrative world of creative language is quite similar to the one through which a narrator in the African oral tradition might travel as he 'spins his yarn':

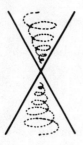

(Zahan et Ganay 21)

The artisan begins fully extended from a centre into space in order to create a narrative world of 'above' and 'below,' 'inside' and 'outside.' Over a period of one hundred years of narrated time the text concentrates into its centre through progressively shorter circles of time and in progressively smaller units of space. The first, central, and final chapters meet in a central 'eye of the needle' and 'I' of the reader. Aureliano Babilonia and the reader *read the same last two pages at the same time and in the same place*. Both 'Babilonia' and the reader stand in the eye of the biblical hurricane while the walls of Macondo fall and the world explodes. At the centre of their reading experience, the solitude in which they find themselves is overcome. The effects of one hundred years of history on consciousness surge forth from the tradition that is Aureliano's language. The appropriation of Aureliano's historical world through the language of the text is accompanied by his self-realization, 'porque en aquel momento estaba descubriendo los primeros indicios de su ser ... profetizándose a sí mismo ... como si se estuviera viendo en un espejo *hablado*' (447; emphasis added). If, as the text concludes, 'todo lo escrito en ellos era irrepetible desde siempre y para siempre,' it is because each reading is a unique experience in time, an experience that the reader will not have a second opportunity to capture.

The experience of the ever-present 'Now' in Macondo is, nevertheless, *always* presenting itself. Experience by its very nature opens itself to new experience. The 'condemnation' to one hundred years of solitude can become a liberation, if the 'solitude of life' is dialectically countered by an appropriation of the one hundred years (Ricoeur 1976,

19, 43). Aureliano Babilonia's self-realization is an open invitation to the reader, who shares his perspective, to do the same. A self-realization is always an apocalypse, for one's illusions and opinions crumble. Such 'disillusion' gives rise to both disappointment and fulfillment. Appropriation implies 'a moment of dispossession of the narcissistic ego' (1981a, 192).

In this way the centre of the narrative world of *Cien años de soledad* is very much a wedge of truth driven into the centre of being. The centre is empty in space yet full of understanding in time. It is filled with both the revelation of one hundred years in a single instant and the reader's achieved self-understanding. The centre is full of the *reverberation* of the voice's presence in Melquíades and it *resonates* with the presence of the reader in the narrative world. I do not believe that this centre of time, language, and the reader's self-appropriation is an absurd failure. What might be absurd would be to attempt an explanation of this centre through a first-order, rational perspective. Such an attempt would be limited indeed, if it failed to recognize the metaphoric foundation of the text in the centre of language, perception, and experience.

The moral dimension of this fabulous world of *Cien años de soledad* is the language with which the careful voice begins his narrative. It is the perceptive understanding with which the doctor who cares for Aureliano outlines the *centro* in such a way that nothing vital will be harmed by violent self-destruction. This is his 'obra maestra' (225). This language full of care and this perceptive understanding meet in the final, moral experience of the fable. The reader is invited to realize he *is* the act of 'care-full' reading that gives life to the text whose world of language we all share. Through a careful reading the text's language and perceptive understanding reverberate with the experience of the reader's own tradition as it meets the temporal concentration of *Cien años de soledad* in the one instant of discovery.

There remains one aspect essential to narrative perspective that has yet to be considered: the historical perspective of the reader who shares the standpoint of the narrating voice in the narrative world. As a reader I have followed the structures of the text closely, for in the text 'estaba escrito [mi] destino' (446). I have dealt with the textual perspectives historically, but in a manner 'contraria a la falsa que los historiadores habían admitido, y consagrado en los textos escolares' (383–4). I have understood history in its effects on a consciousness through which both the world is appropriated and the self is realized, that is 'aquel relámpago de lucidez [en que] tuvo conciencia de que era incapáz de resistir sobre su alma el peso abrumador de tanto pasado' (445–6). I have pointed out characteristics common to an audio-oral perspective of the world: 'y empezó a descifrar … como si se estuviera viendo en un espejo *hablado*' (447; emphasis added). I have pointed to a perspective that can be characterized by the relational tension in the copula. The text and its remembered history begins with 'el diamente más grande del mundo' (74). This diamond is neither the geometrical and spatial configuration of earth nor is it the flowing water of time. It is the mediation of both: 'Es hielo' (74).

The perspective that I have put into play has been, needless to say, a metaphoric perspective. Two factors have decided this reading. My individual training as a reader began in a community marked by an audio-oral noetic and this fact may well have played a role in my reading. This individual factor would allow for innovation. Yet, innovation is not the only deciding factor. I am also working within a tradition and within a community that shares individual experiences of narrative through the criticism of texts and through productive dialogue. To the degree that this community works with and in discourse it can be 'connected with our new kind of orality, the secondary orality of our electronic age, which both resembles and contrasts with primary or preliterate orality' (Ong 1977, 305). If, as the now-popular expression puts it, we can speak of the Latin American literary 'boom,' it is because there are now ears within our community that can hear the explosion (Fernández-Brazo 19).

Other perspectives are certainly valid. A *metonymic* reader perspective might find economic modes of appropriation in the 'eye' of the biblical hurrican that causes the destruction of a decadent world. A *synecdochic* perspective might find the philosophical egg to be a microcosm of the Bible or of literature itself. On the one hand, an *ironic* perspective, like that of Mieke Bal, might still find a hidden meaning in the absurd chaos it encounters when the text explodes to include the reader. On the other hand, an *ironic* concern for visual language, like that of Lois Marie Jaeck, might follow 'some arguments of Jacques Derrida' and examine 'how writing – through repetition – causes the loss of the central presence to which it originally referred, and how the events described in the last three pages of *One Hundred Years of Solitude* are a reflection of the originary loss of centre which the writing of the book occurred.' Such a perspective would certainly erase all traces of a reader reading 'en voz alta' between 'espejos *hablados*.' In proposing a metaphoric perspective, I lay no claim to closure of the text's narrative perspective. As an experience this encounter with the text can only hope to open unto new experience. From the phenomenological standpoint of my perspective, I rest my argument in the mediating centre of language.

8

The Ironic Parable of *Jacob's Room*

Jacob's Room and the name 'Virginia Woolf' move narrative perspective from an 'hombre tímido' and a 'pueblecillo' in Colombia to Cornwall, Cambridge, London, and one who had been 'patted on the head as a child by many an eminent Victorian' (Herrera 349, 346, and Daiches 3). The title introduces an architectural structure not the figure of a person. The reader may be tempted to invert the order and see the room as an attribute of Jacob. The proper name, however, remains an attribute of the noun 'room.' In the title and in the text, objectivity and space are given priority over subjectivity and person.

The forty years between Woolf's birth and the first apperance of *Jacob's Room* in 1922 cannot be characterized in terms of widespread illiteracy throughout England. Of those who voted in the 1906 general election (the year Jacob goes up to Cambridge) a mere 0.81 per cent were illiterate, and of this fraction of a per cent, 68 per cent were to be found in rural areas.[1] By mid-century England had the third largest circulation of daily newspapers in the world.[2] The prefiguration of *Jacob's Room*, however, was not realized in this widespread typographical environment, but in this typographical milieu taken to an extreme. If García Márquez left university in order to write the stories he had heard his grandparents tell, Virginia Woolf enjoyed 'her father's magnificent library [as] her only university and ... made full use of it' (Daiches 2). She read the classics that had been provided by Leslie Stephen, a 'distinguished critic, biographer, philosopher and scholar' (1). Her preliminary competence was not achieved under common circumstances. It was realized in an extraordinary, 'self-contained' world and through an 'unusually rich' education (2). While this background may have made her appear unaware that 'the vast majority of the British population had not enjoyed the classics and could not read a foreign language,' her linguistic competence, achieved through a 'sensibility ... based on intelligence ... [and] the meditative eye,' was acutely aware of the potential of the written word (3). This competence saw her write: 'My theory being that the actual event practically does not exist – nor time either' and 'The test of a book (to a writer) is if it makes a space in which, quite naturally you can say what you want to say' (quoted in Gloversmith 195 and Woolf 1953, 156). *Jacob's Room* is such a space.

The text does not begin in the 'real' world and move to a 'mythical' world. *Jacob's Room* is solidly situated in Cornwall, Cambridge, London, and Athens. It is as historical as Walpole and Victoria and stands before all 'history [that] backs our pane of glass.'[3] If the text is one of those 'books whose virtue is all drawn together in a page or two' and whose sentences 'don't budge though armies cross them,' then surely one of those sentences must be: 'Then they would apply themselves to Jacob and vacillate eternally between the two extremes' (136, 151). To the degree that *Jacob's Room* is a 'character drawing,' it is 'a matter of pins and needles, exquisite outlines enclosing vacancy' (151). The fundamental unity to be found in the text as a whole is the disintegration of an exploded world made available through distanciation in language.

The narrative voice in *Jacob's Room* echoes off its walls and reflects back through the listless 'air in an empty room, just swelling the curtain' (37, repeated 172). The only sound is the creak of one fibre in the wicker armchair 'though no one sits there,' and it is this 'no one' that narrates throughout the text (37, repeated 172). If person is a mode of figuring, here it is constantly disfigured. The voice narrates in every person and therefore cannot be said to narrate in any person. The one person to which all others appear to be equated is a neutral and absolute 'one.' When the voice describes an interaction between *people*, the first person does not function as 'subjective person,' but displays that 'something absolute in us which despises qualification': 'People come together in a room. "So delighted", says somebody, "to meet you" and that is a lie. And then: "I enjoy the spring more than the autumn now. One does, I think, as one gets older." For women are always, always, always talking about what one feels' (140). This 'personal' dialogue does not appear to function between an 'I' and a 'you' but seems to hover in a suspended 'one.' The first-person plural serves as a platform from which to formulate concepts rather than to suggest a shared standpoint. It is also quickly converted to the 'umbrella' pronoun 'one.' After one of the few descriptions of Jacob's inner feelings, the voice quickly clarifies: 'This was in his face. Whether we know what was in his mind is another question' (91). Within a few pages, this *we* becomes: 'Such faces as one sees' (94). The same occurs within the space of a few lines. The reader finds: 'No doubt we should be, on the whole, much worse off than we are without our astonishing gift for illusion,' and one sentence later: 'One's aunts have been to Rome; and every one has an uncle who was last heard of – poor man – in Rangoon' (133). The same is true within the sentence itself: 'Let *us* consider letters ... for to see *one's* own envelope on another's table is to realize how soon deeds sever and become alien' (89; emphasis added).

The first-person narration does not contribute to a dialogue of question and answer between the voice and the reader. The frequent use of 'you' works against it. Most answers are provided by the text and attributed to a 'second person.' These answers are not necessarily preceded by a question. Often the question follows the answer. First, the reader finds an answer to the question of beauty: 'All four were civilization's triumphs, and if you persist that a command of the English language is part of our inheritance, one can only reply that beauty is almost always dumb. Male beauty in association with female beauty breeds in the onlooker a sense of fear' (93). The answer and rejoinder to the question of beauty is already given to the reader whether he has persisted or not. Only then is a question introduced and only for the purpose of clarifying the pre-established answer: 'Have you ever watched fine collie dogs couchant at twenty yards' distance?' (93). Question and answer are inverted. The question serves to clarify the answer not vice versa. The reader is left as an observer whose fundamental role of questioner has been usurped by the voice.

The second person also functions as an impersonal and universal 'one.' Rather than address the reader, it often functions to introduce the voice's own musing reflections as if in dialogue with itself. Only after the voice is silent and the narration finished is the reader invited to participate. Half-way through the eighth chapter the voice muses that 'no one has left an adequate account' of life (92). It complains that, while the 'streets of London have their map ... our passions are uncharted' (92). A question is then asked in the second person and promptly answered with a tour through space that takes 'you' through Holborn to Queen's Square, along the Essex coast, across to the Azores, and finally to the verge of a marsh on the very edge of civilization (92). The reader is not a participant in the 'story' until the 'story' is finished: 'you let him go on with his story, which ends in an invitation to step somewhere, to his room, presumably' (92). Only then is the reader invited to 'fill in the sketch as you like' and *you* is faced with nothing less than the 'chasms in the continuity of our ways' (92, 93).

The reader can, of course, question this passive participation that becomes most apparent when the voice speaks in the imperative. The use of the imperative is not a 'manipulation' of the reader. It is a straightforward command that polarizes the reader into questioning the voice's authority and into disobeying it as much as obeying it. Thus, 'Let us consider letters' invites the reader to consider 'the voices that try to penetrate before the last card is dealt and the days are over' (89, 90). It invites the reader to disobey and consider the 'wires and tubes [that] surround us to carry the voices' and to ask if 'to write letters [is] to send voices' (90). The reader is also invited to disobey and consider how his perception of others will change now that 'telephones ring' when for 'centuries the writing-desk has contained sheets fit percisely for the communication of friends' (90). 'Let us consider letters' is also 'let us consider voice.' The same invitation to disobedience lies in the command: 'Fix your eyes upon the lady's skirt; the grey one will do – above the pink silk stockings' (16). The reader fixes his questions on the voice as much as on the young man or the lady's skirt, whom 'one no longer sees so clearly' once she is on the pier (16). What is this voice that cannot see around a corner and is limited by a wall yet can penetrate another's mind and race back in time to 'the nineties ... the seventies ... the sixties ... the seventeenth century ... arrow-heads; Roman glass' (16)? The second-person narration can also be, then, a subtle invitation to explore from the passive standpoint. It can be an invitation that the reader may or may not wish or be able to accept. He or she may also react against it as if it were a tool for the manipulation of his or her mind, as occurs when 'mind prints upon mind indelibly' (43).

The impersonal 'one' covering both first and second person is, of course, a third or 'non'-person. Paradoxically, this pronoun functions to disrupt the association of reader and voice in the common standpoint that a narration *about* the third person presupposes. 'One' de-personifies or disfigures the 'personal' pronouns. It appears to provide a non-personal, objective standpoint *from* which the voice proceeds. It invites the reader to *observe* a displacement of discourse in space more than to follow an action as it unfolds in the shared time of telling. *Jacob's Room* is a narrative of movement, not of action. Woolf's 'polemical slogan, "Life tells no stories" ' is brought to the fore (Gloversmith 171).

The telling *about* the third person must be reversed if it is to tell a 'no-story' and this 'non-person' is an overwhelming 'no one.' The reader is also called upon to be a 'no one.' The reader is asked: 'Who shall deny that this blankness of mind, when combined with profusion, mother wit, old wives' tales, haphazard ways, moments of astonishing daring, humour and sentimentality – who shall deny that in these respects every woman is nicer than any man?' (9). This question can be answered only with a resounding 'No one' on the part of the reader (9). The voice, of course, immediately reverses the reader's answer with: 'Well, Betty Flanders, to begin with' (9). Characters are also 'no one.' In *Jacob's Room* the 'cat marches across the hearth-rug. No one observes her' (47). This 'no one' tells the reader: 'Nobody sees anyone as he is,' and the statement is as much an affirmation as a negation. The voice is nobody because it is everybody and between the two extremes the reader eternally vacillates.

The narrative voice is inextricably intertwined with its characters. It often attributes thoughts or opinions to a character only after developing them in its own way to a point that the reader is certain they belong to the voice itself. The transition between character and voice is at times almost imperceptible and at other times it suddenly emerges from behind a character's words. A paragraph begins: 'I like books whose virtue is all drawn together in a page or two. I like sentences that don't budge though armies cross them. I like words to be hard – such were Bonamy's views and they won him the hostility of those whose taste ...' (136). Just when the reader is certain that the first person belongs to the voice it is given over to Bonamy. The voice appears and disappears. It submerges in the character's discourse and then emerges to fill 'spaces of complete immobility [that separate] each of these movements' of character discourse (95–6).

The use of person, then, functions to disintegrate the experience of subjectivity presupposed by person. Person is disfigured and subjectivity displaced. The standpoint is shifted into an outer space of objectivity. The universality of the concept provides a standpoint from which to reflect upon the process of perception itself and upon the subject. In terms of a metaphorical perspective the direction is reversed. Here the voice reflects upon the semic field or 'collection of elementary constituents of a concept-entity' (Ricoeur 1977, 201). From the universality provided by a concept, the voice looks back through the disperse 'letters' of the semic field 'written when the dark presses round a bright red cave' (90). It looks past 'the diamond shaped wedge' at the centre of the narrative process and focuses on the 'task of reaching, touching, penetrating the individual heart' (163, 90). This direction of the narrating voice is the same direction followed by Mrs Norman's eyes when she loses sight of Jacob at Cambridge. Here 'her fellow-traveller was completely lost in her mind, as the crooked pin dropped by a child into the wishing-well twirls in the water and disappears for ever' (29). This is the direction the voice takes as it focuses on the 'opal-shelled crab' that slowly circles round the bottom of the baby's half-full bucket (12). This ironic direction is the 'something' that leaves the reader suspended and vibrating as he 'penetrates' to focus on language and perception in the self: 'But something is always impelling one to hum vibrating, like the hawk moth, at the mouth of the cavern of mystery, endowing Jacob Flanders with all sorts of qualities he had not at all – for though, certainly, he sat talking to Bonamy, half of what he said was too dull to repeat; much unintelligible (about unknown people and Parliament); what remains is mostly a matter of guess work. Yet over him we hang vibrating' (70). For both the narrative voice and the reader it is precisely a matter of guesswork. Guesswork is what lies at the primary level of understanding. As a narration from the third person the reader does share the voice's narrating direction. From beginning to end the reader stands behind the no one voice that echoes, 'One must follow hints, not exactly what is said, nor yet entirely what is done' (28) and 'One must follow hints, not exactly what is said, nor yet entirely what is done' (150).

The paradoxical nature of this no one voice telling 'no story' can also be seen at work in the facet of dramatization. Two directions are displayed, one at odds with the other. First, as mentioned above, the voice takes its place in the text not as a narrator but as a voice reflecting upon its own activity. This stance moves the voice away from its traditional act of story-telling and characterizes its function *between* the characters in the numerous spaces of 'complete immobility' that separate their 'movements' (95–6). It is not dramatized as a 'narrator' but as a musing voice itself. One such space opens between a segment in which Mrs Flanders is objectified as a 'pale blue envelope lying by the biscuit-box' and closes with: 'Mrs Flanders wrote letters; Mrs Jarvis wrote them; Mrs Durrant too' (88, 90). The voice muses and reflects upon its own activity: 'Masters of language, poets of long ages, have turned from the sheet that endures to the sheet that perishes, pushing aside the tea-tray, drawing close to the fire (for letters are written when the dark presses round a bright red cave), and addressed themselves to the task of reaching, touching, penetrating and individual heart. Were it possible!' (90). The end of chapter 6 sees the voice reflect upon the 'mind' and 'body' as if they were two separate and divergent entities: 'The body is harnessed to a brain. Beauty goes hand in hand with stupidity' (79). This reflection is itself placed between two sentences that mirror each other: 'The problem is insoluble' at the beginning and 'The problem is insoluble' at the end. The reflective, diaeretic quality that characterizes the voice becomes a basic principle underlying the zig-zag technique of narration. It is this alternating current of thought that moves the mechanism of the text. This diaeretic, reflective quality is also dramatized:

It seems that a profound, impartial, and absolutely just opinion of our fellow-
    creatures is utterly unknown.
Either we are men, or we are women.
Either we are cold, or we are sentimental.
Either we are young, or growing old ...
Such is the manner of our seeing. (69)

This diaeretic movement and conceptual reflection shifts *Jacob's Room* to 'the verge' of non-narrative (92).

The first direction of dramatization characterizes the voice, as voice, in the narration. The second direction of dramatization counteracts the first by moving the characters to the standpoint of the voice. The second chapter sees 'Elizabeth Flanders, of whom this and much more than this had been said and would be said' strewing meal for the chickens and bustling about the orchard (13). The orchard 'was a piece of Dods Hill enclosed' by neighbouring cottages (14). Here the direction of narration moves from character to character as each focuses on the central point provided by Mrs Flanders in the orchard. Thus, Mrs Cranch holds her mat 'for a moment suspended' while 'she observed [that is, spoke] to Mrs Page next door that Mrs Flanders was in the orchard' (14). The pendulum then swings the other way and 'Mrs Page, Mrs Cranch, and Mrs Garfit could see Mrs Flanders in the orchard' (14). The pendulum reaches George Garfit and then swings back as Mrs Garfit says to Mrs Cranch, 'Now she's going up the hill with little John' (15). A semi-circle of characters' views encloses Betty Flanders whose standpoint is slowly elevated as she goes up the hill. Now, Dods Hill is central to the text because 'no words can exaggerate the importance of Dods Hill. It was the earth; the world against the sky; the horizon of how many glances can best be computed by those who have lived all their lives in the same village' (14). Once at the top of Dods Hill, 'the entire gamut of the view's changes should have been known to her; its winter aspect, spring, summer and autumn' (15). These four major units of time underlie the voice's traditional standpoint that the character should have taken up but doesn't. From here, she looks back down into the semi-circle shape of the bay and 'the whole of Scarborough from one end to the other laid out *flat* like a puzzle' (15; emphasis added). Subtly the narration moves into the passive voice and the reader finds: 'It was observed how well the Corporation had laid out flower-beds' (15). First the voice takes a standpoint between the characters, second the characters take up the voice's standpoint.

The scope of the voice's vision also reflects a paradox. If scope is the degree to which the voice can bring parts into a consistent whole, then *Jacob's Room* inverts this facet. Here the voice makes a concerted effort to disintegrate even minimal semantic units. The major unity of the scope lies precisely in 'no one' and 'nothing': 'Nothing settled or stayed unbroken. Like oars rowing now this side, now that, were the sentences that came now here, now there, from either side of the table' (55). Chapters are broken into segments and these, in turn, into divergent themes. Paragraphs are broken by parenthetical reflections. A 'scrap of conversation' here or there is thrown back to the reader 'in broken half sentences' (123, 153). Names are also broken, inverted and reflected back upon themselves as with ' "Mrs Flanders" – "Poor Betty Flanders" – "Dear Betty – " 'or as with 'Cowan, Erasmus Cowan' (12, 39). By the end of the second page 'Jacob' has been broken into 'Jacob' six times and 'Ar-cher' quickly follows (6, 17). Of course, Jacob also 'feeds crows in Flanders' and Archer lies at the bottom of the sea (93). Even the interjection 'Oh!' is broken into 'Oh-h-h-h!' and then reduced to a simple 'O - h' (35, 132).

As mentioned above, mind and body are considered as divergent entities harnessed together. The scope is unlimited in the conceptual space of the mind but quite restricted within the perceptual potential of the body. Body and mind do not appear to function in synergetic unity. Perception is restricted to the limits of 'sight.' When the voice focuses on the birthplace of Western philosophy, it can move from the Acropolis to the 'plains of Troy,' past 'the uplands of Albania and Turkey,' over the 'great towns – Paris – Constantinople – London' and come to rest on the Cornish coast with the salt gale blowing into Betty Flanders's bedroom window (154, 156). The scope can also add depth to the height of the Acropolis and the breadth of Europe. It can enter into Charles Steele's mind just as he 'suspended his paint-brush' and it can read his thoughts to the reader: 'Here was that woman moving – actually going to get up – confound her!' (6). By contrast, when the voice takes up a position next to Jacob at the dinner table, its scope is quite limited. The voice gives only what can be perceived with 'the human eye' (78). Now it is limited to what falls within the frame of a window or a door. Here it looks past the others at the table, out the window, and onto the bay. The window frames the 'escallonia fishing-boats [that] seemed caught and suspended. A sailing ship slowly drew past the women's backs' from one corner of the frame to the other (55). When dinner is over, all get up, pass down the room, hesitate at the door and finally: 'All passed out at the open door' (56). The segment ends when the characters are no longer in view. The same occurs when Florinda is seen 'turning up Greek street upon another man's arm' and Jacob stands 'light drenched from head to toe. You could see the pattern on his trousers; the old thorns on his stick; his shoe laces; bare hands; and face' (91). The rest cannot be seen. It is obliterated by shadows that 'chequered the street' (91). The scope can see from Greece to England and read minds but cannot see past a door, around a corner, or into the dark. This scope is defined by the sense of sight, the concept, and the spatial pole of perception.

The voice is reliably unreliable. It is a consistent pendular swing back and forth between two extremes, each direction of which retraces and undermines the previous. After Jacob sees Florinda with another man, the page ends: 'He has turned to go. As for following him back to his rooms, no – that we won't do' (91). The reader turns the page only to find it begin: 'Yet that, of course, is precisely what one does. He let himself in and shut the door' (92). The reversals and reflections found in all facets of the narrative perspective are essential to undermining the action and allowing a narrative moment to develop. The effect of movement proceeds from this alternating current and eternal vacillat-ing between extremes. The subjectivity of 'person' is shifted to the objectivity of 'non person.' The reader has 'no one' to rely on. The scope's apparent omniscience is undermined by its limited visual sense perception and vice versa. Its function is reversed from that of gathering parts into a consistent whole to that of scattering the facets that con-stitute a unity. The voice does not fully report an action nor does it quite tell a story and therefore it cannot be said to play out cause-effect relations. What it does do is *display* the *effects* of Jacob, that is, the objects that are his property within the room. Each of these objects tells the story. The effects reflect Jacob, the 'one' who was the cause of their being brought into and arranged within the room. There are 'flags in a jar' and 'these half-sentences are like flags set on tops of buildings to the observer of external sights down below' (36, 47). There is a table and 'the sentences that came now here, now there, from either side of the table' (36, 55). There is a photo of his mother, ' "Dear Betty" – "she's very attractive still" ' and cards from societies: 'The little cards, however, with names engraved on them, are a more serious problem than the flowers' (12, 80). There are letters, of course, and 'photographs from the Greeks' and his slippers are 'like boats burnt to the water's rim' (36). All is seen by no one and told by one fibre that creaks in the wicker armchair (37, 151).

The standpoint of this voice lies not in the subjectivity of perception but in the outer space of concept and idea. Much like Sandra, it lies 'back in a trance' as she ranges the world 'in quest of adventure or a point of view' (149, 141). The process of perception – representation – illusion – hallucination is therefore also reversed. Betty Flanders 'had the illusion that the mast of Mr Connor's little yacht was bending like a wax candle in the sun. She winked quickly' (5). Jacob has the illusion that a rock is his Nanny and later the voice tells of a storm that spread over the sea 'jerking the stars above the ships this way and that' (8, 11). Whether the reader realizes 'our astonishing gift for illusion' or not is not the point: 'The point is, however, that we have been brought up in an illusion' (133). It is this reversal in direction that displays the semic field as 'letters strewn about' in disorder creating such 'confusion everywhere' (172, 173). The reader as 'observer is choked with obser- vations' and 'submerged in chaos' (66). He or she must construct a taxonomy – 'a system of classification which is simplicity itself' in order to overcome the chaos (66). The system, of course, is a seating ar- rangement that looks down into the parabolic structure of an 'amphi- theatre' (66). On one page, despite 'our astonishing gift for illusion,' Jacob finds 'what people have said appears to have sense in it' (133). The next page it is all 'nonsense … damned nonsense.' As the narrative nears an end, it looks into the parabolic cave of non-sense.

The temporal dimension of *Jacob's Room* is also split into directions at odds with each other. First, time is objectified by the objects in the room that tell the story of Jacob. No sequence can be expected because he 'left everything just as it was … Nothing arranged. All his *letters strewn* about for anyone to read' (172; emphasis added). The room looks back in time to its past occupancy by Jacob. In the final chapter the reader hears one 'fibre in the wicker arm-chair creak' (172) and looks back through his past reading to the middle of the text where he finds: 'The sitting room neither knew nor cared. The door was shut; and to suppose that wood, when it creaks, transmits anything save that rats are busy and wood dry is childish' (88). If the childish reader persists in his backward search, he will find the one fibre in the wicker arm-chair creak again in chapter 3 'though no one sits there' (37). More than the activity of rats is transmitted by the creaks in *Jacob's Room*. They are hints of presence in an emptiness. They transmit the movement of time from the objective present to a past subject now absent. It is the same retrospection in time that the voice follows when it enters the thoughts of the young man leaning against the railings (16). Retrospection in time is also brought to the fore when the reader realizes that events at the end of the text may be prior to those at the beginning. Reverend Floyd recognizes Jacob as he exits from Charter's shop in Piccadilly near the end of chapter 13 (170). This event, at the end of the text, is prior to Mr Floyd's search for Mrs Flanders's letter in chapter 2. Here, near the beginning, the voice notes: 'Meeting Jacob in Piccadilly lately, he recognized him after three seconds' (19–20).

The second direction of time points from the past to the present. The text moves from Jacob's childhood on the beach to his years of boyhood education, then on to his stay at Cambridge and finally his visit to Greece. As the narrative unfolds the passage of time becomes more precise. Units of time can be measured between, say, Jacob at age nineteen when he goes up to Cambridge, age twenty-five when he visits Miss Perry, and twenty-six in Athens (28, 99, 150). This is the direction the reader takes as he or she reads the text. The reader finds himself in much the same position as Mrs. Norman in the non-smoking carriage of the train. The reader also looks 'stealthily ... over the edge' of the printed page at Jacob, wonders how he is, and watches the scenery shift into the past where the train and the narration has already been (27, 28).

The duration of time begins as a slow pendular swing covering large units. As the narrative progresses the pendulum swings faster and covers shorter periods until it comes to a central point of rest in Jacob's room. The room is to be found, however, at the beginning, middle, and end of the text (36, 88, 172). The sequence from childhood, to youth, to adulthood covers nineteen years by the first two chapters, then only six years by mid-text, and only one year in the final chapters.

As the narration draws to a close, days take the place of years: 'This was on Monday. But on Wednesday he wrote' (145). Days change to: 'Ten minutes, fifteen minutes, half an hour – that was all the time before her' (154). Minutes are followed by: 'Now the agitation of the air ... Now it was dark. Now one after another lights were extinguished. Now great towns' (156). The minutes begin to race with the 'Gallop – gallop – gallop' of a horseless rider; the 'gilt clock at Verrey's [strikes] five' and when the master gunner's second hand points to six (that is, both dead centre and towards the reader), 'a target ... flames into splinters' (163, 164, 151). Jacob and Archer are dead. The narrative vibrates to a halt. The final chapter is the shortest in length and duration. It lasts the time between Bonamy's comment, 'He left everything just as it was,' and Mrs Flanders's reverberating question (172). Nevertheless, it is also the longest. All of the objects point back in time to the entire narration that is present in the room and Mrs Flanders's question echoes in the reader's mind long after the voice is silent.

The pendular swing of time comes to a rest at the end of the text, but the end is also the centre between the two extremes of its vacillating movement. The final lines of the narration find Betty Flanders exclaiming, 'Such confusion everywhere! ... [while] bursting open the bedroom door' (173). In the centre of the text Betty Flanders stands before Jacob's bedroom door and wonders: 'Better, perhaps, burst in and face it than sit in the antechamber listening to the little creak, the sudden stir, for her heart was swollen, and pain threaded it' (89). As early as chapter 3 the reader is given a tour of Jacob's room in Neville's court (36). The pendulum of narrative time vibrates to a rest at the beginning, middle, and end of the narrative yet it stops only once. Time, in *Jacob's Room*, is the 'perfect mastery of machinery' but it contains no future (151). *Jacob's Room* stands at the frontier of time and narrative. It is where space begins.

The narrative world of *Jacob's Room* is either the silent world of the written word or, for brief intervals, a noisy world of telephones and crowds. The telephone is, however, not a medium of audio-oral communication. It is another form of writing. Here one is 'doomed ... to write letters' or to '*send* voices' (90; emphasis added). The letter is 'venerable,' but the telephone only 'valiant' (90). It is with regret that the world turns from the written 'sheet that endures' to the spoken 'sheet that perishes' (90). Writing breaks free from the author's intended acts of communication and creates distance: 'Let us consider letters ... for to see one's own envelope on another's table is to realize how soon deeds sever and become alien' (89). The text begins with Betty Flanders first writing a letter, then reading, and only then speaking. It ends with Jacob writing letters from Greece.

The sense of sight plays the dominant role throughout the narrative. 'What does one fear?' the voice asks and then promptly answers 'the human eye' (78). It solidly affirms: 'Such is the manner of our seeing' (69). The reader is told: 'Fix your eyes' upon the young woman (16). He or she is not invited to listen but is 'choked with observations' (66). If the essence of light is 'to *make visible*,' visibility is the essence of the lights that burn in *Jacob's Room* (M.M-P. 1962, 426). A lamp burns in the forest and on Mrs Flanders's table. In Cambridge 'the lamp of learning' burns bright with Greek, science, and philosophy (37). During the day the sun shines 'dazzlingly ... like an eye upon the stirrups' (21). The vista of Scarborough is explained, 'laid out flat' from one end to the other by Mrs. Flanders's panoramic view, and George Plumer's cold 'grey eyes' have in them 'an abstract light' (15, 32).

Sound in the text is the pendular swing 'of a broom sweeping – sweeping,' but in *Jacob's Room* 'sound [spreads] itself flat' (95, 171). One sound is 'framed' by another as if it were something to be viewed: 'She heard [the thrush] more faintly. Beyond it was the humming of the wheels and the wind rushing' (115). It is more often than not 'the voice of the alarum clock,' a 'clatter,' a 'clamour,' or the 'whip cracking' that is heard (159, 144). The Parthenon stands in 'silent composure' while 'love songs *rasped* out to the strum of guitar and gramophone' (144; emphasis added). The bell that rings at the foot of Dods Hill carries 'Seabrook's voice – the voice of the dead' and with it Archer's 'voice mixed life and death inextricably, exhilaratingly' (14). This sound begins when the undertaker closes his 'eyes, the light so soon goes out of them' (14). Sound does not belong to people. Sound is either the chaotic noise of the street or the creak of an object in the room.

If each facet helps constitute a figure, the characters in *Jacob's Room* reverse the process. Here the voice consistently figures *facettes*. It is Jacob's 'face' that Mr Floyd recognizes in Piccadilly not his 'tall' figure of a 'fine young man' (170, 19). It is Jacob's face that the voice reads when he stands under the arch lamp and it is upon Jacob's face that Mrs Norman dwells (91, 28). Each character is a *facette* of the narrative world spread out in a parabolic crescent. The narrating voice sprinkles them with light and makes them visible.

Of the faces which came out fresh and vivid as though painted in yellow and

red, the most prominent was a girl's face. By a trick of the firelight she seemed
to have no body. The oval of the face and hair hung beside the fire with a
dark vacuum for background. As if dazed by the glare, her green-blue eyes
stared at the flames. Every muscle of her face was taut ... A whiskered face
appeared above her ... All this blazed up and showed faces far back, round,
pale, smooth, bearded, some with billycock hats on; all intent ... until the hiss
was like a swarm of bees; and all the faces went out. (71)

If the optical apparatus we call a 'lighthouse' can be defined as 'parabolic reflectors consisting of small facets of silvered glass,' then the
character world of *Jacob's Room* is such an apparatus.[4]

   The characters are developed in two contrary directions. First, they
can be seen to represent archetypes of different social roles. Mrs Flanders is the typical mother who sits up for her son when he is late in
returning from collecting moths. She is a 'sensible' woman whose qualities of 'wit, ... daring, humour and sentimentality' seem to summarize
womanhood in one sentence (9). She and Rebecca are 'the eternal
conspiracy of hush and clean bottles' (11). On the other extreme, far
from her 'blankness of mind,' is Bonamy (9). He is silent, secretive,
fastidious and has 'a taste [for] literature' and 'sentences that don't
budge' and 'hard words' (136). He has no trouble seeing 'the clear
division between right and wrong' because he is an intellectual (41).
Between the motherly woman and this intellectual *bon ami* are arranged
a semicircle of types. Mrs Jarvis and Sandra Wentworth Williams are
romantics in search of adventure and a point of view. Captain Barfoot
and the impassive policeman at Ludgate Circus are figures of manly
authority. Mrs Pascoe is all eyes. Mrs Papenworth is all ears. George
Garfit is the veteran and Mr Floyd the pastor. Timmy Durrant is a man
of science, Bonamy a man of letters. On each side of Jacob can be
placed Fanny Elmer who is all love and Florinda who has no mind but
plenty of beauty (76, 79). Jacob is the central character, but invisible
because the voice stands between him and the reader. This Clara Durrant discovers, when she starts: 'She saw Jacob. "Who?" asked Mrs
Durrant sharply ... But she saw no one' (170). Jacob's type in turn is
a 'no type.' Jacob has 'little sense of personal association' because, like
the voice, he is objectified (145). He is that 'silent young man' on the
other side of the voice (68). The same can be asked of Jacob as is asked
of Seabrook: 'Had he, then, been nothing? An unanswerable question'
(13).

   The second direction gives a hint of personality. This hint of presence echoes back to the reader when a character is mirrored by the narrative voice. The spectacular view presented by Mrs Flanders from the 'raised circle of the Roman camp' is mirrored by the voice as it swings across Europe from the height of the Acropolis (17). Betty is the 'whole of Scarborough' by day (15). The voice is the whole of Europe by night. Jacob's type is 'no hero.' He is the central and absent facet of the text. He stands central to the crescent and shares the same axis of voice and reader when the pendulum passes this centre. When the voice centres on Jacob it is often difficult to see where one begins and the other ends. Tell-tale objects create a space of transition in which a hint of personality reverberates and echoes back to the reader. Jacob muses over the 'kidney-shaped spots' on a moth's wings: 'The tree had fallen the night he caught it. There had been a volley of pistol-shots suddenly in the depths of the wood ... The tree had fallen, though it was a windless night, and the latern, stood upon the ground, had lit up the still green leaves and the dead beech leaves. It was a dry place. A toad was there. And the red underwing had circled round the light and flashed and gone' (21). When 'voices' sound 'gravely' and the organ replies 'wisely' in Cambridge, the narrative voice begins to reflect:

If you stand a lantern under a tree every insect in the forest creeps up to it – a curious assembly, since though they scramble and swing and knock their heads against the glass, they seem to have *no purpose* – something *senseless* inspires them. One gets tired of watching them, as they amble round the lantern and blindly tap as if for admittance, one large toad being the most besotted of any and shouldering his way through the rest. Ah, but what's that? A terrifying volley of pistol-shots rings out – cracks sharply; ripples spread – silence laps smooth over sound. A tree – a tree has fallen, a sort of death in the forest. (30; emphasis added)

This passage mirrors and inverts the order of the first. Both are the same but quite different. Jacob muses in the past perfect tense; the voice speculates in the present. Both narrate the same events and reflect each other. Both Jacob and voice are 'non-persons,' yet, a hint of personality echoes between the two. The former is patient, interested, and involved while the latter is analytical, distant, impatient, and uninvolved. Despite the differences there still is to be heard a faint note where it *is* Jacob that muses but the voice is also present and where the voice observes but Jacob's musing also lingers suspended. Both the words of Jacob and those of the voice 'hang close to the tree' (90).

They both lie 'sweet beneath the leaf' and at the close of the narrative, 'all the leaves seemed to raise themselves' and then quickly 'the leaves sank down again' (90, 172, 173). In that space opened beneath the leaves or pages, both voice and character intermingle.

The facet of role can also be divided in two directions. On the one hand, there are the active roles of the characters surrounding Jacob and, on the other, the passive role of Jacob himself. The active roles, in turn, form a divergent wedge that points to two extremes: Mrs Flanders and Richard Bonamy. The active roles are in keeping with the type represented. Thus, Mrs Flanders acts constructively to build a home for her children and Bonamy reads and analyses other characters. Bonamy falls 'into thought about Jacob's character' and then: 'Was Clara,' he thought ...'the silent woman? – would Jacob marry her?'' (136, 148). Mrs Flanders, by contrast, is seen struggling 'half-way between forty and fifty. Years and sorrow between them; the death of Seabrook, her husband; three boys; poverty; a house on the outskirts of Scarborough' (13). She is struggling to provide an 'example for the boys' (13). In the final chapter these two extremes are concentrated in the room. Bonamy begins to examine, analyse, and read bills, letters, and invitations. Betty Flanders bursts open the door, begins to collect Jacob's effects, and questions both Bonamy and the reader.

These active roles of intellect and sentiment are not central to the narrative, although they do meet in the centre. Action itself is mentioned only in terms of brutal and systematic killing, on land and sea. Ironically, a simple 'they say' links the destruction of war to civilization's greater achievements: 'These actions [of war] together with the incessant commerce of banks, laboratories, chancellories, and houses of business, are the strokes which oar the world forward, they say' (152).

Whoever 'they' may be, Jacob is not one of them. He is the passive role that is the 'cause' of the narrative act. It is Jacob's displacement from Cornwall to Scarborough to Cambridge, to London, France, Italy, and Greece, that the narrative follows, in its zig-zag pattern. Jacob smiles 'but said nothing' (59). He laughs so much but 'he could not speak' (48). The reader is warned that 'whether this is the right interpretation of Jacob's gloom ... it is impossible to say; for he never spoke a word' (47). He likes 'hearing' music but knows 'nothing about it' (86). He has 'nothing to fear' even though the 'whole of civilization was being condemned,' for he is 'unworldly,' 'gloomy,' and 'not much given to analysis' (108, 134, 81, 135). Jacob 'never asked himself' such questions as 'What for? What for?' (157). Jacob's role, like the letters his mother receives, is to tell 'really nothing that I want to know' (135). Jacob's role is a 'no role.' He is to do nothing but sit quietly on the other side of the voice to be painted and observed. The reader also finds himself sitting and quietly observing as the room is filled with observations 'enclosing vacancy' (151).

No one is privileged in the narrative world of *Jacob's Room* except the voice. The closer the characters come to the voice the more privileged they are. Betty Flanders and Bonamy fill Jacob's room with personality. Together, they enter into almost every facet of Jacob's world. Both receive letters from Jacob in Greece and the character of each is made evident by its views of Jacob. The 'only one of her sons who never obeyed her' reflects the mother, and 'the definite, the concrete and the rational' Bonamy is reflected when, as a friend, he falls into thought about Jacob (21, 142). Their proximity to the voice privileges them as extremes. Like the voice, Mrs Flanders is elevated to view the whole of Scarborough laid out like a map before her. Again, like the voice, Bonamy is 'fonder of Jacob than of anyone in the world' (136). His thoughts become constant, albeit unsteady, points of reference for seeing Jacob at Cambridge (136, 148, 160).

Between the two extremes of Bonamy and Mrs Flanders the privilege of the characters vacillates. Mrs Norman is a mother like Betty Flanders and she sees Jacob 'like her own boy' (28). Her thoughts give a concise report of Jacob's appearance as she sits 'opposite a strange young man in a railway carriage' (28). The voice reads her mind and finds that he is firm, youthful, indifferent, unconscious, nice, handsome, interesting, distinguished, and well-built. The reader is warned that one 'must do the best one can with her report' because it is self-reflective and unreliable (28). It is unreliable precisely because it is a consistent whole presented by a particular person: 'Nobody sees anyone as he is … They see a whole – they see all sorts of things – they see themselves … Mrs Norman now read three pages of one of Mr Norris's novels' (28). The voice reads Mrs Norman's thoughts and she, in turn, reads Jacob. She brings together all the parts of Jacob's character and reports a whole person. The voice, in turn, reverses the facet and *explains* that this *whole* is unreliable because it proceeds from but one *part* of the narrative world. The explanation disintegrates the whole. It moves from 'whole' to 'all sorts of things,' then to 'themselves,' then to 'Mrs Norman,' to 'three pages,' and finally *one* novel (28).

Timmy Durrant is a student like Bonamy but he is more distant from the voice. Neither his 'scientific' calculations of the 'exact time or day of the month' nor his knowledge of shipping impresses Jacob (45). Yet, like the 'no one' voice, Timmy Durrant is 'no sight for him, nothing to set against the sky and worship' and he gives 'no reason for Jacob to turn sulkey' (44, 45). Timmy Durrant's positivistic 'eye' brings out 'Jacob's gloom' (47). Jacob's character, as a whole 'figure,' is left incomplete until all of the *facettes* have been displayed. Jacob has neither full height nor width nor depth until the last sentence is read. Jacob has 'no privilege' until all of the particular characters and objects of the narrative world cast the whole silhouette of his absent figure against the wall of *Jacob's Room*. Each character and every object, then, has the privilege of being a facet in the 'exquisite' outline enclosing his 'character-drawing' (151).

The characters in the narrative world are as reliable as the narrative voice. Mrs Flanders is reliably constructive. She builds a world for her boys despite the loss of her husband. She is faithful to his memory and will not *think* of Mr Floyd's proposal: 'How could I think of marriage!' (18). Nevertheless, there is the thought of Captain Barfoot. Bonamy is another matter. He is an intellectual with a reflective mind. He knows right from wrong. A reversal in reliability is to be expected of him. Bonamy is 'fonder of Jacob than of anyone in the world' until he sits with Clara (136). Before long he wonders if Jacob will marry her and begins to feel a 'force rushing round geometrical patterns in the most senseless way in the world' (148). By the beginning of chapter 8 Bonamy feels the full force of his love for Clara Durrant and his bitterness towards Jacob. The voice sarcastically asks: 'How acquit Bonamy of sentimentality of the grossest sort; of being tossed like a cork on the waves; of having no steady insight into character; of being unsupported by reason, and of drawing no comfort whatever from the works of the classics?' (160). Gone is the definite, concrete, and rational *bon ami* of chapter 7.

Timmy Durrant also introduces a reversal into the narrative. His notebook and scientific observations reverse the direction of synergetic perception and experience in order to analyse it. Point by point he abstracts and explains a simple movement: 'The eyes fix themselves upon the poker; the right hand takes the poker and lifts it; turns it slowly round, and then, very accurately, replaces it. The left hand, which lies on the knee, plays some stately but intermittent piece of march music' (47). This analytical observation effectively reverses the direction of perception adopted by Jacob when he stands by the fire near St Paul's and watches its light reflect off faces suspended in the dark. Jacob, however, offers nothing to rely upon either. He is as reliable as the 'one' and 'no one' of the narrative voice. The reader finds himself in the vacillating swing between two extremes of reliability and unreliability. Beginning, middle, and end – there is 'no one' and nothing definite to rely on. In the experience of *Jacob's Room*, the reader is invited to find 'self reliance.' He or she cannot escape the fact that 'whether this is the right interpretation of Jacob's gloom ... it is impossible to say; for he never spoke a word' (47). It is the *reader* who is invited 'to step somewhere, to his room presumably ... – fill in the sketch as you like' (92–3). *Jacob's room* is a narrative of space. It is an empty space full of objects and a hint of presence in the one creaking fibre of a wicker armchair. It is precisely this one tell-tale creak that, as any sound, can fill 'Jacob's Room' and echo from wall to wall. This one vibrating sound is loudest and echoes strongest when Jacob's memory and the voice's speculation reflect a hint of each other's person. If the reader moves to 'the verge of the marsh' on the very edge of the narrative world, Jacob will be found writing corrections in Morris's book on insects (92, 21). Jacob's recollection begins, 'The tree had fallen,' then moves to the central echo, 'it creaked – creaked ... and creaked again,' and ends in conjunction with the segment at 'she said.' The recollection is one continuous display of dichotomies: inside, out; up, down; light, dark; silence, noise; peace and violence.

Eight events, or rather facets, can be seen at work displaying a spatial configuration that appears to underlie the text as a whole. Each event is a facet in the narrative whole that can itself be divided into four movements. Each movement is a display of counterpoint vacillation between foreground and background. The first movement begins with Jacob walking from the dark 'marshy places' and dark moors to the lighted room (21). The second movement bypasses a mowing-machine *turning* under Jacob's window, then slips through the window into the room and penetrates a box within the four walls of the room. The third movement brings about a complete reversal. The movement from a general setting to a particular box changes to a movement from the particular box to the general setting of the moors. The fourth movement comes to rest on an elevated platform that looks to a world below. With these four movements in mind the whole of the narrative segment can be analysed in terms of its eight facets or points (P).

The passage as a whole begins some time late at night in a marshy place with a foreground defined by the circle of light cast out by Jacob's lamp placed low on the ground. Jacob stands in the dark looking into the circle of light. Only what is available to the character's eye is available to the reader. All foregrounded objects are placed low on the ground: leaves, a toad, a lamp and, of course, the tree itself, which has fallen to the ground. No cause is given for the tree's having fallen. It was a 'windless night' and the 'volley of pistol-shots' is more probably the tree cracking than thunder from lightning. What is provided then, is a 'no-cause.' There is only an *effect* that 'causes' the reader to speculate. A moth appears suddenly from the darkness into the light, flashes, and is gone. The background is the dark forest, while Jacob stands waiting between the dark of the forest and the light of the lamp. This facet, or P1, in the parabolic figure on page 221 below, takes place outdoors.

The next facet (P2) begins after twelve with a movement by Jacob from the dark background, outside, progressively into the lighted room inside. He stands mid-way between the dark marsh and moors behind him, looking in at his mother who is actively passive. She is 'sitting up' but 'playing patience' (21).

The third facet (P3) begins with Jacob moving from the dark outside into the light inside just as suddenly as the moth that flashed into the lamplight. He enters so suddenly that he frightens his mother and wakes Rebecca. The succession of events in this first movement is guided by dichotomies of space and sight: out to in, out to in, dark to light, dark to light. A subtle change comes about near the end of this third facet that indicates a change in movement. The direction of viewing Jacob reverses and is directed back upon itself. At this point, where Jacob stands 'in the hot room, blinking at the light' the reader sits next to Betty Flanders and looks out to 'the depths of darkness' from which he has come (21). A change in direction has been brought about. It is now from in to out; from light to dark. A movement has been achieved between two extremes.

The second movement begins with an answer to a question that has not been asked in the text. Nor is there any indication that it is Jacob who gives the answer, for it might also be the narrating voice. Narrator and character begin to reflect each other and a transition in space and time takes place. It is no longer night but day. Light is now outside and dark inside. The answer is presented in the room where Jacob now sits, analysing the different facets of a moth with the help of Morris's book. The fourth facet (P4) of the parabolic figure below is opened when this inside drops quickly into the background and the outside is foregrounded. Barnet's mowing-machine is now personified and an adverb of constant time introduced: 'The mowing-machine always wanted oiling' (21). The whole machine 'creaked – creaked and rattled ... and creaked again' as the whole narrative turns 'under Jacob's window' (21). Barnet retraces Jacob's steps in the opposite direction and, of course, now it is day. He quickly drops into the background and a voice from 'no where,' belonging to 'no one' mixes the present and the past by mixing adverb and tense: 'Now it was clouding over' (21). Light moves to dark as the sun is clouded and then 'back came the sun dazzlingly' (21). The outside then drops into the background and the direction of light moves from outside to inside 'like an eye' that passes over the stirrups, through the window, upon the bed, upon the clock and penetrates the open butterfly box. The narrative seems to become a Chinese box within a box within the four corners of the globe. The succession of events surrounding P4 and the second movement is brilliant. It sparkles with light and dark. The display of foreground and background moves inside-outside-inside and the light flashes from *dark* in the room to *light* outside to *dark* under the cloud to 'dazzlingly' *bright* and then back into *dark*. The narrative truly grows 'trimly in the diamond-shaped wedge as the gardener had planned it' (163). Such is the movement of Barnet.

The fifth facet (P5) begins the third movement. It is as sudden as was Jacob's entry into the room in the third facet. The direction of the fifth facet is, however, the opposite of that in the third. Here it is not Jacob who enters the room but the voice that flies from the box, out of the window, and onto the moors. Here, what was the background of the first movement, that is, the moors, becomes the foreground of the fifth. The room, in turn, falls into the background. A complete reversal reflects the first movement: moors to room becomes room to moors. Box, room, window, house, and garden are left behind. Space is inverted, turned upside-down as is a face when seen in a parabolic mirror. The fifth facet is this movement of sudden change from the dead butterflies of the box to the flurry of clouded yellows 'eight miles from home' (20).

The sixth facet (P6) follows the flurry of butterflies as they 'zigzagged' low across the purple clover (21). The horizontal displacement of the first movement – out, to in, to out – now becomes a vertical displacement from down on the 'clover,' to up on the 'hedgerows,' to down on the 'turf,' then up to a hawk on high then down to 'a hollow ... beneath a ruin,' and finally follows 'a white admiral circling higher and higher round an oak tree' which is never caught (22). If facets P1 and P2 are limited to what can be perceived through the sense of sight, facets P5 and P6 are not limited. If facet four gives an answer, facet six begs a question: Who saw the hawk drop the bloody entrails?

The seventh facet (P7) moves 'miles away from home' (22). Jacob is low in a hollow watching the white admiral. It does not flash into the light of a lamp placed beside a fallen beech tree but circles higher and higher up a standing oak. The direction of the gaze is from low to high, following the helix drawn by the insect as it moves away from the central character of the text.

The high-flying admiral leads to the final movement. Jacob, who stands in the hollow under a ruin, drops into the background and facet P8 foregrounds a character 'living alone, high up' (22). This final facet stands separate from the rest in that it foregrounds not the old woman herself but her specific function. Again, it is neither butterflies flashing like signs strewn over a semic field, nor is it a character sitting in a room or standing in a hollow that becomes foregrounded. The old woman, who stands opposite Barnet and his creaking mowing-machine in facet four, *tells* stories *to* Jacob. She addresses a character in the narrative world, not the reader without. Temporal considerations now replace spatial dichotomies. As in facet P4, the past tense replaces the past perfect tense of P1 to P3 and P5 to P7. Here it is a definite and constant time of 'every summer' and 'always sees' in counterpoint with an intermittent and indefinite 'sometimes' (22). The passage here comes to its temporal closure. It has moved in succession from 'late' to 'after twelve,' to day to 'early morning,' and finally to 'at dawn' (21, 22). The clock moves backwards. It is not the time of experience, that is, from morning to noon to midnight. It is that of the concept: from night back through the day to early morn and on to dawn. Facets P8 and P4 both deal with a universal concept of time; an 'always' wanting oil and 'always [seeing] two badgers' (22).

The universal time of the narrating voice, then, appears to emerge *from* the spatial play of foreground and background. The characters in the narrative world are directed 'from the particular to the universal' (149). The voice, by contrast, stands 'vibrating, like the hawk moth, at the mouth of the cavern of mystery' that is language at the core of the text (70). The voices's gaze is directed from the universality of the concept down into the centre of the narrative world. The movement of the text back and forth, horizontally between extremes, corresponds with a vertical movement. The vertical movement runs in two directions, each at odds with the other. The direction of the characters and the narrative world is inductive, proceeding from a small point on the Cornish coast to Scarborough, Cambridge, London, France, Italy, and the universality of Greek architecture. The narrative voice, by contrast, slowly moves from a universal 'one' and 'no one' at the outset to take on the particular personality of a definite person. At the end of the text the reader knows the voice as well as Jacob.

Time and space are inseparable. While the inductive and deductive directions of character and voice move vertically, the pendulum of time sways ever faster. As it vibrates faster the horizontal crescent grows shorter and shorter, concentrating the narrative space. The 'racing star' at the end of chapter 11 covers Cornwall, Scarborough, Greece; then races back to London and Cornwall; then swings back to Greece and finally rests in the middle of *Jacob's Room*. WIth each swing of the pendulum another facet is added to the character-sketch of Jacob. With each swing the voice stands out more clearly as a character in the text. At the end of the text the narrative voice does not jump into the narrative world. On the contrary, its silhouette and that of Jacob's step out as *one* from the text's very centre: 'Can I never know, share, be certain?' (90). Yet, is this silhouette any different from that of the reader. Is his or her question not 'How does [life'] bring to light meanings capable of being taken up and understood by another historical being, who overcomes his own historical situation' (Ricoeur 1974, 5)? The text as a whole is a parabolic structure 'strewn' around this central question. It moves first from the Cornish coast to Cambridge. The second movement vibrates and hovers over chapters 7 and 8. Here we find: 'Let us consider letters' and these letters are in *Jacob's Room*, 'there under the lamp' (89, 88). The third movement takes the narrative to 'Olympia,' a 'feeling for architecture,' and 'the problems of civilization' (137, 145). The fourth movement belongs to the reader for it takes place in 'all high souls' (137). The central question of the text is the question of Jacob and is the question of the reader.

Who are the readers of Jacob's Room? Surely Bonamy, for he reads Keats, and Timmy Durrant pouring over his notebook of scientific observations is also a reader (41, 47). They are not real readers, however. Mrs Norman is a real reader. At the beginning of the text, she reads 'half a column of her newspaper; then stealthily [looks] over the edge to decide the question of safety by the infallible test of appearance' (27). She ponders, thinks, muses, and then reads another 'three pages' (28). Then she peers at Jacob over the edge of her novel and notes 'his

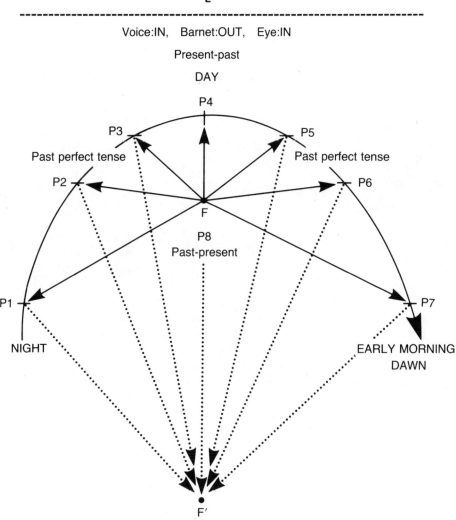

Figure 3 Parabolic Space of *Jacob's Room*: A
P = the succession of narrated facets
L = Letters, the text
F = the standpoint of the suspended voice on high
F′ = the standpoint of the reader

P1

Limited to sense perception

Foreground: inside a circle of light,
low on the ground;
a fallen beech tree

Background: outside a circle, dark
marshy places

P7

Background: home and moors
miles away

Foreground: Jacob low in a hollow,
an oak tree standing;
a butterfly spiralling
up tree

P2

Foreground: Mrs. Flanders; a
lighted room inside

Background: Jacob crossing a dark
lawn; outside (after
12:00)

P6

Background: inside/outside; Jacob

Foreground high/low butterflies.
Not limited to
perception (that is,
Who dropped the
bloody entrails?)

P3

Foreground: Jacob in light, inside
Background: dark moors

P5

Background: inside, butterfly box
Foreground: the moors

P4

Foreground: Barnet turns mowing-
machine under Jacob's
window; answer
creates questions:
Who? Where? When?
Why?

Background: Mrs Flanders

P8

Foreground: old cottage woman
high up and alone;
telling of butterflies

Background: Jacob

Present-past:
'Now it *was* clouding over'

Past-present:
'And if you look*ed* ... you could
always see'

Figure 4 Parabolic Space of *Jacob's Room*: B

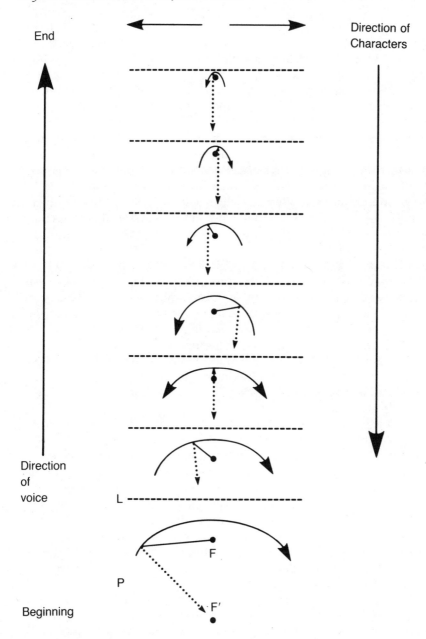

Figure 5 Movement in *Jacob's Room*

indifference' (28). Before she knows it she is in Cambridge and Jacob 'bursts' open the door. At the end of the narrative, Jacob is also a real reader. He finds 'a drum of marble conveniently placed, from which Marathon could be seen' (146). He reads and stops to think about how countries should be ruled: 'And he read again ... And then looking up and seeing the sharp outline, his meditations were given an extraordinary edge ... Jacob read on again ... Jacob wrote ... Jacob got up' (146). What are the characters reading? Do they read the texts they hold or do they look up to read the first-order world around them? What is the reading experience of *Jacob's Room*? Is it the literal first order that is suspended in order to allow a *metaphorical* world to emerge or is it the opposite? How often does the reader not look up in amazement from *Jacob's Room* and ask, 'What for? What for' (157)? Is it not precisely the *poetic* world that is suspended in order to observe the chaos of the *literal* world and in order to reflect upon the process of perception itself and then, finally, to penetrate through discourse to a 'non-sense' found at the very core of mankind? Is it not the metaphorical world that is suspended? Does the reader not look from the *illusion* of a standpoint 'living alone, high up' down at an *ironic* world in disarray and disintegration that looks 'like two boys fighting' (22)? Who is the reader of *Jacob's Room*? Who will answer the question it recommends?

Throughout the narrative, the voice insists upon the reader taking a passive role. He or she is to observe, *no* questions asked. The reader's active role is suspended. The voice asks the questions and answers them. It gives the 'points of view' and changes them. 'Though the opinion is unpopular' it voices it anyway, and then changes it (140). It makes a point and then replies 'with something quite off the point' (140). It speaks into the world of the text and answers to its own echo. Here the narrative stands on the frontier of a lyrical poem where the 'poet, so to speak, turns his back on his listeners, though he may speak for them and though they may repeat some of his words' (Frye 250). The reader is suspended. In *Jacob's Room* the reader is left 'out of the picture' and in this he and she coincide with Jacob's silhouette.

From the outset, however, my point has been that this *is* a narrative, a parabolic narrative and, as a narrative, it must partake not only of the diaeretic, disjunctive, zigzag structure of ironic distanciation but also of an assimilating, conjunctive, grasping together of its scattered parts. It will be recalled that a parable offers 'no' explanation. On the contrary, the disciples demand: 'Explain to us the parable of the weeds of the field' (Matt. 13:36). When Jacob is himself faced with a painting, does the reader not find: ' "A pretty solid piece of work," said Jacob, straddling his legs in front of it. "But what I wish you'd explain ..." ' (123). If, as a parable, the text is to reveal a moral dimension, this dimension is not found in the narration itself. The moral dimension towards which every echo off the walls of *Jacob's Room* is directed is the reader's *awareness* of his or her self.' Every facet of the text reflects an awareness of his and her own activity as a reader. By taking the reader's role away, it is revealed to him and her. The reader, although outside the narrative world, still stands on the same axis as the narrative voice. That voice *strews* words as if leaves across the page. These the reader gathers up through his understanding, through his grasping the parts together. The voice gives *distentio*; the reader gives *intentio*. The text gives a diaeretic succession of spatial events; the reader gathers them in the 'Now' of his or her reading. In this way the final question, 'What am I to do with these, Mr. Bonamy?,' can be answered. If the reader has presumed that the text will end 'in an invitation to step somewhere, to his room, *presumably*,' his or her reply will quite probably be 'off the point' (92, emphasis added; 140). The 'somewhere' he and she are invited to step is quite clear: 'She held out a pair of Jacob's old shoes' (173). *Jacob's Room* gives us a *display* of the brilliance that is language. The reader is invited to wait with Mrs Flanders for Jacob's appearance, for when Jacob appears so does the reader. The reader is invited to 'play patient,' sit up with his *'attentive mind'* and observe the wandering voice (St Augustine, quoted in Ricoeur 1984, 1:20). It is the reader who must provide this attentive mind, the *intentio* that is the muthos of the narration. The moral of the story is the *care* with which the reader reads the text. It is from this reading full of care that each reader, as an individual, makes sense of its 'non-sense.' With care each reader reveals 'Jacob' and the 'voice' and the 'self' through discourse. What can be appropriated is precisely the reader's 'subjective activity' through the 'objective movement' of the text. If the 'responsible' reader truly *cares* about the world at which he 'stealthily [looks] over the edge' of the written page, he or she will surely know what to do with Jacob's empty shoes. When and where the responsible reader realizes this fullness of care for the world, then and there is the moral revealed; then and there the final movement complete. The reader, I believe, is for the text a myth of its assimilation.

Concluding Considerations

A few decades ago, Scholes and Kellogg wrote concerning point of view in narrative: 'In the relationship between the teller and the tale, and that other relationship between the teller and the audience, lies the essence of narrative art' (240). Recently a third relationship has been added: that between the audience and the sign system of the tale. These relationships are neither static nor without direction. Audience, teller, and tale provide different points of departure for the interplay of facets that reveals narrative perspective. A change in one relationship will have repercussions on the other two as well. Taken in its most general sense, the relationship between the teller and the tale is more than a matter of voice and story. It is also a history of narrative production as a mode of world appropriation. Between the teller and the audience can be found a history of reception and the different modes of narrative appropriation today. The relationship between the audience and the tale cannot be characterized by a systematic analysis of narrative techniques and strategies alone. The audience and tale are also mediated by an art of reading and listening, an art of posing questions and proposing answers.

Narrative perspective is the essence of this art. While its relationships are in many ways different from our everyday dealings with life in general, this essence cannot be divorced from the process of language, perception, and experience through which different concepts of its uniqueness emerge. Narrative perspective is realized in language and language is our very mode of being in the world. Narrative perspective offers a channel for language to express itself creatively between audience, teller, and tale. The essential relationships of narrative perspective give rise to awareness, an awareness of the world, an awareness of another mode of being in the world, and a self-awareness. In this narrative perspective is intertwined with perception. The perception of a text, both in its production and reception, cannot be independent of our everyday 're-creation or re-constitution of the world at every moment' precisely because it is such a re-working of a world (M.M-P. 1962, 207). Narrative perspective, then, also offers new and renewed channels for awareness and world creation and re-creation. Finally, the interplay of facets will give rise to an experience that cannot be defined or limited to any one of the parts. The experience to which narrative perspective gives rise is greater than the sum of audience, teller, and tale because it is a dynamic interplay of relations between them. It refuses to be enclosed within a neat definition. In this respect it plays an essential role in appropriation and offers a guarantee against stagnation in opinion. Narrative perspective offers a medium through which the understanding and explanation of a text's mimesis and mu- thos can make of experience an offering to a tradition and community at large. These experiences we offer proceed from different points of departure. One may depart from the work in the world, another from the symbolic dimension of the text, and still another from the reader. The points of departure and the directions taken do not vary only out of individual desire but in answer to the needs of tradition. The needs of tradition cannot be answered by filling a lack or gap alone. What is provided by a tradition must also be esteemed and celebrated if it is to continue mediating past, present, and future. Narrative perspective, then, also contributes a medium through which to exchange experience in the celebration of texts (Valdés 1987, 89).

With this mediating principle in mind I have offered both questions and tentative answers concerning narrative perspective. It is also with this exchange of experience in mind that I have presented a reading of *Cien años de soledad* and *Jacob's Room*. In degrees of difference each text can be understood as a generative pole in the dynamic process that is narrative. The narrative perspective of each can be played out by inclining towards question or answer, reaching out to the world or reversal, ear or eye, assimilation or distanciation. If the narrative per- spective I have played out in *Cien años de soledad* hears the magnetic figure of Melquíades proclaim at the top of his voice, 'Las cosas tienen vida propia ... todo es cuestión de despertarles el ánima,' then it also sees the brilliant display of objects in *Jacob's Room*, each with its tale to tell, each animating the figure of an absent person (59). As an expe- rience, *Cien años de soledad* is nothing less than 'el diamante más grande del mundo' and *Jacob's Room* 'the diamond-shaped wedge as the gardener had planned it' (74, 163). The essence of these diamonds mediates similarity as well as difference. If the concentrated pressure of time and space from which diamonds are born can be proven the trick of a hustler or pest, and if 'fiction' can be proven totally independent of the phenomenology that expresses the linguistic and moral substance of our being, then I too shall believe in narrative perspective as something divorced from our everyday life and the heritage we share in common. Until so proven, I gaze in wonder at the 'diamante más grande del mundo' and listen in awe to those echoes from the cavern of mystery that is language. In this 'la concentración implacable' of colonel Aureliano Buendía also awards me 'la paz del espíritu' (245). To this end I play the facets of narrative perspective. Thus I respond to 'What for? What for?' Thus I find revealed 'Who cares? Who cares?'

Notes

1 The term hermeneutics or interpretation used in a broad sense is not limited to the 'classical discipline concerned with the art of understanding texts,' but forms 'part of a process of coming into being of meaning, in which the significance of all statements – those of art and those of everything else that has been transmitted – is formed and made complete' (Gadamer 1975, 146). Hermeneutics, then, is the art of understanding and Gadamer goes on to clarify: 'All understanding is interpretation, and all interpretation takes place in the medium of a language' (350).

   Central to Gadamer's development of hermeneutics as understanding and interpretation is the notion of appropriation or assimilation (*Aneignung*): 'When we are concerned with the understanding and interpretation of linguistic texts, interpretation in the medium of language itself shows what understanding always is: assimilation of what is said to the point of making it become one's own. Linguistic interpretation is the form of all interpretation, even when what is to be interpreted is not linguistic in nature, ie [*sic*] is not a text, but is a statue or a musical composition ... [These forms] in fact presuppose language' (360). Both Paul Ricoeur and Robert Weimann develop this fundamental notion of appropriation. For Ricoeur it is a dispossession of the narcissistic ego and a repossession of the self as well as making one's own a foreign mode of being in the world (Ricoeur 1981a, 182–93). For Weimann it is 'the imaginative appropriation of the world and the nature of one's existence in it' (Weimann 1976, 9).

2 Gadamer's hermeneutics is a 'linguistic approach' to the issue of understanding as interpretation. Nevertheless, this approach is not to be

confused with a modern, empirical science of language that parts from Ferdinand de Saussure's concern for *langue*. While hermeneutics and semantics might be said to share a common point of departure, semantics 'appears to describe the range of linguistic facts externally, as it were, and does so in a way that has made possible the development of a classification of types of behavior [*sic*] with respect to these signs ... Hermeneutics, in contrast, focuses upon ... the internal process of speaking, which if viewed from the outside, appears as our use of the world of signs' (Gadamer 1972, 82–3).

3 Merleau-Ponty responds to the opening question, 'What is phenomenology?' with the following explanation: "Phenomenology is the study of essences; and according to it, all problems amount to finding definitions of essences: the essence of perception, or the essence of consciousness, for example. But phenomenology is also a philosophy which puts essences back into existence, and does not expect to arrive at an understanding of man and the world from any starting point other than ... "facticity." It is a transcendental philosophy which places in abeyance the assertions arising out of the natural attitude, the better to understand them; but it is also a philosophy for which the world is always "already there" before reflection begins – as an inalienable presence; and all its efforts are concentrated upon re-achieving a direct and primitive contact with the world, and endowing that contact with a philosophical status. It is the search for a philosophy which shall be a "rigorous science," but it also offers an account of space, time and the world as we "live" them. It tries to give a direct description of our experience as it is, without taking account of its psychological origin and the causal explanations which the scientist, the historian or the sociologist may be able to provide ... The reader pressed for time will be inclined to give up the idea of covering a doctrine which says everything, and will wonder whether a philosophy which cannot define its scope deserves all the discussion which has gone on around it, and whether he is not faced rather by a myth or a fashion.

Even if this were the case, there would still be a need to understand the prestige of the myth and the origin of the fashion, and the opinion of the responsible philosopher must be that *phenomenology can be practiced and identified as a manner or style of thinking, that it existed as a movement before arriving at complete awareness of itself as a philosophy'* (1962, vii–viii).

CHAPTER 1 Language of Experience

1 Ricoeur 1981, 70. The term *wirkungsgeschichtiches Bewusstsein* has also been translated as 'effective-historical consciousness.' See Gadamer 1975, 305ff.

2 Reiner Wiehl explains Gadamer's concept of a hermeneutic ontology as a 'multiplicity of histories of interpretations' of Being, and as the 'manifold histories of understanding Being' (466). This historically shaped interpretive thinking about Being, according to Wiehl, 'defines itself as a universal ontology of experience and language' (468).

3 Gadamer shares this essential notion with Wilhelm von Humboldt but it is important not to confuse Gadamer with 'American relativism, derived from Humboldt ... [that presents] a new spirit of empirical research, according to which the different languages are so many different images of the world and perspectives on the world, and none can escape that particular image and that particular schematisation within which he is imprisoned' (1975, 493). Gadamer clarifies that the 'modern philosophy of man, in its confrontation with Nietzsche, has worked out the special position of man and shown that the linguistic constitution of the world is far from meaning that man's relationship to the world is imprisoned within a linguistically schematised habitat' (402). He goes on to state that the 'variety of these views of the world does not involve any relativisation of the "world" ' (406). Each linguistic view of the world, according to Gadamer, has the potential 'to understand, from within itself, the "view" of the world that is presented in another language' (406).

4 Gadamer's notion of a common language may share certain characteristics with a sociolinguist's concept of 'speech community,' yet it cannot be equated to this concept. Gadamer returns to Aristotle's *Politics* in order to state that 'language, in its nature, is the language of conversation, but it acquires its reality only in the process of communicating. That is why it is not a mere means of communication.

'For this reason invented systems of artificial communication are never languages. For artificial languages, such as secret languages or systems of mathematical symbols, have no basis in a community of language or life, but are introduced and applied only as means and tools of understanding. This is the reason that they always presuppose a living process of communication, which is that of language. The convention by means of which an artificial language is introduced necessarily belongs, as we know, to another language. In a real community of language, on the other hand, we do not first decide to agree, but are already in agreement, as Aristotle showed' (1975, 404–5).

This notion does not coincide with, say, Joshua A. Fishman's definition of 'speech community': 'Speech community (a term probably translated from the German *Sprachgemeinschaft*), like variety, is a neutral term. Unlike other societal designations it does not imply any particular size nor any particular basis of communality. A speech community is one, all of whose members share at least a single speech variety and the norms for its appropriate use. A speech community may be as small as a single closed interaction network, all of whose members regard each other in but a single capacity' (232). Fishman is quick to point out that neither of these conditions is necessarily typical of all speech communities studied by sociolinguists. Slight similarity to Gadamer's notion based on Aristotle might be found in Fishman's observation that 'one of the characteristics of large and diversified speech communities is that some of the varieties within their verbal repertoires are primarily experientially acquired and reinforced by dint of actual verbal interaction within particular networks, while others are primarily referentially acquired and reinforced by dint of symbolic integration within reference-networks which may rarely or never exist in any physical sense. The "nation" or "region" are likely to constitute a speech community of this latter type and the standard ("national") language or the regional language is likely to represent its corresponding linguistic variety' (233). While it might be said that both linguist and philosopher are concerned with the 'density of communication or/and symbolic integration' made possible by language, each approaches this common ground from different directions and different points of departure (Fishman 234).

5 Gadamer's understanding of the relation between language and world is closer to that of Humboldt than to that of Saussure. While all agree that the nature of language is arbitrary. Gadamer differs from Saussure in his attitude towards tradition. Saussure opposes the arbitrary nature of the linguistic sign (that is, the arbitrary relation within the linguistic sign of the *signifiant* or acoustic image and the *signifié* or conceptual substance) to the concept of tradition. Freedom lies within arbitrariness and is restricted by tradition: 'La puissance *temps* vient mettre en échec à chaque instant la puissance qu'on peut appeler *arbitraire* <(libre choix)>' (1:164, col. 6), and again, 'cela n'empêche pas qu'il n'y ait dans le phénomène total un lien entre ces deux facteurs antinomiques: la convention arbi-traire en vertu de laquelle le choix est libre, et le temps, grâce auquel le choix se trouve fixé. C'est parce que le signe est arbitraire qu'il ne

connaît d'autre loi que celle de la tradition, et c'est parce qu'il se fonde
sur la tradition qu'il peut être arbitraire' (1:165, col. 1).

Gadamer follows Humboldt in also affirming that the 'might of language'
puts in check the 'power of the individual' (1975, 399, and Humboldt
63–4). Nevertheless, Gadamer points out that in each unique realization
of language a whole tradition, world-view, or attitude is implied and this
attitude towards our surroundings or habitat enables us to have a world
(1975, 250–1, 402–3). Again, it is this universal capacity to have an attitude
towards the 'world' or environment that offers humanity freedom from
the animal condition of being locked within an immediate surrounding or
'habitat' (1975, 402, 403). Tradition, then, also offers humanity a fundamental freedom. Gadamer argues as well that while 'we stand always
within tradition,' tradition, understood as preservation, 'is as much a freely-
chosen action as revolution and renewal' (1975, 250). Tradition may limit
the power of the individual but it also offers humanity a fundamental
freedom.

Saussure, then, parts from the arbitrary nature of the sign and moves
away from the philosophical notion of tradition. Gadamer, by contrast,
directs the human sciences towards tradition. In this way Saussure
dismisses the biblical account of humanity's linguistic relation to the world
while Gadamer directs his attention towards it (1:147–9, col. 6). Gadamer
understands Genesis (chapters 2 and 11) as offering a profound account of
the human freedom from which arbitrariness stems. Thus, '[our] freedom from the habitat is also freedom in relation to the names that we give
things, as stated in the profound account in Genesis, according to which
Adam received from God the authority to name creatures.

'Once we realise the full importance of this it becomes clear why man,
as well as having a general linguistic relationship to the world, also has
a wide variety of different languages. Man's freedom in relation to the
habitat is the reason for his free capacity for speech and also for the
historical multiplicity of human speech in relation to the one world. When
myth speaks of a primal language and the creation of a confusion of
languages, this idea reflects meaningfully the real dilemma that the multiplicity of languages presents for reason, but in what it says this mythical
account turns things on their head when it conceives the original unity of
mankind in the use of an original language later sundered in a confusion
of languages. The truth is that because man is always able to rise above
the particular habitat in which he happens to find himself, and his
speech brings the world into language, he is, from the beginning, free
for a variety in the exercise of his capacity for language' (1975, 402–3).

This appeal to a biblical interpretation is in keeping with hermeneutics as a tradition. While older forms of hermeneutics such as St Augustine's *De Doctrina Christiana* grew out of the need to explain the Bible, Gadamer turns the older form 'on its head' and uses the Bible to explain hermeneutics. I follow his example in the section 'Hablar – Parler ...' in chapter 5 below.

6 In Joseph H. Greenberg's edition of the 1961 Conference on Language Universals held at Dobbs Ferry, New York, Charles F. Hockett states that every human language has learnability. He proposes that a speaker of one language can learn another language probably because of 'Tradition. The conventions of a language are passed down by teaching and learning, not through the germ plasm' (Hockett in Greenberg 1966, 13, 11). While Gadamer certainly shares this view with the linguists, it is important not to include Gadamer in the empirical tradition to which both Greenberg and Hockett belong. The 'Memorandum Concerning Language Universals' that Greenberg prepared in collaboration with Charles E. Osgood and James J. Jenkins states: 'This study of language universals is intimately connected with the establishment of scientific laws in the linguistic aspects of human behaviour. It is thus of general significance for the development of the behavioral sciences. The study of universals leads to a whole series of empirical generalizations about language, some as yet tentative, some well established. These are the potential material for a deductive structure of scientific laws' (Greenberg 1971, 153).

Gadamer describes his efforts and those of the human sciences as follows: 'But now the real problem that the human sciences present to thought is that one has not properly grasped the nature of the human sciences if one measures them by the yardstick of an increasing knowledge of regularity. The experience of the socio-historical world cannot be raised to a science by the inductive procedure of the natural sciences. Whatever "science" may mean here and even if all historical knowledge includes the application of general experience to the particular object of investigation, historical research does not endeavour to grasp the concrete phenomenon as an instance of a general rule. The individual case does not serve only to corroborate a regularity from which predictions can in turn be made. Its ideal is rather to understand the phenomenon itself in its unique and historical concreteness. However much general experience is involved, the aim is not to confirm and expand these general experiences in order to attain knowledge of a law, eg [*sic*] how men, peoples and states evolve, but to understand how this man, this people or this state is what it has become – more generally, how has it happened that it is so' (1975, 6).

Gadamer insists that what he 'seeks to discover and bring into consciousness ... [is] something that does not so much confine and limit modern science as precede it and make it possible' (1975, xvii). His awareness of the fundamental contingency of all human thought, including his own thought, does not permit Gadamer to take up an absolute position because 'the consciousness of contingency does not do away with contingency' (406–7).

7 Weimann 1976, 12–13. Weimann translates *Wirkungsgeschichte* as 'the impact of literature.'

CHAPTER 2 Perception of Language

1 Merleau-Ponty 1964c, 21–2. In works cited, I shall abbreviate 'Maurice Merleau-Ponty' to M.M-P.
2 Barfield 1928, 224. 'For perception, unlike the pure concept is inconceivable without a distinct perceiving subject on which the percepts, the soul- and sense-data, can impinge.'
3 Burke 1967 explores the relationship between the body and language as well. His symbolic act describes the *'dancing of an attitude'* and the 'attitudinizing of the poem [in which] the whole body' may become involved (9). His study focuses primarily on the relation between the author and his work and specifically on the role some physical disorder may have on the text's production. I am concerned primarily with the other end of the spectrum, that is, a reader who is not understood in terms of a 'psychogenetic illness' or a 'mental conflict' (10).
4 Holman and Harmon define synaesthesia as 'the concurrent response of two or more of the senses to the stimulation of one. The term is applied in literature to the description of one kind of sensation in terms of another' (496). Abrams defines it in basically the same terms (171). This definition presupposes that perception is data from the world impinging upon the senses. The world stimulates and the senses react. According to Merleau-Ponty, synesthesia is an action not a reaction. It is primarily the concurrent questioning or reaching out of two or more senses towards an aspect of the world. It is an interchange and communication between all senses.
5 M.M-P. 1962, 111. Together with the dialectic of action-movement, Merleau-Ponty creates a second dialectic between what may be called human

'movement' and the movement of an object. The former is called 'movement' because it has a highly abstract or speculative quality about it.
Although it may appear 'objective' and therefore centripetal, it presupposes
a centrifugal beginning. He calls the movement of an object a 'concrete'
or 'centripetal' movement. See also Mallin, 79.

CHAPTER 3 The Experience of Perception

1 See Iser 1979, 1–20, who offers a concise overview of the methods and
premises underlying today's approaches to literature. He outlines three
positions: the phenomenological, the hermeneutic, and the gestalt, to
which correspond ontological, historical, and operational premises and
which follow methodologies based on the strata model, the question-
and-answer logic, and 'the concept of schema and correction,' respectively
(5). While Iser works from the latter gestalt position and approaches
theories of structure, function, and communication in terms of the 'non-
alignment of or asymmetry between text and reader,' I am working from
Ricoeur's combination of the two former positions (14). In keeping with
Ricoeur's theory of assimilation and distanciation outlined below, I take
a dialectic of 'similarity' and difference, 'symmetry' and asymmetry as
my point of departure.
2 Ricoeur's understanding of phenomenological hermeneutics, or hermeneutic phenomenology, is constructed upon a deep affinity between hermeneutics and phenomenology. He explains that *phenomenology remains
the unsurpassable presupposition of hermeneutics*. On the other hand, phenomenology cannot constitute itself without a *hermeneutical presupposition*'
(1981a, 101). Returning to Heiddeger's *Being and Time*, Ricoeur states that
the phenomenological attitude or the *'choice in favour of meaning is ... the
most general presupposition of any hermeneutics*' (114). The attitude that
experiences a transformation of non-sense to sense is already a choice in
favour of meaning. In this way a 'new model of truth could ... be elicited
from the phenomenology of perception and transposed into the domain
of the historical-hermeneutic sciences. Such is the consequence that
Merleau-Ponty drew from the Husserlian phenomenology' (119). Much
like phenomenology, however, 'hermeneutics similarly wishes to withdraw from the objectifications and explanations of historical science and
sociology to the artistic, historical and lingual experience which precedes
and supports these objectifications' (119). Thus, phenomenology is, in
Ricoeur's words, also 'an exegesis, an explanation, an interpretation'

and hermeneutics is also 'every question concerning any sort of "being" [*étant*]' (120, 114).

Mario J. Valdés describes phenomenological hermeneutics as follows: 'Hermeneutics is a theory of interpretation of written documents wherein the status of the interpreter is considered in the commentary. Phenomenological hermeneutics is a contemporary revision of the nineteenth-century discipline wherein the Romantic notion of establishing the author's genius has been replaced by a full consideration of the reading experience as the point of departure of the enquiry. The work of Heiddeger was essential for development of phenomenological hermeneutics, since it made possible the philosophical premise of being-in-the-world, which has proved to be the solution to the subject-object impasse' (Valdés 1987, 27). For a development of the principles underlying phenomenological hermeneutics and the role it plays in the study of literature see Ricoeur's *Hermeneutics and the Human Sciences* (1981a) and Valdes's *Phenomenological Hermeneutics and the Study of Literature* (1987).

3 The *Cours de linguistique générale* is not only a platform from which to launch an empirical science but also an exercise in hermeneutics. By this I mean that the text is to a certain degree also a presentation of Saussure's students' understanding and interpretation of the views he gave orally in the form of academic lectures. It is the synthesis of an array of different perspectives brought together not only after the dialogue between the students and the professor had taken place, but after Saussure's death. What the reader of Saussure is faced with, then, are a few notes by Saussure and a combination of readings or rather listenings transcribed by Albert Sechehaye and Charles Bally with the help of Albert Riedlinger. As Joseph H. Greenberg points out, we are not dealing necessarily with the views of Saussure alone. In carrying out their task the students conceive of it as one of 'welding the materials at their disposal into a single coherent doctrine. We now know that they freely interpolated wording of their own where they felt it to be necessary ... Under these rather special circumstances, it is obviously not always easy to say what De Saussure really thought on a number of issues. Moreover, it is clear that he himself had not yet worked out a completely articulated doctrine' (Greenberg 1971, 331). In this particular quote Riedlinger's notes are not reflected by the wording of the *Cours de linguistique générale*.

4 See Austin 1962 and Searle 1969. Austin's speech-act theory, according to Oswald Ducrot, clarifies that in producing any sentence we accomplish three acts simultaneously: 1. A 'locutionary act, to the extent that

238 Notes to page 53

we articulate and combine sounds and evoke and link syntactically the notions represented by the words. 2. An illocutionary act, to the extent that the production of the sentence constitutes in itself a certain act (a certain transformation of the relationship between the interlocutors) ... 3. A perlocutionary act, to the extent that the act of enunciation serves more distant ends that the interlocutor may very well not understand even though he has mastered the language perfectly. Thus, by questioning someone, we may have as a goal doing him a favor, embarrassing him, making him believe that we respect his opinion' (Ducrot and Todorov 343).

John R. Searle (who does not accept Austin's distinction between locutionary and illocutionary acts) developed the speech-act theory further by concentrating on illocutionary acts (23). The locutionary act, then, centres on the production of the utterance itself, the illocutionary act centres on transforming the relationship between those involved in the dialogue, and the perlocutionary act centres on the impact or effect the utterance will have.

5 Ricoeur distinguishes between an epistemology and a taxonomy. An epistemology is the aspect of language that grasps things together according to an understanding in order to subsequently explain them. A taxonomy is the aspect of language that lends itself to the inventory and combination of elements and units arranged in terms of binary oppositions. Semiotics is the model that governs the investigation of taxonomies and has as its basic unit the linguistic sign. Semantics, according to Ricoeur, is the science of the usage of signs as they occur in the basic unit of discourse, which is a meaningful sentence (Ricoeur 1974, 79–96). Todorov's remarks concerning point of view reflect the importance of opting for Ricoeur's notion of epistemology over the structuralist concept of a taxonomy: 'The category of point of view is becoming less important ... Literary criticism, which one saw in point of view the secret of the literary art, is discovering that the category includes a series of distinct features, that it has after all only descriptive value, and that it cannot serve as a criterion for success.

'Efforts have long been made to find a single opposition around which to organize all the features connected with the relationship between the narrator and the represented universe. From these efforts, syncretic terms have a reason to group several categories in one or to postulate their solidarity ... The difficulty is *evident*: each [opposition discovered] covers several independent categories' (Ducrot and Todorov 329, emphasis added). I agree that the semiotic difficulty is 'evident' in the etymological sense of the word.

6 Ricoeur is referring to I.A. Richards's pioneering work in the area of metaphor. Ricoeur notes that Richards's term 'metaphor' includes both the tenor or 'underlying idea' and the vehicle or 'the name of the idea under whose sign the first idea is apprehended' (1977, 80).

7 Ricoeur 1977, 251. The reference is to Wheelwright's 'perspective.'

8 Ricoeur 1981a, 211–12, and see 1981b, 246: 'There is a *structural analogy* between the cognitive, the imaginative, and the emotional components of the complete metaphorical act.'

9 Ricoeur 1984–8, 2:187n. Ricoeur is here using Mario Valdés's notion of realizing the intentionality of a text through the act of reading. Valdés, along with Jauss and Iser, explores the crucial intersection of mimesis 2 and mimesis 3. See Valdés 1982, chaps 3–5, and 1987, chap. 2.

CHAPTER 4 The Concept of Narrative Perspective

1 Roman Jakobson's famous 'Closing Statement: Linguistics and Poetics' outlines six constitutive factors in any speech event to which correspond six functions of language. The six constitutive factors are (1) an *addresser* who sends (2) an *addressee* (3) a *message* that is operative within (4) a *context* referred to and that is also expressed in (5) a *code* fully or at least partially common to the addresser and the addressee. The (6) *contact* is a physical channel and psychological connection between addresser and addressee that allows them to enter into and maintain communication. To each of these correspond, respectively, (1) an *emotive* function that aims an expression of the speaker's attitude towards what he is speaking about, (2) a *conative* function that orients towards the addressee by way of grammatical expressions such as the vocative or the imperative, and (3) a *poetic* function that centres on the message for its own sake. In terms of the two basic modes of arrangement used in verbal behaviour, '*selection* and *combination*,' the '*poetic function projects the principle of equivalence from the axis of selection into the axis of combination*' (358), (4) a *referential* function that orients towards the context, (5) a *metalingual* function that centres on the code itself, although not necessarily in the manner of logicians and linguists, but also in the role the code plays in our everyday usage, and finally (6) a *phatic* function that strives to maintain and prolong communication (see Jakobson in Sebeok 353–7).

2 Rimmon-Kenan 1983, 85. I shall abbreviate 'Shlomith Rimmon-Kenan' to 'S.R-K.'

3 Barfield 1928, 21, 32, and 224.

4 The choice of metonymy over metaphor is in keeping with Rimmon-

Kenan's spatial criterion. In his discussion of metonymy as proposed by Gaston Esnault, Bernard Pottier, and Algirdas Greimas, Paul Ricoeur notes that 'metonymy follows the order of things and proceeds analytically, whereas metaphor plays on comprehension in a synthetic and intuitive manner' (1977, 201). Even here, however, he is careful to point out that 'new metonymies ... bring into play an "active selective perception" ' (202).

5 See Ricoeur 1984, 2:29–30, for an analysis of the confrontation between the notion of 'understanding' and of 'deep structure.'

6 See Benveniste 1966, 1: 225–36, 260. Although the concept of contrast is essential to Emile Benveniste's argument, he does not limit the consideration of 'person' to structural relations of opposition and difference alone. He also bases the concept of 'person' on the experience of human beings who 'figure' (that is, make an appearance, count, reckon) in the living situation of a dialogue. The 'I' figures as subjectivity in the situation of a dialogue and the 'you' figures as a non-subjective figuration in the same situation. The 'he, she, it' is a non-person in that these are absent from the dialogue situation and therefore do not figure in it (1: 228). I understand Benveniste's argument as both ontological and structural because he deals with 'beings' brought together and sharing a living situation of speech. While Benveniste states, 'Une théorie linguistique de la personne verbale ne peut se constituer que sur la base des oppositions qui différencient les personnes; et elle se résumera tout entière dans la structure de ces oppositions,' he returns to the situation of a dialogue from which the 'théorie linguistique' is drawn and upon which it reflects (1: 227–8). This prior level cannot be characterised in terms of difference and opposition alone. Once he returns the theoretic principles to the lived experience of meaningful speech situations, then he must (and does) contend with the ontological and transcendant nature of *figuration*. The consideration of 'person' as 'figurations' (that is, those who appear in the situation of a dialogue), then, also points to a phenomenology of perception. His understanding of *personae* in the etymological sense as 'figurations' allows for the creative dimension of language as well. This understanding not only suggests the figurative or tropological aspect of discourse similar to Merleau-Ponty's notion of the body as a literary work of art, but also suggests Ricoeur's notion of 'la métaphore vive' as both trope and *figure*, or 'human face' (M.M-P. 1962, 151–2, and Ricoeur 1981b, 229) I shall develop the notion of 'person' as 'figuration' in narrative perspective below.

7 Valdés argues for a tripartite description of the narrative text that brings together the historical dimension of production, the formal dimension

as a continuity in time of a sequence of words, and the reading dimension that is the text's realization (1987, 33, 39) I must agree with this description and state with him that ultimately the text as an object of literary study 'depends on how the text relates to our human interests and purposes' and that it 'is much more than that which does not put in question its empirical facticity' (1987, 39).

8 Valdés 1987, 55, and Weimann 1976, chap. 1. This notion of present meaning as a mediation of past significance and 'future consequence' comes from Paul Ricoeur's mediation of the Gadamer-Habermas debate in terms of retrospection and prospection. See Ricoeur 1981a, 100.

9 Luk 1962, 91–2. Paul Ricoeur's chapters 'A Plea for Writing' and 'Against Writing' reflects this mediating principle. See Ricoeur 1976, 37–44.

10 Valdés and Miller 1985, iv.

11 Marx 1973, 89, 484–91. See also Weimann 1976, 11.

12 See Friederici 1973, 323–441.

13 See Germán Arciniegas's chapter 'Don Quixote and the Conquest of America' in *Latin America: A Cultural History*, trans. Joan MacLean (New York: Alfred A Knopf, 1967) 76–87.

14 See Enrique Anderson Imbert, 'La colonia, cien años de república,' in *Historia de la literatura hispanoamericana* (México: Fondo de Cultura Económica, 1954), 1:74: 'Las tres partes de *La Araucana* aparecieron, sucesivamente en 1569, 1578 y 1589; y por primera vez España sintió que América tenía ya literatura.' The three oldest editions of *Lazarillo de Tormes* appeared simultaneously in Burgos, Alcalá, and Antwerpen in 1554. See the preliminary study of Díaz-Plaja (1974), xxiv.

CHAPTER 5 Figuring out Narrative Perspective

1 Valdés 1987, 54–5: 'I have characterized literary criticism as a form of celebration within a community; this is an international community of individuals who participate in the tradition of textual commentary. In order to participate one must first recognize the community, and in order to engage in the multi-voiced conversation one must recognize the validity of other voices. If we are to engage in conversation, we must be willing to listen as well as to speak ... [We] are members of a community whose main purpose for being has been and is ever to enlarge the dialogue into an oratorio of past significance in present meaning.'

2 Ricoeur 1976, 69. Ricoeur uses the terms 'semantic face and non semantic face.'

3 Borges, 'Las ruinas circulares,' in 1980, 1:435, and Valdés 1982, 28–9.
4 This configuration is similar to what Jean Pouillon calls 'un roman "avec," ' which gives the feeling of 'être dans la peau d'un personnage.' He opposes this to 'un roman "par derrière;" ... plus loin,' which I deal with in terms of a parabolic or spatial configuration below. See Pouillon 1946, 80–1 and 85.
5 White 1978, 12. 'But what Piaget's theories do suggest is that the tropes of figuration, metaphor, metonym, synecdoche, and irony, which are used in conscious processes of poiesis and discourse formation, are grounded, in some way, in the psychogenetic endowment of the child, the basis of which appear sequentially in the fourfold phasal development which Piaget calls sensorimotor, representational, operational and logical.'
6 Whorf 1956, 143–4. For a conceptual response to the Sapir-Whorf hypothesis see Max Black, *Models and Metaphors: Studies in Language and Philosophy* (Ithaca, NY: Cornell University Press, 1962), 244–57. Black's criticism of Whorf is directed primarily at his metaphors. He tries to render Whorf sufficiently precise to be tested, in spite of the 'formidable obstacles' of inconsistency, the 'vaporous mysticism,' and the 'exaggeration' (244–5). He claims that Whorf is confused when he affirms that language and thought both are and are not the same: 'I have already argued that Whorf identified the "conceptual system" and the "world view" with the language in which they were expressed, while also confusedly thinking of them as distinct' (254–5).
7 White 1978, 73. For an explanation of deconstruction criticism in terms of an ironic mode of discourse see chapter 12, 'The Absurdist Moment in Contemporary Literary Theory.'
8 Ong 1982, 72. At the risk of over-anticipating the next chapter, I intend to 'look at a room' and to listen to 'high-fidelity' (in an etymological sense) through an investigation of perspective in Virginia Woolf's *Jacob's Room* and Gabriel García Márquez's *Cien años de soledad*.
9 Ong 1977, 315, 287, 279, 291, 287–8, and 293.
10 Ong 1977, 120, 310. See Brathwaite 1984. See also Harris 1970. Harris's lecture is inspired by Merleau-Ponty's words: 'The act of the artist or philosopher is free but not motiveless. Their freedom ... consists in appropriating a *de facto* situation by endowing it with a figurative meaning beyond its real one' (3). This is a movement from a first-order to a second-order metaphorical perspective. Harris situates the Anglophone Caribbean experience within the context (with both similarities to and

differences from the Hispanic culture) of Latin American consciousness that he exemplifies with the realism of Gabriel García Márquez (24–5).

11 Ong 1977, 337. Ong describes human consciousness *metaphorically* as an 'open closure' and the ' "I" interfaces with everything.'

12 See Kline (1967): '**speak**, intr. and tr. v. – ME. *speken*, fr. OE. *specan*, fr. earlier *sprecan*, rel. to OS. *sprecan*, OFris. *spreka*, MDu. *spreken* (var. *speken*), Du. *spreken*, OHG. *sprehhan* (var. *spehhan*), MHG., G. *sprechen*, "to speak," ON. *spraki*, "rumor, report," and cogn. with W. *ffraeth* (for **sprakto-*), "eloquent." All these words derive fr. base **sprek-*, "to speak," which, however, orig. meant "to make a noise, shout, cry, crackle," fr. I.-E. base **sper(e)g-*, **spher(e)g-*, "to strew, sprinkle; to sprout, burst," whence also OI. *sphúrjati*, "it crackles," Gk σφαραγεῖν, "to crackle," L. *spargere*, "to scatter, sprinkle." See **sparse** and cp. words there referred to. Cp. also **speech, spokesman**.'

13 I am not speaking of fable in the sense that Menakhem Perry uses fabula in the fabula/syuzhet dichotomy: 'Fabula is defined as consisting of motifs in their natural chronological sequence which a reader may reconstruct while *syuzhet* is the actual sequence of these same motifs in the text, the order in which the reader encounters them' (39) nor am I considering the fable in Mieke Bal's terms of a sequence of events within the grammatical order of the text. I do accept her notion of fabula's cyclical shape (5, 21, 22).

14 *New Oxford Bible* (1973). I am following the example set by Hans-Georg Gadamer (1975, 402–3) Here I call upon the Bible as an example of 'written tradition' in order to explain my understanding. Also see note 4 of chapter 1, above.

15 Ricoeur 1976, 59: 'Here a poem is like a work of music in that its mood is exactly coextensive with the internal order of symbols articulated by its language.' For a development of this analogy see Schneider 1946. Animal, symbol, and music come together in the audio-oral world of 'fabulari.'

CHAPTER 7 The Fabulour Metaphor of *Cien años de soledad*

1 United Nations 1978, 6. I have argued above that statistics are often used to create an illusion of historical objectivity (p. 12 above and Gadamer 1975, 268). I am making no such claim here. I have selected these statistics in order to address the question: Which medium of discourse is most likely to have had repercussions, at the level of prefiguration, on the mode of discourse and the techniques of narrative perspective?

2 'Colombia,' *Encyclopedia Americana* (1984) and 'Colombia,' *Encyclopaedia Britannica* (1972).
3 García Márquez 1982a, 447, 446. Unless otherwise specified, quotes will be from *Cien años de soledad*.
4 Angel Rosenblat, *Nuestra lengua en ambos mundos* (Estella: Salvat, 1971), 41–76. Rosenblat attacks the growing tendency to bow under the pressure and power of authority commanded by the written word. He insists that spelling and writing must respect the spoken language, as has been the case in *Castellano* since Nebrija.

CHAPTER 8 The Ironic Parable of *Jacob's Room*

1 Great Britain 1906, 9.
2 United Nations 1949, 512.
3 Woolf 1976, 65, 47. All quotations will be from *Jacob's Room* unless otherwise indicated.
4 'Lighthouse,' *Encyclopaedia Britannica* (1911).

References

Abrams, M.H. 1957. *A Glossary of Literary Terms*. New York: Holt, Rinehart and Winston

Anderson Imbert, Enrique. 1954. *Historia de la literatura hispanoamericana: La colonia, cien años de república*. México: Fondo de Cultura Económica

Arciniegas, Germán. 1967. *Latin America: A Cultural History*. Trans. Joan MacLean. New York: Alfred A. Knopf

Austin, J.L. 1962. *How To Do Things with Words*. Cambridge, MA: Harvard University Press

Bal, Mieke. 1985. *Narratology: Introduction to the Theory of Narrative*. Trans. Christine van Boheemen. Toronto: University of Toronto Press

Barfield, Owen. 1928. *Poetic Diction: A Study in Meaning*. London: Faber and Guyer

Benveniste, Emile. 1966. *Problèmes de linguistique générale*. 2 vols. Paris: Gallimard

Booth, Wayne C. 1961. *The Rhetoric of Fiction*. Chicago: University of Chicago Press

Borges, Jorge Luis. 1980. 'Las ruinas circulares.' In *Prosa Completa*. 2 vols. Barcelona: Bruguera

Brathwaite, Edward Kamau. 1984. *History of the Voice: The Development of National Language in Anglophone Caribbean Culture*. London: New Beacon

Burke, Kenneth. 1967. *The Philosophy of Literary Form: Studies in Symbolic Action*. 2nd ed. Baton Rouge: Louisiana State University Press

'Colombia.' *Encyclopedia Americana*. 1984 ed.

'Colombia.' *Encyclopaedia Britannica*. 1972 ed.

Culler, Jonathan. 1979. 'Jacques Derrida.' In John Sturrock (ed.), *Structuralism and Since: From Levi-Strauss to Derrida*. Oxford: Oxford University Press

Daiches, David. 1942. *Virginia Woolf*. Norfolk: New Directions

Derrida, Jacques. 1967. *Of Grammatology*. Trans. Gayatri Chakravorty Spivak. Baltimore: Johns Hopkins University Press

Díaz-Plaja, Guillermo. 1974. Introductory study to *Lazarillo de Tormes*, ix–xxxix. México: Porrua. Volume contains two novels: *Lazarillo* (anonymous) and Francisco de Quevedo, *Vida del Buscón Don Pablos*.

Ducrot, Oswald, and Tzvetan Todorov. 1979. *Encyclopedic Dictionary of the Sciences of Language*. Trans. Catherine Porter. Baltimore: Johns Hopkins University Press

Eddie, James E. 1973. Foreword to Maurice Merleau-Ponty, *Consciousness and the Acquisition of Language*. Trans. H.J. Silverman. Evanston: Northwestern University Press

Fishman, Joshua A. 1971. 'The Sociology of Language: An Interdisciplinary Social Science Approach to Language in Society.' In Joshua A. Fishman (ed.), *Advances in the Sociology of Language*. The Hague: Mouton

Fernández-Brazo, Miguel. 1972. *La soledad de Gabriel García Márquez (Una conversación infinita)*. Barcelona: Planeta

Forster, E.M. 1927. *Aspects of the Novel*. New York: Harcourt, Brace and World

Friederici, Georg. 1973. *El cáracter del descubrimiento y la conquista de América: Introducción a la historia de la colonización de América por los pueblos del viejo mundo*. Trans. Wenceslao Roces. México: Fondo de Cultura Económica

Friedman, Norman. 1967. 'Distance and Point of View: An Essary in Classification.' In Philip Stevick (ed.), *The Theory of the Novel*. London: Collier-Macmillan

Frye, Northrop. 1957. *Anatomy of Criticism: Four Essays*. Princeton: Princeton University Press

Gadamer, Hans-Georg. 1972. 'Semantics and Hermeneutics (1972).' Trans. P. Christopher Smith. In David E. Linge (ed.), *Philosophical Hermeneutics*, 82–94. Berkeley: University of California Press, 1976

– 1975. *Truth and Method*. Trans. Garrett Barden and John Cumming. New York: Continuum

García Márquez, Gabriel. 1982a. *Cien años de soledad*. Estudio Introductorio por Joaquín Marco. Madrid: Espasa-Calpe

– 1982b. 'La soledad de America Latina.' In *Nobel Prizes, Presentations, Biographies and Lectures*. Stockholm. Almquist & Wiksell

Genette, Gerard. 1980. *Narrative Discourse: An Essay in Method*. Trans. James E. Lewin. Ithaca: Cornell University Press

– 1982. *Palimpsestes: La littérature au second degré*. Paris: Éditions du Seuil

Gide, André. 1933. 'Le retour de l'enfant prodigue.' In *Oeuvres complètes d'André Gide*, 5:1–27. Paris: Nouvelle revue française

Gloversmith, Frank. 1984. 'Autonomy Theory: Ortega, Roger Fry, Virginia Woolf.' In Frank Gloversmith (ed.), *The Theory of Reading*. Brighton: Harvester

Great Britain. 1906. *British Sessional Papers: 13 February – 21 December*. XCVI. London: House of Commons

Greenberg, Joseph H., ed. 1966. *Universals of Language*. 2nd ed. Cambridge, MA: MIT Press

– 1971. *Language, Culture, and Communication*. Stanford: Stanford University Press

Gullón, Ricardo. 1970. *García Márquez o el arte de contar*. Madrid: Taurus

Guzmán Campos, Germán. 1968. *La violencia en Colombia: parte descriptiva*. Cali: Progreso

Harris, Wilson. 1970. *History, Fable and Myth in the Caribbean and Guianas*. Georgetown, Guyana: National History and Arts Council, Ministry of Information and Culture

Hawkes, Terence. 1977. *Structuralism and Semiotics*. Berkeley: University of California Press

Herrera, Roberto. 1985. 'Gabriel García Márquez: el hombre.' In Ana María Hernández de Lopez (ed.), *En el punto de mira: Gabriel García Márquez*, 345–56. Madrid: Pliegos

Holman, C. Hugh. and William Harmon. 1986. *A Handbook to Literature*. New York: Macmillan

Humboldt, Wilhelm von. 1988. *On Language: The Diversity of Human Language-Structure and Its Influence on the Mental Development of Mankind*. Trans. Peter Heath. Cambridge: Cambridge University Press

Iser, Wolfgang. 1978a. *The Act of Reading: A Theory of Aesthetic Response*. Baltimore: Johns Hopkins University Press

– 1987b. 'Narrative Strategies as a Means of Communication.' In Mario J. Valdés and Owen J. Miller (eds), *Interpretation of Narrative*. Toronto: University of Toronto Press

– 1979. 'The Current Situation of Literary Theory: Key Concepts and the Imagination.' *New Literary History* II, no. 1:1–20

– 1985. 'Feigning in Fiction.' In Mario J. Valdés and Owen Miller (eds), *Identity of the Literary Text*. Toronto: University of Toronto Press

Jaeck, Lois Marie. 1984. '*One Hundred Years of Solitude*: The End of the Book the Beginning of Writing.' 16th Annual Meeting of the Canadian Comparative Literature Association. Guelph: 4 June

James, Henry. 1934. *The Art of the Novel*. New York: Charles Scribner's Sons

Jauss, Hans Robert. 1978. 'Theses on the Transition from the Aesthetics of Literary Works to a Theory of Aesthetic Experience.' In Mario J. Valdés and Owen J. Miller (eds), *Interpretation of Narrative*. Toronto: University of Toronto Press

– 1982. *Toward an Aesthetic of Reception*. Trans. Timothy Bahti. Minneapolis: University of Minnesota Press

– 1985. 'The Identity of the Literary Text in the Changing Horizon of Understanding.' In Mario J. Valdés and Owen Miller (eds), *Identity of the Literary Text*. Toronto: University of Toronto Press

Kline, Ernest. 1967. *A Comprehensive Etymological Dictionary of the English Language*. Amsterdam: Elsivier

Leitch, Vincent B. 1983. *Deconstructive Criticism: An Advanced Introduction*. New York: Columbia University Press

León-Portilla, Miguel y Angel Ma. Garibay. 1972. *Visión de los vencidos: Relaciones indígenas de la conquista*. México: Universidad Nacional Autónoma de México

'Lighthouse.' *Encyclopaedia Britannica*. 1911 ed.

Lotman, Jurij. 1977. *The Structure of the Artistic Text*. Ann Arbor: University of Michigan Press

Lubbock, Percy. 1957. *The Craft of Fiction*. New York: Viking Press

Luk, Charles. 1962. *Ch'an and Zen Teaching*. Vol. 3. London: Rider

Mallin, Samuel Barry. 1979. *Merleau-Ponty's Philosophy*. New Haven: Yale University Press

Marx, Karl. 1973. *Grundrisse: Foundations of the Critique of Political Economy*. Trans. Martin Nicolaus. New York: Random House

Merleau-Ponty, Maurice. 1945. *Phénoménologie de la Perception*. Paris: Gallimard

– 1962. *Phenomenology of Perception*. Trans. Colin Smith. London: Routledge and Kegan Paul

– 1964a. *L'Oeil et l'Esprit*. Paris: Gallimard

– 1964b. *Sense and Non-Sense*. Trans. Hubert L. Dreyfus and Patricia Allen Dreyfus. Evanston: Northwestern University Press

– 1964c. *Signs*. Trans. Richard C. McCleary. Evanston: Northwestern University Press

– 1968. *The Visible and the Invisible: Followed by Working Notes*. Trans. Alphonso Lingis. Ed. Claude Lefort. Evanston: Northwestern University Press

– 1969. The Relations of the Soul and the Body and the Problem of Perceptual Consciousness.' In Alden L. Fisher (ed.), *The Essential Writings of Maurice Merleau-Ponty*. New York: Harcourt, Brace & World

– 1970. *Themes from the Lectures at the Collège de France 1952–1960*. Trans. John O'Neill. Evanston: Northwestern University Press

Miller, Owen. 1985. Preface to Mario J. Valdés and Owen Miller (eds), *Identity of the Literary Text*. Toronto: University of Toronto Press

New Oxford Annotated Bible with the Apocrypha. 1973. New York: Oxford
University Press

Norris, Christopher. 1982. *Deconstruction Theory and Practice.* New York:
Methuen

Ong, Walter J., SJ. 1977. *Interfaces of the Word: Studies in the Evolution of
Consciousness and Culture.* Ithaca: Cornell University Press

– 1982. *Orality and Literacy: The Technologizing of the Word.* London: Methuen

Perry, Menakhem. 1979. 'Literary Dynamics: How the Order of a Text
Creates Its Meaning.' *Poetics Today* 1, nos. 1–2:35–65, 311–61

Pouillon, Jean. 1946. *Temps et Roman.* Paris: Gallimard

Ricoeur, Paul. 1974. *The Conflict of Interpretations: Essays in Hermeneutics.* Ed.
Don Ihde. Evanston: Northwestern University Press

– 1976. *Interpretation Theory: Discourse and the Surplus of Meaning.* Fort Worth:
Texas Christian University Press

– 1977. *The Rule of Metaphor: Multi-disciplinary Studies of the Creation of Meaning
in Language.* Trans. Robert Czerny, Kathleen McLaughlin, and John Costello,
SJ. Toronto: University of Toronto Press

– 1979. 'The Function of Fiction in Shaping Reality.' *Man and World*
12:123–41

– 1981a. *Hermeneutics and the Human Sciences: Essays on Language, Action and
Interpretation.* Trans. and Ed. John B. Thompson. Cambridge: Cambridge
University Press

– 1981b. 'The Metaphorical Process as Cognition, Imagination, and Feeling.'
In Mark Johnson (ed.), *Philosophical Perspectives on Metaphor.* Minneapolis:
University of Minneapolis Press

– 1984–8. *Time and Narrative.* 3 vols. Trans. Kathleen McLaughlin and David
Pellauer. Chicago: University of Chicago Press

– 1985. 'The Text as Dynamic Identity.' In Mario J. Valdés and Owen Miller
(eds), *Identity of the Literary Text.* Toronto: University of Toronto Press

Rimmon-Kenan, Shlomith. 1983. *Narrative Fiction: Contemporary Poetics.* London:
Methuen

Saussure, Ferdinand de. 1967. *Cours de linguistique générale: Édition critique.*
4 parts. Ed. Rudolf Engler. Wiesbaden: Otto Harrassowitz

Schmidt, James. 1985. *Maurice Merleau-Ponty: Between Phenomenology and
Structuralism.* Houndmills: Macmillan

Schneider, Marius. 1946. *El orígen musical de los animales-símbolos en la mitología
y la escultura antiguas: Ensayo Histórico-etnográfico sobre la subestructura totemística
y megalítica de las altas culturas y supervivencia en el folklore español.* Barcelona:
Consejo Superior de Investigaciones Científicas

Scholes, Robert E. and Robert Kellogg. 1966. *The Nature of Narrative*. New York: Oxford University Press

Searle, John R. 1969. *Speech Acts: An Essay in the Philosophy of Language*. Cambridge: Cambridge University Press

Sieber, Harry. 1978. *Language and Society in La vida de Lazarillo de Tormes*. Baltimore: Johns Hopkins University Press

United Nations. 1949. *Statistical Yearbook/Annuaire Statistique*. Lake Success, NY: Statistical Office of the UN

United Nations. 1978. UNESCO. *Estimates and Projections of Illiteracy*. New York: Division of Statistics on Education

Valdés, Mario J. 1982. *Shadows in the Cave: A Phenomenological Approach to Literary Criticism Based on Hispanic Texts*. Toronto: University of Toronto Press

– and Owen Miller, eds. 1985. *Identity of the Literary Text*. Toronto: University of Toronto Press

– 1987. *Phenomenological Hermeneutics and the Study of Literature*. Toronto: University of Toronto Press

Vargas Llosa, Mario. 1971. *García Márquez: Historia de un deicidio*. Barcelona: Barral

Weimann, Robert. 1975. ' "Reception Aesthetics" and the Crisis in Literary History.' *CLIO* 5, no. 1:3–29

– 1976. *Structure and Society in Literary History: Studies in the History and Theory of Historical Criticism*. Charlottesville: University Press of Virginia

– 1982. 'Perspectives on Realism.' Centre for Comparative Literature, University of Toronto. Spring:1–43

– 1983. 'Appropriation and Modern History in Renaissance Prose Narrative.' *New Literary History* 14, no. 3:459–95

– 1985. 'Textual Identity and Relationship: A Metacritical Excursion into History.' In Mario J. Valdés and Owen Miller (eds), *Identity of the Literary Text*. Toronto: University of Toronto Press

White, Hayden. 1973. *Metahistory: The Historical Imagination in Nineteenth-Century Europe*. Baltimore: Johns Hopkins University Press

– 1978. *Tropics of Discourse: Essays in Cultural Criticism*. Baltimore: Johns Hopkins University Press

– 1981. 'The Value of Narrativity in Representation of Reality.' In W.J.T. Mitchell (ed.), *On Narrativity*, 1–23. Chicago: University of Chicago Press

– 1985. 'The Rule of Narrativity: Symbolic Discourse and the Experiences of Time in Ricoeur's Thought.' *Revue de l'Université d'Ottawa / University of Ottawa Quarterly* 55, no. 4:287–99

Whorf, Benjamin Lee. 1956. *Language, Thought and Reality: Selected Writings of Benjamin Lee Whorf*. Ed. John B. Carroll. Cambridge MA: MIT Press

Wiehl, Reiner. 1986. 'Heidegger, Hermeneutics, and Ontology.' Trans. Brice R. Wachterhauser. In Brice R. Wachterhauser (ed.), *Hermeneutics and Modern Philosophy*. Albany: State University of New York

Wood, Robert E., ed. 1970. *The Future of Metaphysics*. Chicago: Quadrangle Books

Woolf, Virginia. 1976. *Jacob's Room*. London: Granada

– 1953. *A Writer's Diary: Being Extracts from the Diary of Virginia Woolf*. Ed. Leonard Woolf. London: Hogarth Press

Zahan, D., and Solange de Ganay. 'Études sur la cosmologie des Dogon et des Bambara du Soudan Français.' *Africa* 21:13–23

Index

Abrams, M.H. 78
Act of Reading (Iser) 114
actants 93, 94
action 39, 46, 47, 71, 102, 103, 123,
    133, 139, 150, 151, 162, 201, 206,
    213; as act 91, 122; character 73,
    171; as direction 24, 25; *distentio
    animi* 65; and language 104; logi-
    cal act 127; logic of 94; mimesis
    and 67, 88; and movement 155;
    perspective 133; phronesis 67;
    position 95; prefiguration 70;
    and reaction 120; reader 178;
    synergy 66; and time 69, 71, 81;
    voice 80, 81
actors 91, 93
advent 39, 48
aesthetics: *aisthesis* 124, 125, 126;
    Bloomsbury 148; cultivation
    of 124; differentiation 125; and
    experience 113, 124, 125, 126;
    of negativity 124; object 114,
    118–23, 126; of reception 110;
    of representation 110; percep-
    tion 124–8, 163; perspective 163;
    pleasure 125; point of view 78;
    of reception 124, 125, 128

Africa 152, 167, 193; illiteracy
    in 165; narrative strategies 167;
    narrative world 193; oral
    noetic 149, 165, 193
America 152, 193
Anatomy of Criticism (Frye) 69
aneignung. See appropriation
application 127; as *applicare* 124
appropriation 104, 121, 147, 150,
    155, 162, 164, 194, 195; as
    aneignung 111; as assimilation 54,
    111, 132, 147; and conscious-
    ness 112; defined 55; as distanci-
    ation 148; event 54, 55, 92; Marx
    on 110; and metaphor 61, 64;
    narrative 226; perspective 63,
    164, 227; as play 156; and pre-
    figuration 109; reader 64, 109;
    and refiguration 162; and self-
    appropriation 141, 153, 155, 195
Aracataca 165
Arciniegas, Germán 152
Aristotle 64, 70, 74, 98, 188, 231n.4
Arnheim, Rudolf: *Art and Visual
    Perception: A Psychology of the Cre-
    ative Eye* 115
art 110, 115, 199

UNIVERSITY OF TORONTO ROMANCE SERIES